STANDUP GUYS

A Generation of Laughs

by

John DeBellis

BookLocker.com, Inc.
2012

920 Spot Books
www.920spot.com

First Edition

Cover designed by Lucie Tran

"I really liked it. Don't know how you remembered all that stuff. The writing was pretty sharp, which leads me to believe you must have had some outside help. Some big words and even some traces of humanity! Couldn't have been you. In any event, please pass on my congratulations to the author and tell him, her or perhaps your Dad before he passed. It's a wonderful book." —Larry David

"This amazing read reminds me of how it might have been for artists hanging out in cafes in the early 20th Century; drinking and laughing, trying to discover our authentic selves in the world of standup. In this crazed existence, DeBellis reveals dead-on how getting laughs practically, if not completely, validated our reason to exist. On a personal note, I'd like to thank the author for so brilliantly reminding me of my tortured, insatiable need to be judged by strangers going on now for over forty two years. Someone had to take the hit. This book perfectly describes my favorite obsession." —Richard Lewis

"I don't think any of us would have become the comedians or entertainers that we've become without passing through that crucible. And also I wouldn't trade anything for the fun we had. God we had fun. We were too stupid to know how hard it was. I miss seeing everybody all the time. Standup Guys authentically mirrors that time period." —Bill Maher

"John DeBellis is one of the many comedians I met in New York City and didn't sleep with. If the 1940s produced the greatest generation, the 1970s and 80s arguably produced the funniest generation. John documents this wonderfully in his book; add "phenomenal memory" to his list of talents, which includes 'terrific joke craftsman'. I was transported right back to the bar at Catch A Rising Star, sitting on a stool with my various notebooks and playing "Is this funny?" I can't believe that was thirty years ago and I was only six." —Rita Rudner

"Standup Guys was so real that I was waiting to get heckled by the book. The writing is witty and smart and it authentically captures what it was like to be a comic during that magical time, when standup was our life, and not yet our livelihood, and the friendships we formed were destined to last a lifetime." —Richard Belzer

"I can honestly say the paper this book is printed on is of pretty high quality and the cover is relatively durable." —Gilbert Gottfried

"John's book brings back that special era vividly and makes me feel like asking for cab fare again. For eight bucks a night we lived like court jesters that had taken over the kingdom. If you want to know what it was like being a standup comic back in the 70's and early 80's then this is the ultimate read." —Robert Wuhl

"As a standup comic, I was so able to identify with John's vivid description of the comedy world in the 70's and 80's and this daring and bold wave of risk-takers. This was a generation of fresh, young comedians that spawned comedy clubs throughout the country and enticed people to go out to see them and laugh. I'm proud to be part of this club and very grateful that I'm not as neurotic and dysfunctional as some of them here in this book." —Kevin Nealon

"John's book relives all those great, early, explosive years of New York comedy: the brotherhood, the backstage fun, the beer, and even the broken bones. It was a blast." —Joe Piscopo.

"John's hysterically funny, historically significant document makes me nostalgic for those crazy days of failure and nights of hope. Being 'one of the guys' was a perk, because these guys were all true originals. I learned, I laughed, I loved the freedom we had to work out who the hell we were in public because we couldn't be alone with it. The voices that evolved on those teensy stages have impacted TV and comedy for decades, so I guess we were doing something right." —Melanie Chartoff

"The most amazing thing about this book is that it is so wonderfully descriptive and detailed, and so perfectly captures the essence of our early days in standup comedy, that I wonder how John DeBellis was able to take enough time away from watching Yankee games on the Yes Network to actually write it."—Bobby Kelton

"The book was great. It brought back a lot of memories, all of them good. When the Strip opened in 1976 if wasn't for the Standup Guys I don't know if we would have lasted. Thanks to everybody, John, Glenn Hisch, Piscopo, Bobby Kelton, and Larry David who came from Catch and the Improv, which gave us the time to develop acts like Jerry Seinfeld, Ray Romano, Paul Reiser, Larry Miller, Dennis Wolgberg, George Wallace etc. Thanks Guys." —Richie Tienken (owner of the Comic Strip)

"I am too busy with all the free Internet porn to read the book, but I am sure I would have liked it. Okay, not really. I loved the book and enjoyed being part of the comedy scene you describe so well."—Wil Shriner

"Wow, what a fun ride! Every time I picked up this book it was like stepping into a time machine." —Steve Mittleman.

"The clubs were like being in a Marx Brothers film. If the Marx Brothers were still alive they would turn John's book into a movie. It is simply that funny." —Mark Schiff

"I loved this book! It was like reliving the beginning of my own comedic life through John's memories of the times. I could not put the book down...well, I couldn't put it down because I spilled jelly on the cover and it stuck to my hands." —Glenn Hirsch

"The book depicts an era of the development of the comedy boom and the camaraderie that existed in a kind of brotherhood society. It was a time when we'd share ideas and help one another. The book

brings you into those moments of creativity and some of the crazy and hilarious events we all experienced in that wonderful place in our lives. It allows the reader to be that envied 'fly on the wall'. I am proud and privileged to have been part of it. A great read. Bravo, John." —Buddy Mantia (member of the Untouchables comedy team)

Dedicated to my daughters, Alina, Kendal.
Page, and Lane and to the memory of
Ronnie Shakes, Glen Super, Andy Kaufman,
Marjorie Gross, Dennis Wolfberg, Rodney Dangerfield
Rich Jeni and to all the standup comics who have passed on.

TABLE OF CONTENTS

Author's Preface

There were so many people, comics, staff and even very funny anecdotes that were not included in the book in order to keep it at a reasonable length. The anecdotes are as accurate as my memory would permit and the dialogue close enough to capture the essence of the moment. Time has a way of altering our perceptions and perhaps affecting the precise order of when things actually occurred. That said, in certain instances, I purposely took things out of sequence to highlight a particular moment or message.

In the few occasions when I mentioned club owners in a derogatory manner, the comments were not aimed at the owners of the Improv, Catch or The Comic Strip, but rather at the owners of the fly by night comedy clubs. Other than that, I've chosen not to air out any dirty laundry. It was never my purpose—to do that would have changed the tenor of the memoir.

I did my best to be as inclusive as possible. It's one of the reasons I decided on self-publication. Publishers would have insisted that I center the story only on those who are famous. That would have ripped the soul out of the book. This memoir isn't about being famous, it's about artistic integrity, innocence, the struggle to improve, the love of the art form and most of all the camaraderie. I thank you all, even those who aren't mentioned in the memoir, for without every single one of you, that time may not have been so magical.

Prologue

On TV screens across America, Bill Maher is seen sitting in his dressing room getting the final touches before he takes the stage for the premiere of his new HBO show, *Real Time*. As he speaks to the makeup woman, there's a knock on the door.

"Yeah, come in," Bill says, but before he can even finish that statement, the dressing room door opens and Larry David enters.

"Opening Night. Opening Night," Larry David sing songs teasingly as he enters, smiling, his arms spread in good cheer.

"Larry David! Larry David's come by," Bill says shaking Larry's hand.

"This is fantastic!" Larry exclaims.

"Isn't that sweet," Bill barely gets out.

"Ah come on," Larry interrupts.

"I knew *they* were coming," Bill says pointing to two of his comic friends in the room. Larry greets them; handshakes are exchanged. Their conversation continues.

"That's a surprise. You know that was very sweet of you."

"You know, absolutely, absolutely. And John DeBellis says hello— and to wish you good luck."

"I love him. I did my first gig with him. How's he doing?"

Suddenly, Larry's face freezes in shock. "You don't know?"

"Don't know what?"

Larry looks around at the other guys. There's no response. It takes few seconds for him to respond.

"Uh...uh...oh shit!"

"What?

"Uh...he's got...he's got cancer. Pancreatic cancer! You didn't know that?"

Bill starts to laugh. "Oh this is your...that's funny, but this..."

"No," Larry insists as he turns to the others. "Did you hear it? Did you know?"

Ron Zimmerman (one of Bill's comic friends) nods his head, yes, he's heard.

"Oh my God," Bill says realizing Larry is telling the truth. And he's visually upset.

"It's such a shame," Larry sadly murmurs.

"*This* is the moment you choose to tell me this?" Bill groans eyeing his watch. "I'm going on in like two minutes, Larry. Like two minutes I got to go on!"

Bill rises from his chair.

"Did I screw things up?" Larry innocently asks.

"No…no…why telling a performer right before he goes on that a close friend is dying, why would that be?" Bill snarls.

Larry sheepishly replies, "He's still got a couple of months."

"It's you Larry!" Bill shouts.

"You asked me how he was," Larry argues, playing the victim.

"They knew apparently," Bill says looking at his friends. "But they didn't choose this moment to tell me because they're not selfish!"

"I'm not selfish! I came down to wish you luck. How am I selfish?"

"You are the man who glorified selfish in America. What was Seinfeld? What was your show? It's about glorifying selfishness. That's what's wrong with this country. Selfishness. Yes, Larry you did that! You ruined America," Bill barks.

A production assistant peeks in, indicating it's time to go on. "Okay," Bill acknowledges.

"I'm sorry, I didn't know it was going to screw you up. I wouldn't have said it," Larry insists.

"That's alright. Be a dick for me at this moment!" Bill retorts as he turns to leave. "Thank you, Larry. Thank you so much. Fuck you!"

Bill exits leaving Larry talking to himself, trying to figure out what he did wrong.

The next morning I received a wake-up call from my ex-wife who thought I was dying. Half asleep I screamed, "Larry said that on HBO and you believed him? It was LD. You know him for almost thirty years! He's like a brother! If I were really ill he'd never say that! Then it wouldn't be as funny!"

Neither LD nor Bill warned me about the bit, which made it funnier to me. They didn't have to. They knew that I'd love it. The week before, LD had done me a huge favor and I wanted to repay LD. I was unable to think of what to give a multi-millionaire, but I knew exactly what to give the ultimate hypochondriac. I had a notary public witness a letter I sent to Larry willing him all my body parts. So who cared if the world thought I was dying or even dead and cremated—my brother comics and I thought the whole thing was hilarious and to our group that was really all that mattered.

As of this writing, I am not dying, nor do I have, or ever had cancer, or even had to use Viagra. But before any of that happens, I figured I'd better write it all down. The stories and memories of a period in time, like no other, spurned a close bond that is still unbreakable, even when one's premature demise is used as fodder on national TV. We belonged to a unique group who, more important than even loving each other, understood each other and for a certain time in our lives found a place that was custom made just for us!

"My parents didn't think being a comedian was a career. They thought it was like I was learning to whittle. 'He'll just go through this. He'll move on to lanyards and sailing and things like that, right?' But I knew from the first time: I'm doing this for the rest of my life."

-JERRY SEINFELD

A Made Comic

In 1976, I was in my early twenties; my bald spot not yet a reflection in someone's eye. Up until then, I had done all the things comics do to prepare themselves for the "life"—I had a childhood filled with pain and disappointment.

Before starting a trek across the country in my Dodge van, I returned home from school in Boston when a friend set me up with a blind date. She was actually very attractive, if you're the type who use X-rays as pin-ups. She suggested we go to the Improvisation since she only lived a few blocks away… in Hell's Kitchen. It was a dangerous area. The second it turned dark, hookers appeared on every corner of Ninth Avenue, networking, handing out their business cards—little square packets that looked like foil-covered raviolis.

After squirming through the Improv's narrow entrance, its walls covered with black and white photos of comedy and show business greats performing, we entered the showroom—a dark cavernous place, filled with so much smoke that roaches died of lung cancer.

The club squeezed in about three hundred people without breaking too many ribs or leaving the "bridge and tunnel" girls' fake eyelashes stuck to the walls. No two chairs matched and each table varied in height—cockeyed from matchbooks wedged under their wobbly legs. The only wall free of layers of black oily paint, gum and torn sections of wallpaper was the famous exposed red brick wall behind the stage, where the *Improvisation* sign rose above most of the comics' heads. (A short breed, the average height of a comic is considered kneeling.).

The stage wasn't much bigger than an airplane's flotation device, and rested in the left corner of the room near the emergency exit, which comics often opened to punctuate a joke or an ad lib. Leaning against the outside wall was a piano so out of tune it sounded like it was strung with Bob Dylan's vocal chords.

That night, behind a microphone, worked a young fiery Elayne Boosler, the perpetually insane Andy Kaufman, an insecure, nervous Larry David in his green army coat and some brilliant comics you may not have heard of: Ed Bluestone, whose huge eyes widened with every

1

image-filled one liner; Larry Ragland, a black comic who did such a good Sammy Davis impression that one of his eyes actually looked like glass; and Bob Shaw, whose piece about a guy accidentally taking pills and distorting his speech was the funniest five minutes I've ever heard.

After a few too many drinks and watching my date get so drunk she thought the waitress was her yoga instructor, I felt inspired and soon had the waitress belly-laughing. I was so funny that she actually told me the date of the next Improv audition —that was the moment I realized I could incorporate my future plans of avoiding responsibility and be what I was destined to be: a standup comic!

"I would go to small clubs between auditions. I was at The Golden Lion and never got on. One night I said to the manager, 'How come you never put me on?' And he said, 'Because your material is shit and you have no personality.' So I came back the next night. I figured I'm nineteen or twenty years old and I could afford to hang out another twenty years. I'd outlast him."

-MARK SCHIFF

******

I was too nervous to remember how I got my audition number. The combination of fear, excitement and an argumentative imagination made me also forget I'd been sitting on a hot sidewalk for five hours. I only had another three or four hours left to eat, get more nervous and memorize my act, which consisted of jokes I wrote the day before and painstakingly honed while waiting in line. I spent a small portion of that time getting to know my fellow insecure auditioners, convinced the only thing keeping them from committing suicide was someone reading the suicide note and not laughing—or laughing and stealing the joke.

Now, the only thing more annoying than an always-on comic is a young comic. They pounce on you like giant Jehovah Witness mosquitoes questioning you about setups and punch lines. Around that time I started therapy and after a year, got in touch with my inner child. All I heard him say was, "Do you think this is funny?" A standup comic's inner child, even by the most stringent standards of pro-life

2

advocates, would not be mature enough to be considered a fetus. Comics are essentially children without adult supervision.

Almost all of the auditioners who went on before me either got no response or were heckled and humiliated into running offstage—and left to pursue another career or a better drug dealer. Normal people would find this painful to watch, but I knew I was a comic when the fewer laughs the guys before me got, the better I felt. Even a bad audience can be a positive thing—it gives you a built-in excuse for doing bad—and if you do well you can temporarily feel superior to your jealous peers.

I don't remember who the comic was before me, or seeing him get *the dreaded light* from the MC that signaled his time was up—or even seeing him leave the stage alive. I just remember this coal black room with flashes of color from peoples' clothes, an unusual amount of coughing and being drawn to this bright white light surrounding the stage as if I had died and was going through this tunnel to stardom. Little did I know that for most of us, the "star" in stardom actually meant starvation. I found myself standing before a microphone, struggling to get it out of the wobbly stand, my jittery hand causing it to tremble more than my leg. My eyes blinded by a spotlight, seeing only blackness, were barely able to pick out tables filled with the enemies' daring faces. I had crossed the threshold into Comic's Hell— the first time on stage before a paying audience at the famous Improvisation—at the mercy of my jokes—jokes that hadn't even made the transition from napkins to real paper.

"The very first time I did standup, I was a freshman in college in 1974. I did four minutes. I got two laughs. That's about a joke every two minutes. Now it's thirty years later and it's about the same ratio. I'm very proud of that."

-PAUL REISER

I remember my first line getting a laugh, then came a few others before walking off to the customary applause and feeling of nausea. It seemed like one of those times in life when the action doesn't merit the response—like putting on a condom after you lose your erection. The nausea quickly disappeared, replaced by a taste of the "life." There was no turning back. Not only had I been bitten by the standup bug, I was infected—my body was ravaged by future setups, punch lines, toppers, savers and of course, excuses. I am a standup comic—hear me say, "It was a terrible audience!"

I didn't pass the auditions that night, but that didn't deter me—nor prevent me from writing a suicide note just in case I never passed, or passed and was unable to write any more jokes. I heard on the audition line that the club owners wanted to see you a few times before making you a regular because it usually took several auditions to lower the young comic's self-esteem far enough to make him completely subservient to the sadistic whims of the all powerful MC. This brings us to the night I became a "made" comic and deemed a regular at *Catch a Rising Star*.

My audition number was handed to me by Terry Columbo, an Italian Hannibal Lecter, his thick neck surrounded by chains made of gold, bright enough to give you sunburn. Again I waited for what seemed like hours, which in reality was hours, but this time I actually had written a few jokes that had gotten laughs from coffee house audiences.

At the time, the best and most famous MC in New York was Richard Belzer, who thrived on verbally assaulting the audience, and putting fear into the comic's blinking eyes, making us feel even inferior to mimes. I was on my way to the bar, when "The Belz" himself, who wasn't the MC that night, but was dressed completely in black (always ready to attend the funeral of a young comic, I imagined), turned to me and said, "Hey, kid, you wanna buy a joke?" I didn't need to buy one, nor did I need to chance making an unfunny response to The Belz, so I gave him what all comics want: a laugh, then quickly turned to the bartender. I had escaped with my comic life, which The Belz, with his razor sharp wit could destroy in less time than it takes the MC to give you the dreaded light: *You're time is up, get the fuck off!* How many standup comics does it take to screw in a light bulb? One, but he'll only change it if it's the light to get the comic before him offstage...

About an hour later, I went on stage, stumbled through my graded-on-a-severe-learning-curve "A" material, and got a few good laughs from the bloodthirsty crowd. The hostile Monday night audition crowd was mostly from Jersey and the outer Boroughs. The men dressed to match the hair on their chests and were loud, rude and so drunk they lacked the coordination to clap—a few not yet used to the freedom of having their handcuffs removed. The women's clothes shined like neon signs and their perfume was invasive, if not toxic. That night, my biggest laugh came from this joke: **"I asked my father if I did certain sexual things by myself would I go blind? And he said**, *Yes, because if I catch you I'll poke your eyes out."* It wasn't exactly Shakespeare, but who cares, he's dead and I'm alive (at least at this writing).

As I walked offstage and into the bar, Bob Shaw, the MC—the comic with the funniest five-minute piece ever—caught up to me and said, "John, you should be doing this for a living." I didn't know what to say, but this wasn't the time to do the old standup standby and laugh. Slowly, words spilled out of my parched mouth. "Did I pass?" Bob smiled and said, "Yes, come in tomorrow night." Before I could get out the first of a thousand "thank you"s, the next act left the stage. Bob quickly turned and ran into the showroom, his ponytail smacking me in the face—an unintentional symbolic gesture preparing me for my first year of standup comedy.

Meeting My Peers

"I went to the club and I couldn't believe it. There were twenty or thirty guys just like me."

-BILL MAHER

Top row: Larry David, Rebecca Reynolds, Elayne Boosler, Bob Shaw, Richard Belzer. Second Row: John DeBellis, unknown.

The next night was a rainy, comparatively quiet Tuesday at Catch. I was told to come in late because if I made it on, it would be towards the end of the show. Around eleven-thirty (the weekday shows started at ten-thirty), I sheepishly walked into the club, the newest regular. Unlike the Improvisation, which was darker than a Bronx shooting gallery, the bar at Catch was bright and brothel-gaudy. On one side, there was a long green wall covered with head shots of comics and singers and on the other, a long, Mafia-black bar that loomed like an evil reef waiting to cut the skinny stage legs off of a new comic asking for cab fare.

6

Not knowing where to go or stand, I walked up to the bar and ordered a Coke. Before I could ask what was expected of me, Elayne Boosler walked over and told the bartender I was a new regular—which meant the soda was free—and introduced herself. I've always found meeting celebrities awkward. They know you know who they are, but feel it's the polite thing to do. It would be like Jesus ripping a hand off the cross, leaning down to shake your hand and saying, "Hi, I'm Jesus Christ, you know, the Son of God? I'm a little tied up right now—what do you say we talk in three days?"

Speaking of a god of sorts, when I was first at SNL, I was called into an office where three people were watching performers' tapes. One of them was Woody Allen. I stammered my way into the room dressed in a wrinkled shirt with a large coffee stain. Before formal introductions could be made, Woody Allen stuck out his hand for me to shake and said, "Woody Allen." Momentarily paralyzed by the surprise of meeting the greatest comedy mind ever, whose humble and sincere demeanor made the moment even more surreal, I shook his hand—mentally commanding every sweat gland in my palm not to emit fluids. I tried to time the break-off-the-handshake perfectly, so I wouldn't hold on too long for him to think I was a potential stalker, or too quickly for him to think I found him physically repulsive. Happily, the handshake ended time appropriate, with both of us breaking simultaneously. But suddenly the ball was in my court and I had to say my name. Not wanting to withhold any secrets from my idol, I considered telling him my full name, John Joseph DeBellis, but feared I might stumble over an extra word—and besides, what if for some unexplainable reason we became chummy and he decided to call me J.J.? I hated that nickname. Yet how could I tell my hero never to call me that—even if we *were* best friends?

"John DeBellis...n-n-n-ice to meet you," I finally stuttered. He smiled. Yes, Woody Allen smiled and replied, "Nice to meet you, too." Then, I scurried over to an empty seat, which thankfully had arms I could grab onto to keep me from melting onto the floor. I spent four hours in the same room with Woody Allen, listening to his critiques. One of those tapes turned out to be of Gilbert Gottfried. Woody thought he was hysterical, which he absolutely was, but he also thought he was a Cherokee Indian. I didn't dare correct him. How could I tell the master that Gilly was not an American Indian, but just a Jewish kid from Lower Manhattan? After four hours (I would have stayed for several weeks without food and water if Woody had stayed), he said, "Goodbye," and left. A few minutes later, he returned to get his Yankee hat he left on the coffee table. He excused himself for standing in front of me to pick up the hat and once again, said, "Goodbye, nice meeting you." I repeated his words exactly—you can't improve on genius.

After Elayne introduced herself, she said she'd try to get me on stage. Apparently she'd been in the audience during one of my auditions and I made a positive impression. She was called on stage to introduce the next act, which saved me from trying to make coherent small talk. I stood at the bar by myself, sipping my Coke, not knowing the extent of the free drink perks and if it was transferable to alcoholic beverages. I felt like I just walked into an A.A. meeting drinking an open six-pack and smoking crack. I thought everyone was staring at me, thinking, *how dare that imposter come into our home.* Just before Elayne returned after introducing the next act, another comic approached me, holding out his hand. I shook it, but this time I needed to be introduced. "Glenn Super," he said. I think it was Glenn's quick smile that disarmed me, plus the fact that I didn't know he was a comic. Apparently, Elayne must have told Glenn I was a new regular. We spoke for a while, lasting longer than most of my first conversations with anyone, except maybe a shrink, because soon we got around to talking about baseball, which meant the Yankees.

Before I even had a chance to think about it, Elayne said I was up next, which was pretty immediate, because the act was about to leave the stage. Maybe she planned it that way so I wouldn't have time to worry about bombing. I don't remember much about my first set at Catch A Rising Star—I was too traumatized to know whether or not I tanked in front of the two customers left in the room. I vaguely recall getting on stage and telling a few jokes, getting a few chuckles and walking back to the bar hoping they wouldn't kick me out or tell me never to set foot in any comedy club again. I didn't know it at the time, but several comics had been sitting in the back of the room watching my set. As they came out, Elayne Boosler introduced me to Larry

David, David Sayh and a few other friendly faces whose names I can't remember. I later learned that it usually took a while for new comics to be welcomed into the comedy circle, but word had spread about my writing ability, which gave me instant credibility. (Yes, I was the man who wrote the "poke your eyes out" joke). It's not that comics are an unfriendly bunch, it's that there are very few places where they feel like they really belong—besides a diner at 3 a.m., hovering over a craft-service table or long-term therapy—so they are very protective of their domain. I hardly spoke that night, but I hadn't laughed so hard since I heard about my Uncle Pauley pretending he was deaf and insisting his Miranda rights be read to him in sign language. Money can't buy you love, but a good laugh can buy you a few moments when you actually feel loved.

Although I was to become close friends (which he will probably even deny on his headstone) with Larry David, my first impression of him was that he was different in a way I couldn't put my finger on, but if I could, Larry would make sure I first wiped my hand clean. He spoke in a strange rhythm, sort of a cross between Jackie Mason and Mr. Ed, and the questions he asked were offbeat—it wasn't so much his subject matter as it was his unique phrasing and unchecked directness, which at first hid his remarkable intelligence.

David Sayh, with his *I dare you* twinkling blue eyes and his quick smile, was one of the few comics who did well with women, especially during his almost daily separations from his (now ex) wife. On the night of one of their worst fights, I called and spoke to his wife, who informed me that David had once again left for good. When he returned the next day there was a huge sign on the door that said: "Fuck You David" and on the bottom, in small letters, "P.S. John called."

About thirty minutes after my debut at Catch I met comedian (to this day one of my closest friends) Bobby Kelton, who had these small bags forming under his eyes, not quite big enough to be considered carry-ons. At some point he had the bags removed by a plastic surgeon cousin. He came into the Improvisation carrying his new de-bagged headshot and proudly replaced his old eight by ten glossy. Later, while he was doing a set, I used all the skills I'd learned in art school and drew bags beneath his eyes. For years he couldn't keep a bright-eyed

9

head shot up for long—soon I'd come along and add back the bags. Larry, Bobby and I became inseparable (trying to spell "inseparable" reminds me of why Larry and Bobby would never let me play Scrabble with them). To this day Larry yells at me for my bad spelling. I wrote an article for a magazine, which involved LD and when he read the final draft he screamed out at me, "How the hell can you let a piece go to anyone like this!" LD is a lover of words and very precise. I also love words. I just don't love the letters it takes to spell them.

Larry, Bobby and I spent most of our offstage time together talking comedy and baseball and arguing/debating some inane issue such as: 'Would George Washington rather have had a bridge or a tunnel named after him, and if he preferred the latter, would it have been the Holland or Lincoln tunnel?' If you ever witnessed the three of us ordering, you'd think that we were imitating Congress trying to pass an omnibus spending bill.

I also became good friends with the first comic I met that night, Glenn "Mr. Bull Horn" Super. Glenn was a ball of energy, but unlike most hyper comics who spin off in more directions than a speeding ballerina, he actually knew where he was going and went there without mimicking Peter Falk's serpentine in "The In-Laws." If I did a clinical study of comedians, I bet 90 percent of them suffer from Attention Deficit Disorder; the other 10 percent probably wouldn't be able to concentrate long enough to finish the test.

Glenn died in 2001 of cancer, two or three days after 9/11. I visited him the day before he passed away. Lacking strength, he hadn't shaved for several days and his dark scraggly beard made him look Middle Eastern. One of the last things he said to me was "John, if I live a couple of more days, I'm going to be arrested as a terrorist." I laughed, but I wanted to cry. Perhaps crying is what truly is at the core of every comic's laughter. I miss Glenn and will always remember him the way most comics want to be remembered—using his last few breaths to get a laugh.

When the show at Catch A Rising Star was near its finish, the substitute MC took over. Elayne would pick out a comic out of a pack of new standups starved for stage time and who didn't mind working to a sole audience member too drunk to know his table from his chair.

Elayne then joined my new comic pals and me at the bar when Richard Lewis walked in. She introduced me to Richard, who, I was shocked to find out, had heard about me from Bob Shaw. If Bob saw a comic he thought was funny, like most comics back then, he spread the good word, instead of today's breed, bent on finding fault in other comics' material, delivery, persona, temporal lobes or Facebook photo. After a few laughs, Richard asked if I wanted to go to the Improvisation to meet the manager/part owner, Chris Albrecht. At first I suspected that he'd heard I had a car and just wanted a ride, but when we got to the club, Richard was true to his word—or words—comics don't ever say just one word. They tend to stretch a yes or no answer into a filibuster.

Over the next several months, I spent many nights driving Richard from Catch to the Improv and then home. Sometimes, on the ride to drop Richard Lewis off, Rick Overton, who lived near me, would join us. Rick, at that time, was a member of the comedy team Overton and Sullivan. Some people see the good in everything, or the bad in everything. Rick, (very much like comic Uncle Dirty), saw everything in everything, meanings within meanings, that to the novice human would be meaningless. He could be curious, serious and absurd all within the same expression. He was generous with his laugh, which was full and leaped out of his mouth like it was being freed. While Larry David, Bobby Kelton, Bob Wuhl, and I would be in the bar arguing about sports or who would be a better liver donor, Rick Overton could usually be found outside doing some kind of martial arts with sticks that made him look like an orchestra conductor having a psychotic break.

Richard Lewis, on the other hand, was more complex, an incongruous mix. He was compassionate, understanding and quick to help a young comic, yet his elusiveness suggested he was temping for himself. Even as Richard arrived at a place, he gave you the feeling he was leaving, or even worse—that he had to get out of there before it exploded. He was as naturally funny as he was neurotic. Because of his good looks and quick wit, unlike most of us skittish comics, he had no problem meeting women. He was also helped by his full head of black shiny hair that obeyed his comb rather than committing suicide like my follicles. The girls he brought to the clubs were so beautiful that none of us could imagine being with anyone so gorgeous unless we unfolded their picture. If Freud didn't roll over on his couch trying to figure out Richard Lewis's billboard-sized neuroses, he'd fall off fantasizing about his girlfriends.

I don't remember what we talked about on that first night, but I did discover I could drive in the fetal position. Richard noticed my odd posture and a few weeks later suggested a therapist he thought might at least help my driving form and his safety during future free rides. His name was Alan Lefkowitz and he became known as the comic's therapist, which meant he had to field calls of desperation at strange hours, had a noisy waiting room that resembled a club's nightly lineup, made very little money and had a shortened life span. I was a little hesitant about seeing a shrink. When I was in art school, I had a few sessions with a nasty shrink who suggested that being a man was just a phase that I was going through. Little did I know he was right—I gave up my manhood to become a comic—or rather, a perennial adolescent.

My soon to be shrink, Alan Lefkowtiz, had the greatest explanation of why childlike introverts, such myself, became standup comics. He said, "Comics are counter-phobic. The thing they are most afraid of in life is *getting laughed at,* so by going on stage, they are taking control, making people laugh when they want them to laugh.' They turn the dread of humiliation into power and love, or at least the possibility of a date. I guess he was right. As a kid, the first person I made laugh was my Aunt Virginia. It was then that I realized I had power, real power— the power to make her lose control of her bladder. The show I performed for her always ended the same way: with a standing ovation—sort of—she'd rise, shrieking "Stop it, Johnny, I'm gonna wet my pants," and rumble towards the bathroom. I was eight at the time, and my Aunt Virginia was, well, it's not polite to tell a woman's age, so let's just say she was two hundred pounds, but looked one hundred and ninety—okay, one ninety-five, kids tend to glamorize things. It was there that the roving standup germs found a new host and spread through me, controlling my every thought, producing an itch whose only relief was to get laughs.

For years I've heard people say standup has to be one of the hardest things to do. From the outside looking in it might seem that way, but for a comic the hardest thing to do is *not* be a comic. The showcase clubs gave us the opportunity to be who we were, despite whom we were, and to do what we loved to do every night. Sure there were nights you didn't get on, nights when the MC put someone on twice instead of putting you on once and nights when your performance was so embarrassing you were taken off the organ donor list. But you got over it because your comic buddies' laughter refreshed your standup soul, trivializing your individual set and making you feel like you were an important part of the bigger funnier picture. There would be a half-decade of going home to an empty unmade bed, listening to what seemed like an eternity of silence between laughs, but as lonely as that was, I knew that I wasn't really alone. I was a single cell connected to thirty or so comics who at that moment were feeling the same thing.

That night Richard Lewis and I were on our way to Improvisation, which like Catch A Rising Star and eventually The Comic Strip was about to become an integral part of the best five or six years of my life. In a few minutes I was going to meet Chris Albrecht, who would become my first manager, first agent, a ground breaking TV executive, head of HBO and more importantly, the first pitcher on the Improv softball team. Sitting in the car with Richard, it really hit me. I was actually going to be a comedian. And at that moment, I felt like a brand new depressed person.

"I was a regular at The Comic Strip and had started hanging out at Catch. I was standing at the bar hoping Belzer would ask me to go on, but he kept passing me by. At one point he even called up the Improv to find out what comics they could send over. I still couldn't get Richard's attention. So I went into the closed off entrance way, where the pay phone was and called—and told him I was in the bar ready to go on."

-LARRY MILLER

The Law of Comic Relativity (and my childhood)

"I was an only child who suffered sibling rivalry from my imaginary friend."

-JOHN DEBELLIS

"John, a lot stupider guys than you went to college."

–MY GRANDFATHER

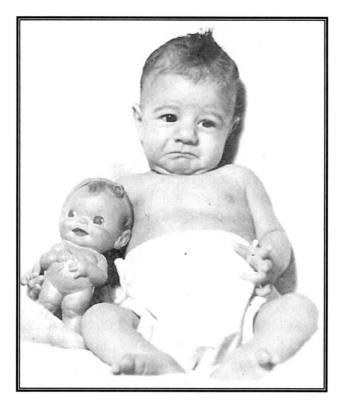

John DeBellis

Comics start their first days in the womb in competition with the placenta and then feel truly inferior when they are the first to be evicted. We feel like victims before we even knew we existed.

The majority of us come from what shrinks consider to be very dysfunctional families, on par with surviving a foster home run by cannibals—which would be tragic unless the child wanted to become a comic. Then, the special blend of toxicity, pity and neglect would be the ideal fuel for the standup's soul.

"I was afraid of my dad, and my mom was a close second. I got close to zero of the daily requirement of emotional vitamins. Aside from that, life was rosy."

-STEVE MITTLEMAN

I am the kind of susceptible soul that tolerates pain by misdirecting it into comedy. Like a good share of my comic brothers and sisters, my parents weren't purposely mean to me—although their *unintentional* behavior could be quite painful. The hurt inflicted upon me was mostly indirect, except for when I was beaten with a barber strap, hit with a wooden spoon and pushed down a flight of stairs—sometimes all at once. Sure, I may have had a few bruises and dented bones, but I never felt unloved, just *mis-loved*, or perhaps in need of body armor. Their love came to me in ways that had to be interpreted, unwrapped and deciphered like a World War II code even the Nazis couldn't break. As hidden as their love may have been, I knew it was there—like a soldier surrounded by unseen fallout after a nuclear bomb. Waiting. Wondering. Expecting the worst.

I was born on a snowy March morning with all the traits and instincts of a future comic: expecting to be spanked at any moment for not putting away the umbilical cord. When comics gets spanked, we not only feel the physical pain and guilt for having done something horribly wrong—we feel guilt for causing our parents to beat the hell out of us for our own good. I'm certain there's a formula for that kind of behavior and I've labeled it "The Comic Law of Relativity." It goes like this: the more violent (emotional or physical) the family abuse, the edgier the comic's material.

In my act, I say, "When I was an infant, my mother used to leave me home alone all day while she worked as a babysitter." A few lines later I add, "I always came last with my mom. She wouldn't breastfeed me because she said she needed the milk for the cats... and they were my neighbor's cats." Obviously, it's not how she actually behaved, but it is how insignificant I felt. In my family's pecking order I was not only the low man on the totem pole, I was at the bottom, buried underground, waiting for the dog to raise his leg.

My mother was never a demonstrative or physically warm person. When she did hug me on special occasions—such as when I was choking on a bone—she timidly held me like she was wearing a HAZMAT protective suit and I was a radioactive porcupine. Her behavior provided great fodder for my act: "When I was a kid my mother used to try to avoid physical contact with me. When she carried me around she used to hold me by my eyelids." Or, "Last night I made love to a virgin and when it was over she said she's had better." A great closing line, which came almost directly from my mother and got a lot of laughs Whenever I'd start to feel good about myself for some achievement, she'd always damper my temporary positive self-image by saying, "There's always someone better than you." And yet, when I did things bad she never once said, "There's always someone worse than you."

My father was not a vicious man, but often did things that bordered on sadistic. For one birthday he gave me a gas airplane that flew, but told me I wasn't old enough to play with it and packed it away in the attic for ten years. I wrote a line for my act that symbolized his "give and then take it away" modus operandi, but added a cruel touch: "When I was an infant, for my birthday, he gave me a swing set and then he put it in front of a brick wall." My father was also notoriously cheap. In my act, I said, "My dad wouldn't pay for my polio vaccine. Instead he had a kid with polio come over to my house and bite me in the arm." Or, "When I finally went to school he wouldn't pay for my books or anything. Instead he got me a job. Everyday he'd rent me out to other parents who didn't want to hit their own kids."

Larry David's father, Morty, on the other hand, was not cheap and was one of the nicest dads I ever met. He was known for never letting anyone pay the check. One afternoon I went to the Flame Diner with Larry's older brother Ken, and just as we were about to leave, Morty walked by and saw us through the window. He came in and said, "Hello," grabbed the check and left. Now as great as Morty was, like most comics, Larry, I'm sure, had a few issues with his father—and definitely his mother—that came out in one of his hilarious early lines:

"The only time I saw my father is when I saw his hand sticking out the door asking for more toilet paper."

-LARRY DAVID

Straight observation comics such as Jerry Seinfeld, Paul Reiser, Bobby Kelton, Larry Miller, Glenn Hirsch, David Sayh etc., for the most part, have underlying pain, but in most cases, it's not as virulent. And thus their acts, though still very funny and smart, are milder, evoking truths rather than a caustic imagination. Larry David's act was a peculiar combo of observation, one-liners and performance pieces. His observations were offbeat and full of pain and rich in imagination. From what I gathered from his and his brother, Ken, he had a childhood of inner torment, probably caused by his unconventional, bizarre thought process.

Comics, no matter what style, have parental issues that pointed them in the direction of comedy, which adds to my theory—the more violent the imagery in the act, the more deep-seated the comic's parental issues are.

Ed Bluestone was out to dinner with Elayne Boosler and her mother. Wherever it was it must have been chilly, so Elayne's mom asked Ed to give his jacket to her daughter. Ed's response: "Fuck you." As you may have guessed, I loved Ed's act. He was quick-witted and his sense of humor was dark. He had what I think was a landmark bit about doing things to upset the widow at her husband's funeral, like tell her, "I'm not sure, but I think I saw the body move." I consider him the father of the sick one-liners. He was also responsible for the very famous cover on <u>The National Lampoon</u> that showed a picture of a dog and gun and read. "If you don't buy this magazine, we'll kill this dog." I can only imagine what Ed's childhood was like, but Richard Lewis, the neurotic's neurotic has vocalized the pain of his own in both his act and his wonderfully revealing book, "The Other Great Depression."

******

The first eight years of my life I lived in a triple-level house, with my mother, father, both grandfathers, a grandmother and my Aunt Virginia, who (as previously stated) more than anyone was responsible for me becoming a comic. My mother was one of fourteen children, so the house was filled with daily visits of uncles and aunts, whose teasing made me feel like I was the punch line of Ed Bluestone's jokes. Every move I made came under adult scrutiny, their eyes watching, their minds willing me to drop breakables or trip over anything within the three dimensions of my body. And of course, I broke lots of things, including a couple of my own bones a few times. My clumsiness was observed with a magnifying glass—not unlike what happens on stage as an adult—only now, it's the critical eye of an audience. Somehow my life always played second fiddle to my neuroses. To most this self-image would doom a person to destruction. To a standup comic, it builds comedic character.

After eight years and a fall off a chair onto a cinder block that nearly caused my arm to be amputated, my family moved away from West New York (New Jersey) to Dumont, New Jersey—forty-five minutes and a million blades of grass away. To them it was the country, but to me it was an hour a week of lawn duty. After proving to a new batch of friends, which included my cousin Butch, that I wasn't just another dirty face that could actually hit a Wiffle Ball, I actually felt at home—like I almost belonged.

I started a new grammar school in fourth grade and befriended the other outsider in the class, Clifford Drakeford, the only black kid in school. He gave me my greatest birthday present—although it took me thirty years to appreciate it. Surrounded by brand new toy soldiers, sporting equipment and baseball cards, Clifford handed me an envelope containing thirty cents, all the money he had in the world. Sadly, Clifford moved away during sixth grade and I never saw him again and today if I asked my friend Gilbert Gottfried (cheaper than Jack Benny's character) for thirty cents, he would make me feel like I just asked him for all the money in the world!

I was a straight-A student. In fact, in second grade, I was the first in my class to get a hundred merits, whatever the hell that meant. In sixth grade, everything changed. Girls started developing qualities that made me overlook the fact that they were girls. Fantasizing about them was even better than beating my cousin Butch and his sidekick Jimmy Alterie in Wiffle Ball. During the next few years, I had intense crushes on several girls, but my shyness coupled with a self-image of myself being a shorter version of Quasimodo with small pox, made it impossible to speak to them, except through jokes. Jokes that may have ricocheted off my math teacher's toupee, but never actually landed me a girl—only lots of detention and bad grades. And while my friends dreamed about being ball players, lawyers, doctors, firemen and mobsters, I tormented myself over whether or not I had the goods to be what I desired most: a standup comic.

Even as a four year old, if I wasn't eating cheese, raw onions and drinking wine with my grandfather while watching the Yankees, I was cemented to the 12-inch, black and white screen, watching comedy shows like Jack Benny, Burns and Allen, Abbot and Costello, Milton Berle, The Show of Shows, Red Skelton and Phil Silvers. I loved the anti-establishment chaos of the Marx Brothers and was transfixed by the rebelliousness of W.C. Fields—even though I had no idea what anti-establishment, transfixed or rebelliousness meant. As I grew older, Sunday nights meant the Ed Sullivan Show, where I saw standup comedy performed for the first time and became addicted watching Alan King, Jackie Vernon, Bill Cosby, Phyllis Diller, Richard Pryor, George Carlin, Robert Klein, the Smothers Brothers, Lonesome George Gobel, Pat Cooper, Jackie Leonard and last, and always least, Rodney Dangerfield. Years later, as a teenager, captivated by a larger Ed Sullivan on our 21-inch, black and white console, I thought I'd seen God (wearing glasses) when I saw Woody Allen. He went from subject to subject seamlessly; his jokes were short, crisp, intelligent and layered with brilliant imagery. Then came the Tonight Show with Johnny Carson, who, was a devotee of standup comics—without a hint of envy—and because of the plethora of comics he introduced—was the true God of comedy. Aside from my old favorites, Carson introduced comics I'd never seen such as Don Rickles, Dick Cavett, Joan Rivers, David Brenner, Gabe Kaplan, Jimmy Walker, Freddy Prinze, Bill Dana, Pat Paulson, Professor Irwin Corey and more.

At one point during eighth grade, I had a huge crush on a girl. In an attempt to win her favor, I entertained both her and her boyfriend—and several other girls and their boyfriends—making up funny bits patterned after one of my favorite standups at the time, Bill Cosby. Being funny didn't get me the girl, but it *did* get her to notice my existence—well, to at least look in my direction anyway. Too shy to be the class clown in high school, I tried to be cool by doing what I thought was the second best thing— hanging out with guys who prided themselves on getting the lowest grades. One semester in Geometry I received a 36, only to lose my crown as the king of stupidity when my friend showed up with a 6 on his report card. Unlike some of my pals, I didn't drop out—or have a date for the prom. I improved my grades to a paper cut above passing, by acing my final exams. During the last two years of high school I quieted down, but still managed to be funny around kids I felt comfortable with, like my lab partner, Linda Diccico, who helped me blow up the chemistry hood.

I graduated high school 336th out of 338. The guidance counselors avoided me in the halls, as if seeing me put their jobs on the line. I knew what I wanted to be, but was terrified of failing, compounded by the thought of humiliating myself in front of an audience. Avoiding my dream after high school, I went to two art schools, the last being in Boston, and obsessed the whole time about becoming a comedian. Several bottles of Strawberry Hill or Boones Farm Apple wine couldn't stem the fear of going on stage. Again, my grades plummeted, only this time it was because all I cared about was making my hippie classmates laugh their pot highs away. Not that the grades actually mattered, since I worked at the school to pay my tuition and had keys to every room— which made it easy to sneak into files and change transcripts. Even that I did for a laugh—I changed a few lower.

It wasn't until I'd landed at the Improv and Catch A Rising Star that I truly felt like I belonged anywhere. My parents, who never pushed me to be anything other than what I wanted to be—which I always knew but never told them—weren't disappointed that I'd never become another Picasso or Van Gogh. I think they were just relieved I'd never be the next Andy Warhol. My father wanted to be a singer and my mother, a writer, so somehow I melded both together and became a comic—known for his writing ability and who loved performing before or after singers. In going against the grain of their practice of destroying my self-image, they finally encouraged me, which was unusual, as most comics' parents didn't understand the drive.

"I seemed like the loser of the family at the time. So to them it was just another thing I could fail at. Back then it would be insane to tell anyone that you were becoming a comedian."

-GILBERT GOTTFRIED

As I mentioned, I am an only child. Many comics are, and those who aren't, are in a sense only children on stage—trying to control what they subconsciously see as a hostile environment, salivating at the thought of blowing the room apart with laughter. During the first year or two I was on the mat more than I was a standup guy. On the nights after I bombed and my comic pals weren't around to inebriate my feelings in banter, I'd go home to an empty bed with a mind crammed with bad jokes, terrible timing and the blistering sound of silence, which was occasionally interrupted by an audience member shouting "GONG." I'd eventually fall asleep thinking I'd never make it and end up a waiter at Poachers or the Green Kitchen, two comedian hangouts, waiting on my comic friends.

A few years later, there were nights when I had killer sets and went home to my terminally empty bed with a mind flooded with laughs, applause and even occasional shouts of "MORE." After a few hours of reliving every setup, punch line and laugh and trying to figure out how my applause rated on the Richter scale, my comic soul would turn to fantasy—imagining a hysterical audience and the approving wink of

Johnny Carson. Then I'd ask myself, "If I'm really that talented, why the hell am I ending up alone again?"

Milton Berle once said, and I'm paraphrasing, that as a comic, there was a part of him that would always be alone, engulfed in a sadness no one could ever touch. I know that exists in me and I can see it in most of my comic friends. When comics laugh with each other, there's a certain twinkle in their eyes that rises from deep within that can only be shared and understood by another comic. And for fleeting moments, the door to that empty spot is opened and we can see we're really not alone.

The Lewis Lineage

"I went on stage, by the way, because I felt more comfortable with strangers than my own family. That's also why I'm in psychotherapy for the last 28 years."

–RICHARD LEWIS

"In a therapy session where I was finally able to feel at one with my depression, I told my shrink that I felt unsuccessful, unattractive and inadequate. He gave me a compassionate look, smiled and said, "John, on the negative side, those are terrible things to feel about yourself, but on the positive side, it shows that you are a very good judge of character."

– JOHN DEBELLIS

For comics, going to a shrink may have started with Woody Allen and will probably end when the earth collapses back into a black hole. In the seventies, you could count on one finger (assuming you weren't using all of them to shove cocaine up your nose) how many comics hadn't seen at least one shrink, once a day. On a walk from the Catch to The Comic Strip, I asked Rodney Dangerfield if he'd ever seen one. He replied, "John, I've seen a million Austrians." To my generation of standups, the big bang of the comic shrink universe started its eternal trail with Richard Lewis. After the third or fourth time I drove Richard home, is when he decided that I either needed a therapist or someone who knew how to tie a noose. As I mentioned earlier he suggested his therapist, Alan Lefkowitz, the Patron Saint of starving comics. Without Alan's help and insight, many a comic would not know who to blame their depression on. If you saw him, with his full beard, hippy attire and anti establishment attitude, your first guess would be that Alan was a former SDS member on the run. Richard was so well adjusted— compared to me, he was Buddha on ecstasy. When I found out that Larry David was now seeing Alan, I took Richard's advice. After all, I wanted to be a healthy human being just like them. For me, real therapy began with Alan. I once went to see a very famous quack that spent my entire first and only session with him with his back towards me, looking up at the ceiling and picking his nose. After he told the ceiling tiles, "Your time is up," I ran out of his office, vowing I'd never go back. The Lefkowitz standup line started with Richard Lewis, passed through Larry David, myself, then, onto Glenn Hirsch, Buddy Mantia, Steve Mittleman, Freddy Stoller, Joe Bolster— and more comics than all the one-liners delivered by Rodney, Phyllis Diller and Woody Allen combined.

Alan, like his clients and his religious beliefs (similar to "If there's an order to the universe, then God suffers from A.D.D.") are unorthodox. For me, and my comic friends whose entire financial empire, on a good day, could get an hour on a parking meter, Alan charged what we could afford. Most of us not only owed him our emotional lives, but also our ability to stay above the malnutrition line. I was put into group therapy—probably because my self-esteem was so low that being told I was worthless would be an ego boost. Except for Richard Lewis, me and one other comic, no one survived group therapy. Buddy Mantia and Brant Von Hoffman each only lasted one session and not because they were cracking jokes. Perhaps telling someone your problems and then having to listen to theirs is too much of a human experience for most comics to endure, (especially for two comics so handsome they could pretend to listen to a beautiful woman and never ever consider that she was pretending to have an orgasm).

The one who lasted in-group past the initial session, as well as several years in my group, was Steve "No Chin" Mittleman whose nickname reflected his lack of a jaw line. He had a solid, visible, jawbone added a few years later with plastic surgery on the TV show, "Extreme Makeover." Steve was tall and lanky, with muscles so weak they would be strained floating in zero gravity. His blue eyes looked like they considered crossing but lost interest along the way and his most prominent feature, his nose, divided and conquered his face. Yet, Steve was by no means ugly. He was an emblem of empathy. His mug was warm and friendly and all of his flaws added up to a face commercial agents thought was a perfect product foil. It lent instant believability to his self-deprecating act—and although girls often rejected him, they still found him attractive. If I had to be in-group with another comic, it would be Steve. We only competed over one thing—whose life was more pathetic. On most nights the downward spiral would stop at a draw. For example, there was a period when Steve had no place to live. The lease on his studio had run out, and I was living in a huge two bedroom I shared with another comic, Brant Von Hoffman.

My bedroom was gigantic by New York standards. It easily fit a full size bed, dressers, a desk and a couch. My usually unmade bed was wedged in front of the lone window, where I hung a shade so thick and dark it could block out the glare of a nuclear blast. Next to my bed was a night table that I saved from the city dump and a few feet away rested a dying couch that unfolded or broke into a bent bed where a person could lay on their stomach and almost touch their toes. When you entered the room, on the right, was an old wooden desk with a top large enough to cart away Pavarotti's body.

For a few months, while Steve pretended to look for a day job I let him sleep on the couch. He needed to rise at 6:00 a.m. to make it to the unemployment office in order to corner the premium minimum wage jobs. In art school, where aside from gaining an appreciation of cubism because it mirrored my life, I took a course in mind control. I never came close to managing it. For me it was like trying to slow down the blades of a blender by spitting on them. I was able to train myself to rise without an alarm clock. Of course, getting up at one in the afternoon made it easier. So I assured Steve that I'd wake him up without fail—and given my reliable body clock, I woke Steve every morning. Only every morning Steve would fall back to sleep immediately, while I spent hours contemplating my own stupidity—which didn't stop me from repeating the process each and every day. Obviously, Steve and I both needed therapy.

Buddy Mantia, a member of the Untouchables comedy trio, continued seeing Alan in private sessions, but on one occasion, Alan asked *me* to come into Buddy's session to help clarify some issues. Reaching a point of frustration, Alan turned to me and said, "John, tell him he's crazy!" So I turned to Buddy and said, "You're crazy." As I spoke, Alan opened the door and found Glenn Hirsch waiting for his session and said, "Glenn come in here and tell Buddy he's crazy!" Which Glenn, of course, did and then, without prodding, Glenn and I shouted in unison, "Buddy, you're crazy!" Alan motioned to Glenn to have a seat and told Buddy his time was up. Buddy and I stayed just long enough to tell Glenn *he* was crazy. Laughter bounced around the room until Buddy and I stepped out into the hall and decided it was, in fact, Alan who was crazy—for not charging us.

A few years ago I directed a film, which took so long to be released the distributors told me they were waiting for the Messiah to send back his R.S.V.P. The first day of filming we shot a scene with the lead character, played by T.R. Knight, in his first therapy session in the very room in which I had my first therapy session with Alan—who, still crazy, didn't charge a location fee.

Although it's probably hard to believe, therapy really helped—it enabled me to appreciate the daylight hours while sleeping through them. To most, I'm sure I seem as neurotic as ever, but I did learn to set boundaries with people—and sometimes myself. I've yet to figure out how to keep people from stepping on them. The biggest change therapy made was for me was to open myself up to a wider spectrum of life like going from a black and white film to hi-definition color.

Richard Lewis moved to L.A. and continued therapy for several years. Larry David no longer sees a shrink although he is now successful enough to afford personal sessions with every living descendent of Freud and Jung—and even Dr. Phil.

There's an old line, "How many shrinks does it take to change a light bulb? One, but the light bulb has to really want to change." It can now be asked, "How many shrinks does it take to change a comic's mind? One or maybe thousands, but only if the shrink can make the comic think he has a mind worth changing."

Richard Lewis and Alan Lefkowitz are responsible for thousands of functional comics who once had the emotional depth of a vacuum and now, not only survive, but actually thrive in a life spent in a slightly less narrow-minded search for laughs.

A New Regular

Chris Albrecht, Judy Orbach

"The Improv was the only major club that was run by no one over the age of twenty-five."

-CHRIS ALBRECHT

When Richard Lewis and I arrived at the Improv that first night we were greeted heartedly by part owner/manager, Chris Albrecht. He was friendlier, more cheerful and shorter than I had imagined—and younger. He had a devilish full-toothed smile that broke into an infectious laugh. To a comic it's the kind of laugh that even if it's not *your* jokes that provoke it, you laugh along as if every joke is yours, and your (comic) friends laugh as if every joke is *theirs*. Laughter spins like a whirlpool, but no comic realizes that he is not the center of attention. That happened most with my friend and fellow comic Glenn Hirsch, who we called Gleeb because an MC once mistakenly introduced him as Gleeb Hush.

Glenn Hirsch

Glenn worked the door at the Improv after he had lost his job at Barney's because he went into a dressing booth, sat down on a bench, pulled his pants down and read a newspaper, so people passing by thought he was answering nature's second call. One night Chris foolishly left Glenn and me in charge of the Improv. We proceeded to split up couples, seating them on different sides of the room and putting people at tables without chairs. Best of all, we set up a table on stage and seated a couple behind Joe Piscopo while he was performing. Typical New Yorkers, the couple watched the show and only got upset because sitting on stage made the service slower. Joe remained cool and did his normal act except when he had to pass drinks to the people behind him. Afterward, Joe, polite as ever, left the stage carrying a few empty glasses.

Our antics were nothing compared to the business Andy Kaufman lost while manning the Improv's phones. People would call up for reservations and Andy, using different accents, would transfer them from one of his characters to another until people hung up in frustration. Without a doubt, Andy Kaufman had the most unusual and the funniest act I've ever seen. I visited his grave a few years ago, and much like himself, his tombstone was modest; but his brilliance was immortal, tugging at my gut from beyond. I smiled, remembering the first time I'd seen him perform when I was a paying customer. I didn't know what to make of his act until suddenly, without reason, he made me laugh until tears fell onto my check, smearing the bar bill I couldn't afford. Now he was doing it to me again, only this time the tears fell onto his grave and I was glad I didn't run out on that check that evening.

On that first night at the Improv, Chris took Richard and me to the bar for a free drink (I don't think any comic ever paid for a drink at the clubs or left a tip). Chris, who had spoken to Bob Shaw and Elayne Boosler, almost immediately made me an Improv regular and told me to come in every night. To me, it was that night that marked the official beginning of my career as a real life, dyed-in-the-polyester, standup comic. It was through Chris as my manager that I got my first TV staff writing job on Saturday Night Live, which came just in the nick of time, because I lost the first job he got me when they said I wasn't allowed to give any more blood. As my representative he met Bridget Potter, then V.P. of ABC and later V.P. at HBO, who hired him at HBO—where he later became CEO and under his guidance created some of the best TV shows ever. Although our careers have gone in different directions, our hair has gone down the same path, which is now empty. Yes, our retreating hairlines have completely surrendered.

I began to suspect that I was going bald when I leaned out of my car window and was pulled over for mooning people.

The next night I decided to go to the Improv first. I met many of the same comedians and several new ones, whose names I mixed up countless times over that first year at the clubs. I never had the greatest memory. In fact, my very first memory was of me forgetting something. And I'm even worse with faces. When I look in the mirror my first thought is always, "Where have I seen that guy before?"

The Improv bar was always dark. The light bulbs that weren't missing had so much dust on them no light could pass through. Most of the comics sat in torn vinyl booths that ran alongside the windows, which like the windows, needed tape to keep from falling apart. Comics are like poorly dressed roaches. If you go to a nightclub and you want to find the comic when he isn't performing, look for the darkest area of the bar or backstage, and if he's not there, then look for the free food. And if the free food is in the darkest area, then you know the club owner is probably a former comic (or a descendent of Nietzsche's roaches). Comics, like vampires, are nocturnal; they wear lots of black and avoid mirrors, but unlike vampires, spend much of their waking hours in diners. You see, if a comic can't eat for free, then they'll eat at the place where the food *should* be free. We had such a place: Poachers. It served breakfast until closing at 6 pm. For ninety-nine cents and the ability to suspend your sense of taste, we got two eggs, toast, bacon and *fresh* orange juice made from concentrate (you could tell it was orange juice from the color, not the flavor). Oh, and of course they served a bottomless cup of coffee made from quicksand. When you swallowed the thick java, it tried to take you down with it. Believe it or not, the only kind of eggs they didn't serve at Poachers was poached eggs! But for 99 cents, you didn't ask questions. There is, however, a story which might be folklore, about a comic sending back his 99 cent eggs and being physically thrown out of the eatery (or, I should say indigestery). Poacher's was a place that the Board of Health was terrified to enter, but we certainly weren't afraid. We got our 99 cents worth, refilling our coffee cups and talking over one another until the java destroyed the walls of our ulcers.

When I stepped in the Improv that first night as a regular, I instinctively searched for a dark corner, but before I could find a place to hide, I was usually greeted either by Glenn Super, Ellis Levinson or Larry David and asked to join them in a booth. I sat in that same booth about four months later with Kitty Bruce, Lenny Bruce's daughter, who at the time was having problems with her boyfriend—the star of "Chico and The Man," Freddy Prinze. A few minutes into our conversation, we somehow, saw through a cloudy window that Freddy was about to enter the club. It was the dead of winter and a pile of comedians' ratty coats, which wouldn't have kept anyone warm if they were on fire, sat stacked beside Kitty. She didn't want to speak to Freddy, so she quickly buried herself beneath the odiferous garments. Here I was—a *new* comic—a species the amoeba evolved from— and Freddy Prinze, for some reason, decided to sit across from me and start a conversation. I was with one of the biggest stars in comedy, but instead of enjoying every minute and trying to extend the conversation to include myself so by its end I would be the new producer of "Chico and The Man," I was desperately trying to cut the conversation short so Kitty didn't suffocate. I was also worrying that if this mega star found out I was hiding his girlfriend under a pile of stinky coats, my career would be over – no more performing to drunks at 3 am. The coats wiggled a little, but Freddy didn't notice. Being a nice guy, he kept talking, trying hard to put me at ease and to entertain, while Kitty struggled to keep still—and keep her lungs free of the asbestos wafting from the torn seat's stuffing. Finally, Elayne Boosler who was the MC that night, called Freddy over to ask if he wanted to do a set. Freddy rose and walked into the room to access the crowd. Elayne, seeing that I had followed Freddy into the showroom like the train of a wedding gown, helped Kitty burrow out and escape.

Elayne was always helping young comics and giving advice, but she was tough on us if we started believing our own feeble excuses like "the fluorescent lighting isn't good for my act," or "I can't follow a comic who followed a comic who was kind of dirty," or "the crowds always boo on Mamie Eisenhower's birthday." She showed me the ropes, insisted I hang out every night, even during the early weekend shows, which were booked with heavyweights—comics like herself who'd paid their dues and were the best in the city. She explained there might be a cancellation and I could get a spot in front of a packed house—which would have scared both the audience and me to death. She told me to go on no matter how late, or how bad the crowd was, or even if there were only two people in the audience—and one was performing the Heimlich maneuver on the other. She said that stage time was the key and whenever possible to open the show, because the crowd was still cold and that's what it was like when you opened for a star on real paid gigs. Elayne was the first comic I ever sold a joke to, which was a huge ego boost because she was such a funny writer herself. I remember the joke, which I'd written in the bar: "You know you're getting fat when you step on your dog's tail and he dies." I know Elayne wouldn't mind me telling you that; she was always fast to praise and give credit.

It was heavyweights like Elayne Boosler, Richard Lewis, Richard Belzer, and Bob Shaw and stars like Robert Klein, David Brenner, Gabe Kaplan, and Rodney Dangerfield who told us that there was enough room for everyone and that helping each other didn't make us less selfish, which is every comic's birthright. It made us better comics, and made the journey ahead more fun; it improved the art form and gave us a good reason to stay up late.

Late Night Comic

John DeBellis performing at 2AM

"John... I can't go up. There's only three people out there...too much pressure."

-LARRY DAVID (I think he was joking)

"I'd hang out til three in the morning every night and sometimes I wouldn't get on for a couple of weeks."

-GILBERT GOTTFRIED

When I became a regular, my semi-regular spot was anywhere from 2 to 4am, a time when if you were lucky, you got a happy drunk or a cocaine addict whose snorts could be mistaken for laughs. The shows ran much later back then. For some reason, New Yorkers needed less sleep, or maybe it was because the streets were so unsafe that they waited for the muggers to go to bed before they left the clubs. Also working those hellish time slots were, in no particular order, my brothers in bombing: Larry David, Marjorie Gross, and Mark Bilgrey.

"It's 1 am and I called Lucien (manager of The Comic Strip) and asked if there was an audience and he said, "There's one guy, but he's a laugher". So I jumped in the car and drove to the club."

-PAUL REISER

My first Improv spot occurred at 3:30 am. I remember standing in the back of the room, watching an audience member intermittently laugh and doze off, and telling the MC, "When you bring me up, bump into the drunk and wake him up." When the MC finally handed me the microphone, I stared into the blinding stage lights until my eyes adjusted and I saw my audience: a table with four people in various degrees of consciousness and a smaller one with a loner who looked like he would still be mean and nasty if he were in a coma. Even though writing was my main strength, I'd only been writing for a month and had no idea what a premise, segue, or topper meant. My performance skills—if they could be called that—were abominable. I lacked experience and had no training—at least if I'd studied Acting 101 I could have impersonated a tree. I squeezed the mic tighter than a desperate man trying to stave off impotence. I tried to gather myself and look composed, but my legs trembled and my hand shook like I was on death row trying to use chopsticks to eat my last meal. I paused for a long time, trying to find a line from my act suitable for an opener at this hour. I finally revved up my chosen line. It emerged with less emotion than a cadaver to an audience who by then had probably forgotten how to listen in English. My joke paid off in a spattering of impatient body movements.

My next joke actually evoked a slightly better response: a yawn. During the rest of my five or ten-minute spot, I heard the screech of chair legs against the floor, the tinkle of ice against glass and a word that sounded like "boring." I finished my set and walked off stage to the beat of six hands clapping like they were shot full of Novocain. Disappointed and brimming with self-pity, I wondered if I could find another profession where I could use suicidal thoughts as inspiration, but my comic comrades guided me to the bar, making up all kinds of positive rationalizations that displayed their creativity. It was a horrible Improv debut, but the feeling of being one with my late night comic peers neutralized that. I bombed night after night, but they kept putting me up on stage, insensitive to the audience's feelings, pocketbooks and alcohol limitations—and especially to the comics who had to follow me.

"It was just awesome playing and devoting my life to learning and refining and growing as a comedian, while being miserable at the same time. Unfortunately, my happiness was based on if I got on stage, and how well I did...."

-STEVE MITTLEMAN

******

Four or five months had passed and I was working a late night crowd of three or four and I ad libbed, "At least the attendance here is higher than my sperm count." I got a big laugh, which enabled me to get a few more laughs...before I bombed. But you have to crawl before you can crawl faster. When being a standup comic was just a fantasy, the thing I feared most were the hecklers—those evil people who lurk in the audience like a pack of inebriated Jack The Rippers waiting to pounce on young comics, and rip their gassy guts out, line by line, shouting, "You stink," "Next," or worst of all, "Gong." As a newbie standup I quivered at the thought of being so badly heckled that I received the dreaded *get off the stage light* and heaven forbid, no cab fare home. Whenever Rodney Dangerfield came in to do a set, if the audience was rowdy, to gain control, he'd make one of us stand in the back of the room, hidden from their view, and yell out, "What do you do for a living?" and he'd reply, "Get guys for your sister." I unfortunately hadn't written any saver lines that could help me escape the barbs and carnage. So how was I, a guy whose comic believability at that time was the equivalent of a blow-up doll faking an orgasm, going to handle hecklers? Simple manipulation. Turn the audience against the heckler. It came to me one night while being foully heckled by a guy in the audience. I ignored the loud mouth and let him spit out a few more insults; then I stopped, looked around the room, then back at him, and said, "Sir, there are people trying to watch the show. You're ruining it for them." I wasn't trying to be funny. I just wanted to survive. The audience took my side and I was able to succeed or bomb on my own without anyone's help. It was a baby step on my way to learning to deal with hecklers. Ed Bluestone turned the audience on hecklers in his own unique and much funnier way. Ed would make some harmless remark to the heckler and then would turn to the audience and say, "I could have gotten hostile, but instead I dealt with the cocksucker."

It was a Wednesday night, and for some reason I went on substantially earlier than my normal 3 am slot at the Improv. The room was half full with people who were only half drunk, so I actually had half a chance to have a halfway decent set. I was actually doing well, getting laughs that weren't forced out of embarrassment, when I heard this scratchy voice from the back of the room saying "Why do you just talk about yourself?" How can anyone who's ever heard the words "standup comic" think that comedians talking about themselves is even a tiny bit unusual. I tried to ignore the heckler's ignorant comment, but the voice persisted, "So, how come you just talk about yourself?" Now, I was dumbfounded, which was about my intellectual peak at that moment and the voice continued, "Why don't you talk about politics or the world—something besides yourself?" The last comment brought up thoughts of old girlfriends, but his voice was too masculine. I didn't know what to say, which is how I usually communicated with women, but this was definitely a guy—an older man from what I could assess from his coarse voice.

I moved forward on stage, ducked under the spotlights so I could see my adversary. Standing in the back of the room was a fellow comic—who'd been on the Tonight Show, The Ed Sullivan Show, even on The Merv Griffin Show. He was a comic who I thought was very funny and who in his act, though talking about other things, related everything in the world back to himself... Professor Irwin Corey. He had wild, almost white cannibalistic hair—like a thousand reptilian tongues springing out in every direction. He was using his real, slimier tongue to destroy any seeds of confidence this young comic might possess sometime in the decades to come. I started to fight back saying clever things like, "talking about myself is funny," which wasn't funny at all, "a lot of comedians talk about themselves" and " I don't think I talk too much about myself," scraping the bottom of the barrel marked *Desperation*. And then, out of nowhere, an unintentional stroke of brilliance escaped from my quivering lips: "Rodney Dangerfield talks about himself." The mere mention of Rodney, whose talent made him justifiably a household name—a true mega-star—incited envious rage in the Professor, who blasted a primal scream so loud I couldn't hear my heart stop.

Rodney was not only hysterical; he was very kind to young comics. He'd always ask "John, do you need any money?" and I would lie and say, "No." How could I take money from a man whose comedy had already given me so much?

Rodney Dangerfield and Robert Wuhl

A very shy man, if a fan walked up to him and said he looked good, Rodney would nervously pump his shoulders, twist his head while fingering his shirt collar and say, "Pressure, pressure." He once did something for my mother, which truly touched my heart. She went to Vegas with her senior citizen girlfriends and noticed Rodney was playing at one of the hotels. She called him. He told her to bring her five girlfriends to the show and order whatever they wanted—he was paying for it. He sat them at a table up front and then in the middle of his act did a few jokes I'd written for him. I think one of them might have been, "I have such bad luck—the other day I went to the racetrack and when they shot off the opening gun, they killed my horse." If just doing the jokes weren't enough, he stopped his set, pointed out my mother and told the audience that her son, John DeBellis, had written those jokes for him. What a moment that must have been for my mother. Finally, she could be proud of something besides my successful friends. Then, after the show, he made it even better when he sat at her table and talked at length with the senior brigade—mostly about how to win at Bingo, I suppose. Rodney deserved all the acclaim and admiration he got and Irwin Corey deserved all of the envy he felt. I may have lost the audience but I'd gotten to the Professor, who might have just been having a bad night, which I now know to be the case. Recently, as a board member of the Comedy Hall of Fame, I interviewed him for their archives. Now 94 years old, he was generous with his time, kind hearted, appreciative of the art form—and the plights of young comics. He was also still very funny. His aged eyes hadn't lost their twinkle. Although I decided not to mention the night he heckled me, I ended the interview by asking why he never talked about himself in his act. "Because the world is funnier than I am," he replied, and then he asked if I had any pot.

The Len Maxwell School of Comedy

It was only a few months ago that I, a man who barely graduated high school, gave a lecture at Harvard. While praying the microphone wouldn't short out from my dripping sweat, I realized I was actually sounding articulate. Not only could I follow my own logic, which is usually like trying to find a contact lens in a tornado, but also the students stopped listening to their iPods and texting on their cell phones. Even the brilliant man who'd hired me found himself listening intently. What profound words captured the imagination of this Pulitzer Prize nominated writer? I was simply telling the students how to structure a comedy routine—one not thrust forward by the obvious inertia of a high concept, one, which included a beginning, middle and end.

No one can make you funny. They can only help you become funnier—or make you realize you're not funny at all. Writing jokes for me came as natural as hopelessness. During my usual comic's day, I'd spend four to six hours writing jokes about my pathetic life, hoping to get people to laugh—at me, with me, against me and maybe even during my act. I'm a comic. My goal is to universally get less respect than Rodney Dangerfield ever got and get paid handsomely for it.

Since my character was that of a loser, the worse I felt about things, the more avenues I had for material. After the first few years my writing sharpened, my funniness improved and my ratio of successful jokes blossomed. The accumulation of disappointing experiences added substance and attitude to my stage character, but unfortunately my act remained as unfocused as my pictures are on Match.com.

After performing my usual 3 am slot at the Improvisation one night, an older man—a few years younger than I am now but with thicker hair than I had then—called me over. His name was Len Maxwell and he was known to us as the man who introduced Woody Allen to his managers, Jack Rollins and Charlie Joffe—and for dating women half his age, but making up for the years by dating two at a time.

The only Broadway plays I could afford to go to, in those days, were the ones Len paid for. He treated Larry David and me (Lenny often said LD was the funniest man in the world—and he wasn't just talking about his act) to big dinners spiced with an overdose of his philosophy and witty banter. But the highlight of those evenings was hearing Larry and Lenny arguing, often over things they agreed upon. It was completely ridiculous and unimaginably hysterical.

I think Larry David and I formed a friendship, because we were both prolific at negative-obsessing, clumsy around women (I was told I had two left testicles), Yankee fans, but most importantly, we loved comics who were originals—comics who either started a trend or took it to greater heights. My style was more traditional in that my material consisted of mostly one-liners—short crisp jokes, using a minimum of words in the set-up and punch line. They were usually only a sentence or two long. My lines were offbeat, sick and took a moment of thought in order to get the joke. Larry's act combined different styles coupled with his insane head, which formed an act that was totally unique, hysterical to us comics, often misunderstood and every once in awhile would end in either a fight or shouting match with the audience.

I spent a lot of nights after the show at Larry's apartment, which was, just around the corner from the Improv, talking about our sets. Every week LD had a new theory on how to perform his standup: looking directly at a friendly audience member, not looking at the audience at all and, my personal favorite, not wearing his glasses so they appeared like a blur to him.

We often talked about writing. Larry told me about a few inventive methods he used. I remember one in particular, where he silently asked himself a question and then answered as if he were a different person. I, on the other hand, just ran things through my brain over and over again until I could actually feel a click or a buzz in my head and an image or part of punch line would emerge. Sometimes I'd start with a simple set up like "He's so ugly that" or "How ugly is he?" I'd write dozens, sometime hundreds of punch lines—some of them so bad I wouldn't put them on Joseph Mengele's tombstone—until I wrote either a whole joke or a fragment. Many times I found the punch line by simply combining fragments. Other times, completely different jokes appeared. Some days I sat for four hours without one funny thought materializing until the third hour, if at all. But even while I'm writing today, I often wonder about the crazy conversations that went on in Larry's mind.

Len ended up teaching me more about comedy than anyone. He was an intimidating presence even after he was confined to a wheelchair for a few decades—and continues to be in spite of his death. Seriously, if I were drowning, he could make me feel guilty for coming up for air. Len had black hair, as dark as the soul of a comic who steals your jokes and light blue eyes as intense as a Van Gogh acid trip. He had an air of authority, which he wore like it was tailor-made; I, on the other hand, wear confidence like it was tailor-made for someone else. I'm sure when and if Len talked to God, he gave Him advice. When he spoke, as painful as it might be, comics listened. When I first met him, I awaited my punishment; my lifetime ban from ever thinking I was funny, but instead was startled by the positive nature of comments. He told me he liked my lines and compared my joke writing to an old comic friend who initials are W.A. He also said my act was just a bunch of unconnected jokes that weakened their believability, thus making my character less dimensional than a noon shadow on white pavement. I'm paraphrasing here, which means I changed his words to make them sound less degrading.

The next day, I met him for lunch and he told me the basics of how to string together one-liners, which, on their own seemed unconnected. If I created a seamless story line, he assured me my act would sound conversational. He also taught me how to edit unnecessary words from lines and even lines completely out of lines and that jokes should be strong enough not to need an explanation later. Len was a ruthless editor. Years ago, I gave him a plaque that reinforced that belief. It said, "If Len was God he would have made us with one lung and one kidney."

His wisdom didn't take right away, like most things with me I have a learning curve so severe that I need a helicopter to lift me to its top. But it eventually stuck. Len told me that if you listen to people talk, conversations don't go in direct lines. People bounce in and out of the subjects and stories before returning to the story—or the point they originally started out to make. Len and I looked through my act and found three or four lines related somewhat in subject matter and made them the through line, spacing them out and finding a strong joke to tie in and end the piece. The next part was the most difficult, finding jokes that had nothing to do with the story and making them fit by going off on tangents

Below is a sample from a routine about a recent trip to Los Angeles. *Recent,* in comic talk, means it's a bit that's probably been in your act for a very long time, but you tell it like it just happened.

"I just returned from a business trip to L.A. To begin with, I'm not a big fan of Los Angeles. It's too slow for me. L.A. is the only place where boredom is considered an ambition. [L.A. joke]

As I entered a studio lot, I ran into an old girlfriend, who I hated seeing. When we went out, she used me the entire relationship! She broke up with me the minute she came out of the coma. [Girlfriend joke]

We started to talk and she told me she had given up acting and was trying to make it as a singer, which I laughed at.

She has the worst voice in the entire world, when she sings deaf people can't even look at her lips. [Bad voice joke] She was once hired to sing the national anthem... after sporting events to clear the stands. [Another bad voice joke]

So, for old-time's sake, she invited me back to her place for dinner, where she prepared a vegetarian meal for me. I don't eat meat under any circumstance. Not for any health reasons. I don't believe that animals should be killed for food. I think they should be killed for fun. [Veggie joke]

We had a few drinks with the meal and we started to fool around. It turns out she was on the rebound. The rebound! Her boyfriend died. He was an idiot-- he was a detective and he was after some grave robbers, so as a decoy he buried himself...but the robbers never showed up. [Idiot/dying joke)

So we made love... and when we did, she insisted on being on top... She said in case she wanted to leave... she didn't want to disturb me. [Sex joke]

Afterwards, she dragged me to a party. Like I said, I'm not a fan of L.A., especially Hollywood, which is the phoniest place on the planet. It's the only place in the world where you can see people in wheelchairs wearing jogging outfits. [L.A. joke, continuing the through line] Babies are born there with blonde hair and black roots. [Another L.A. joke] When I entered the house where the party was held, this weird guy immediately greeted me. Now in New York, weird is different. Guys will claim to be God. Well, this Guy was typical Hollywood. He claimed to be God's child from a previous marriage." [And another L.A. joke] "Do you know in L.A., when you make it with your wife, it's considered foreplay? [And another]

Anyway, after that, some other guy walked up to me and tried to sell me vitamin enriched LSD. [L.A./drug joke] I said no. I tried LSD once and it was the worst experience I ever had. I looked in the mirror and there was no change. [Follow-up drug joke]

Supposedly, we're all made in God's image. I figure in my case, it must have been shortly after he had a stroke. [Ugly joke]

So, anyway, I make my way to the back of the room. Now, I'm minding my own business when this old gypsy lady approached me. She asked me if she could read my palm, which I should never have done. She told me my love life and financial status was going to take a turn for the worse; and then she kicked me in the groin and robbed me." [Loser joke]

The bit goes on from there, ending with me being alone late at night in L.A., whereas now, I'm alone in New Jersey desperately trying to remember the L.A. bit.

Not all comedians use this kind of mechanics and joke style, (in fact, today most don't), nor should they. No rules are unbreakable and most are certainly bendable. Nothing is chiseled in stone, except possibly your grave marker, which by then you can't change even if it were written in chalk. But if it contains as many clichés as this paragraph, your will should stipulate your tombstone to be plowed over. The point is: it's okay to learn to do it this way, as long as you eventually apply your own style.

There were other things that Lenny preached that, at first, seemed as unnatural to me as not taking antidepressants. One was not to judge how my set was going or had gone, or to judge other comics by how the audience responds because the audience doesn't know. Now don't get me wrong, neither Lenny nor myself are anti-audience or audience immune. He was simply saying there are times when you are good but the audience may be tired, may have been blown out by another comic, may not catch comedic subtleties, or can't bend over low enough to see themselves in you. However, there are a few cases, such as the one I'm about to describe, where it's none of the above.

I was once conned by a few friends and the owner of the Baked Potato (the oldest Jazz club in L.A.) to perform while the band was on a break. My comic buddy, Vinny Marz, who would have been a giant of a midget had he been an actual midget, worked nights as the cook. He would feed me free giant potatoes that were actually potatoes, even though they were loaded with fried vegetables, chili peppers and enough cheese to clog the arteries of me and the two guys sitting close by. So when the owner asked me to do a set, I couldn't refuse without risking losing my potato privileges

When I reached the stage, the spotlights were so bright they could make a blind person see and a sighted person blind. Most Jazz musicians, I know play, for the pure love of the music or to dare each other to find the hidden melody, so seeing the audience would just be a distraction. For twenty-five minutes, I didn't hear a laugh, grumble, snicker or a cough. I didn't even hear someone complain they came to hear Jazz—nor an act that might cause them to dislike sound. I tried to convince myself the audience was either laughing at a pitch so high only dogs could hear it or they'd been vaporized by the lights. I may not have cared what the crowd thought of my act, but my sweat glands sure did. It was as if the water in my body couldn't get away from me fast enough—guilt by perspiration. After twenty-five minutes, I realized that no potato was worth that kind of humiliation. I left the stage to applause that was softer than the house cat's purring. When I got to the bar, my friends were laughing hysterically like they were in a time warp hearing me have a good set. About ten minutes later, their laughter faded to silent gloating grins and I asked what was so damn funny. The entire audience was made in China. They were there on some kind of junket and no one understood a word of English! So in this instance, Len was really right. The audience didn't know, nor did they care.

There were other times when I was bombing and the only laughs I heard were coming from disparaging parental voices in my head. Sure, I could have shouted out a few body function jokes or easy sex lines, accenting them with some choice four-letter lingo, but instead, I chose to go down with my ship. In Lenny's words, I was succeeding or (mostly) failing on my own terms, throwing caution and cab fare to the wind. Lenny, never let up on that point and pounded it into my thick skull like a full-frontal lobotomy delivered with an air hammer. To pander is to have lost. It's giving up on yourself and possibly the ability to dig deep enough to find your own special road to a destination you will have truly earned. Len also politely suggested in his definitive, absolute, unequivocal way, that if a line needs to be punctuated by profanity in order to work, then it's not a good joke. I saw Len's logic and to this day have never used profanity on stage, but there were times when I bombed and felt like cursing out Lenny. He nudged me into a specific direction, which enabled me to figure a few things out on my own. One is that if you shut off a cheap easy avenue to laughter on stage, your mind will find better, smarter and funnier words to travel on. I've also learned that when I write a joke and I actually laugh at my words, it never, ever, works in front of any audience. Most importantly, even if the audience laughs hysterically at every joke, it doesn't mean you were good. It may mean they are just an easy audience ripe for the kill or on laughing gas. Judge yourself on how you performed not on the result.

If some thought Lenny harsh, controlling, judgmental and self-aggrandizing then they missed that he was funny, generous, kind hearted and a good friend. He always told the truth (even if it was just his opinion), and made me work harder, helping me become much, much better than I ever would have been if he hadn't taken the time and energy to give me "His" all. To this day, whenever I write anything or come up with a clever retort to hecklers while on stage, I always wonder, "Would Lenny think this was funny? "

So the night I stood at Harvard with Richard Dreyfus, who I had the honor of doing the lecture with, and David Black, the wonderful writer who hired me and has championed my work, I brought Lenny with me in spirit, which was like having a guilty angel standing on my shoulder screaming into my ear, "It's the artist's job to educate the audience, not reflect it!" But without Len's challenges and knowledge, I would never have spoken at such a prestigious university and they actually liked and understood what I think I said. But what do they know? They're only Harvard students and David Black has been nominated for a Pulitzer Prize, only once. I, on the other hand, graduated from the Len Maxwell School of Comedy and can structure a comedy routine I'm pretty sure Len would approve of...I hope.

The First Year to Parental Bliss

All the heavy weight comics, club owners and several stars told me how difficult the first year of standup would be. For me, it was extraordinarily painful. First hitting me on the surface and then digging deep inside like I was being baptized in boiling water. Many nights the best I could hope for was earning a smile, and sometimes getting that from an audience member would turn out to be more difficult than talking a girl into coming to my apartment while the building was on fire. There was always a part of me that dreaded the thought of doing a set. After a bad show the night before, the fear of performing would cling to me all day long, weighing down every thought, turning negativity into hopelessness. During those first few months, I approached the stage tentatively, drenched in fear, as if I were going to dinner at a cannibal's house and bringing myself as dessert. Once I set foot on stage most of me was absent. My attitude was so apologetic I had as much presence as the invisible man's shadow. My timing was either too fast or too slow, and I said the set up after the punch line. Sometimes I stumbled over words. I scrambled them so badly they probably sounded like backwards hiccups. The silence after a joke seemed to last forever. I didn't want to say the next line. Instead, I wanted to swallow my tongue before it swung the rest of my ego—and me to the floor. I imagined murderous faces staring back at me as if I'd just sold their daughter into slavery—at a discount. My heart pounded against my chest like it was trying to push me over from the inside. I could probably go a month without drinking any liquid and there still would be an endless stream of flop sweat pouring over the contours of my face like white water rapids.

"The first year of standup was so difficult, after 3 weeks I ran out of flop sweat."

-STEVE MITTLEMAN

Sometimes I'd abandon my material or any chance of getting laughs and succumb to the voices in my brain shouting, "You're awful.

48

You'll never be a comedian!" At that point I gave up and just wanted to get off stage without getting heckled and find a place to hide in the bar—behind the friendly mobsters who hadn't threatened to kill me yet. The only thing that saved me was the fun we had afterward at the Green Kitchen. The camaraderie dulled the pain—enabled me to dream of the days when the negative sets would eventually turn into positive ones.

Three quarters of that first year ended on a low note, but every now and then I'd have a decent—or even a good set filled with more laughs than silences. Sometimes an audience member would approach me after a set, spewing compliments that pumped my ego until I realized he was either drunk or completely brainless; making me wonder if my target audience could be found at Lobotomy Anonymous meetings. I watched many comics struggle through that first year. The ones who stuck with it and went on despite one humiliation after another almost always ended up with good sets outnumbering the bad ones. I wasn't around for Larry David's first year, but for the first year I spent doing shows with him, it was like watching a rat find its way through a maze, racing forward, thinking it found a way out only to crash into a wall. In Larry's case the wall would have heckled him and been challenged to a fight. LD's learning curve resembled a zigzag with sharp rises and sudden drops. Some nights every piece glided along with the audience happy to accompany him on an outrageous ride. Sometimes that ride stopped abruptly—if he thought he saw someone's lips mouth a disparaging syllable or imagine he heard a chair's sarcastic squeak. In seconds his set would turn into something resembling a Nazi debate ending with only a microphone left on stage. I witnessed Larry, after being introduced, take one look at the audience and then say, "I can't do this," and walk off the stage.

I also remember when Larry reached a level of consistency – sets that contained long laughs and a few applause breaks. It was the first show on a Saturday night. He was doing his "Samoans aren't people, they're pancakes" bit. The audience laughed at every joke and nuance and LD kept taking it further and further to the edge of logic. His other pieces, such as "male kangaroos suffer from pouch envy," exploded and grew and branched off into something completely alien. I could actually see a smile on his face that didn't look like the result of a stroke. He still had inconsistencies, but they were at a higher level and even his shouting matches with the audience seemed, for the first time, less painful—even curable. He'd reached a level that seldom disguised his genius.

Mark Schiff was another comic who from day one had a funny, almost angry presence and needed time to find and perfect that correct persona. He'd launch irreverent sparks of comedy that were wilder than Don King's hair. But in a few years, Mark became one of the funniest guys around.

Gilbert Gottfried, seemingly, lingered in his first year for half a decade, perhaps because he was still in his teens when he started. Then he spent most of that time stuck as the last act in the show, usually designed to clear the house (except for other comics who stayed to watch his weird brilliance). His breakthrough came when he started to do his alter ego, Murray the Agent, whose squinty eyes looked inward, letting only his imagination connect with the audience. Gilly made contact by avoiding it all together. He took simple ideas and twisted them like he was wringing a chicken's neck until all that was left was hysterical pain."

******

"The first year wasn't difficult. <u>I was on a mission</u> and there was no looking back, unless of course, a beautiful woman was following me."

-RICHARD LEWIS

There were, however, a few comics who didn't find the first year particularly difficult. Aside from Richard, Robert Wuhl had an aggressive inner confidence that attacked the audience and barked them into laughter. His first year was condensed into a few months and by the end of his first year, it was as if he had been working for three. David Sayh's rookie year was filled with steady growth, landing him on The Tonight Show in what was probably record time. His first set on The Tonight Show was magic: a brilliant combo of rawness, innocence, street smarts and slick material—an impossible dream that became impossible for even him to duplicate. His second and third time on the show were good, but they didn't match that first night—it was a set so perfect that it preordained him for disappointment.

After two years Bobby Kelton left New York for Los Angeles. While in New York his growth as a standup was steady, but nothing that made us think he would soon be ready for a much bigger stage. Every six months, or so, he'd return to New York to work the showcase clubs. On his first trip back his material was stronger, his performance smooth, but what really made the difference was his confidence, which really showed in his relaxed stage presence. Very little, if anything, rattled him.

"One night I was on stage at Catch and some wise guy ran onto the stage, saying his friend offered him $100 to do it. I said, "As long as you're ruining my show you should spit it with me." The crowd roared and his friend walked up and gave us each fifty bucks. It was more money than I had made in 6 months."

-BOBBY KELTON

Less than a year later Bobby went from being an amateur to do the first of twenty-two appearances on the Tonight Show.

Steve Mittleman had the most amazing comic growth spurt I ever saw. During a group therapy session he announced he was going to enter New York's Big Laff Off, scheduled for broadcast on Showtime. I thought he had about as much chance of winning as I had of initiating a bidding war between two sperm banks. He wasn't getting any opportunities to work full houses, his sets were inconsistent—and often more painful than a circumcision performed by a blind moyle.

"When jokes didn't work, I took it personally, and the audience took it personally. They actually felt bad for me. You think I would've started getting sympathy laughs"

-STEVE MITTLEMAN

Seemingly out of left field, Steve became incredibly focused. On the first night of the contest he had a terrific set and won. We still seriously doubted that he could win the entire contest. Except for Rodney and Rita Rudner, I never saw any comic work with such tunnel vision. He performed two or three sets a night on weekdays and as many as he could get on weekends. At each level of the contest, he got progressively better. On the final night Steve was so confident it didn't matter if God Himself was backstage placing bets against him. That evening he reached comic nirvana. Every set-up led the audience astray; every punch line pulled the carpet out from under them. He had an amazing show—the kind comics could spend an eternity dreaming of performing. After struggling to put it all together for several years, in that short period of time, he went from an amateur to a true standup guy and suddenly worth a hell of a lot more than cab fare and free drinks.

I took Elayne's advice and hung out at the clubs every night, even when I didn't have a spot, knowing that there was always a chance a comic might not show up and they'd need a replacement At first, I sat in a booth at the bar pretending I couldn't wait to perform for a primetime audience and kill, while praying all the comics scheduled would show up. My anxiety quadrupled whenever I made the mistake of going into the showroom and seeing three hundred or so audience members laughing their heads off. I hadn't experienced anything close to that kind of response yet. Petrified of failing, I was grateful a more experienced comic was always present when someone couldn't make it across town on time. But as the weeks and months went by, I gained more courage and sat in the back room watching Richard Lewis, Elayne, Bluestone, Bob Shaw, Richard Belzer, Brenner, Klein, Rodney and all of the other heavyweights work full houses. I even saw, Barry Diamond, LD, Hirsh and Kelton do their first primetime spots and thought if they could do it, it didn't mean I could, but it also didn't mean I couldn't either. I'd finally grown a thick enough comic crust that even if I bombed I wouldn't become a casualty. Finally, after my first year, I got my opportunity for a primetime spot and it was well worth the wait.

I'd been performing standup at the showcase clubs for a little over a year and still wouldn't let my parents come see me. I told myself it was because I wasn't ready yet and they'd make me so nervous I would bomb. I also didn't want them hearing my material—which at that time was mostly comprised of difficult childhood jokes. Several comics, with totally different acts, had similar fears of disappointing their families.

"My grandmother was watching Bill Cosby and was going on and on about how funny he was and so talented. So I said to her, thinking this was my chance to impress her, "I auditioned for a show in L.A. and got the audition because Billy Cosby said I was funny." And my grandmother said to me in typical Jewish fashion, "Yes, but you didn't get the job."

-GILBERT GOTTFRIED

Alan, my therapist, ordered me to bring my parents to my show. He said if I didn't, not to bother coming back to therapy the following week. That should have been enough incentive for me to quit therapy, but I was at a point when I realized I was too insecure to overcome my defects by myself—and so I reluctantly agreed. I asked Chris Albrecht for the 9:40 spot during the first show on a Saturday night at the Improv, which was the best slot on the best night of the week. I explained why I had to have that slot. Chris knew my parents because at the time he was living with my cousin Cheryl and so he agreed without hesitation.

It was a nerve wracking week. Most of my shows proved mediocre and as Saturday night approached, my sets took a turn for the worse. I went to my comic friends for reassurance and advice, which was like walking up to a guy, who had just fallen off a twelve story building and asking him how to get over my fear of heights. LD, as usual, was an honest voice of doom. Jack Graiman said something like, "What's the worst they can do, cut you out of the will?" Barry Diamond cracked, "So you'll bomb, we'll still love you!" Glenn Hirsch relayed his own horrible fantasies of working in front of his mother. Glenn Super, however, was the lone positive voice. He had performed in front of his folks in different incarnations since he was a kid. He pointed out that

Chris wouldn't have agreed to give me the 9:40 slot so quickly if he hadn't thought I'd do well.

I awoke Saturday morning and had a breakfast of dry toast washed down by a jug of Brioschi (Italian Alka Seltzer) and spent most of the day in bed beneath the covers. I finally arrived at the club around 9:20, when the first act would go on and headed straight for the bar, thinking a few Bloody Mary's would give me some much needed courage. Chris saw me and started teasing about how good the audience was, how it would be my fault if I bombed and it would ruin the show since it was the best spot. Of course he was joking; trying to lighten the mood, only I wasn't hearing it that way. After I finished my second drink, I peeked at the crowd. Chris had put my parents just where I'd asked—where I couldn't see them. There's nothing scarier for a young comic than to see a friend or relative in the audience. I returned to the bar and while I finished my next drink, told the MC, Bob Shaw, to bring me up quickly because my parents were there. He suggested he use more time in between to give me less time to bomb and then, right before the act got off, he patted me on the shoulder and said I'd do fine—it was a good house.

The act exited and Bob ran on stage—and brought me up a second or two after the audience stopped applauding for the prior performer. Handing me the mic, he gave me a reassuring smile and left me there, alone, beneath the lights where my parents could see the child they'd raised in all his nervous grandeur. I greeted the audience and then went into my first line, apologizing for being late because I got a flat tire by running over a guy with a glass eye—and it resulted in an explosion of belly laughs. So did the next line and the next. Now, my nervousness slipped away and I became my material. Every hesitation, frown and ironic look was perfect and rang true—this was really my life and my life off stage was fake—just an anxious dream. The laughs built to rolls and not once did I fall into the pattern of thinking I couldn't do any better than that last line. My mind gave over to my character and the set was explosive. When I finished, the audience rose in applause. It had been the best set I'd done up to that point—still one of my best ever— which still amazes me since my material was not nearly as good as it is today.

As I ran off stage, the audience was still clamoring and clapping, some patting my back as I walked by. I flew to the bar, not believing I had done that great. Chris greeted me with a huge smile and my folks appeared, both of them glowing. I never thought I could cause that reaction in them unless I'd brought home something radioactive.

A member of the audience asked for my autograph, which completely caught me off guard. It was my first autograph request—and it happened right in front of my parents. Of course I segued straight into my shy, undeserving side and wrote: "Writing autographs makes me envious of illiterate people. Best wishes, John DeBellis."

When I walked into therapy the following week, Alan gave me a great big hug and a smile of infinite proportions.

"You knew I'd do that well," I said.

"Of course," he replied. "Your parents are too important to you. There's no way you'd let them down."

On that Saturday night at exactly 9:52 pm, my comic life had grown. I finally knew what it was like to kill an audience, like Shaw, Boosler, Bluestone and Lewis. Although I didn't repeat that powerful performance for a long time, since I hadn't really reached that level as a comic yet, it made me see what I could do and it was only a matter of working hard every day until I would soon be able to repeat it over and over again.

First Trip to L.A.

The first year of doing standup I lived in my parents' basement. My grandfather, an ex-mobster by trade, helped me build a room in the left corner of the cellar. We framed out a doorway and a window and made walls—insulating them behind dark wood paneling that went out of style before we hammered in the first nail. Going to the lumberyard with my eighty year old grandfather was not your typical senior citizen outing. He demanded I carry the door while he directed me to put it in the van—without paying for it. He also ordered me to grab a doorknob on the way out and then decided the insulation stacked on the loading dock was meant to be ours, too—all gifts from the lumber yard.

For some reason when my parents bought their house they built a second kitchen in the basement directly below the upstairs one. It had a refrigerator one generation past an ice box, cabinets riveted into the cement walls and painted surplus green to emulate an Irish battleship, and a stove so old it had to be lit with a flame thrower. The bright green Formica table was surrounded by matching chair cushions torn and wrapped more times than a mummy. The ceiling boasted a huge fluorescent light. If you managed to look up without burning your retina, you'd see it was squeezed between two water pipes that tended to leak now and then.

Moving back home after living on my own in Boston for four years and attending an art school whose rules were more abstract than the paintings, was not easy; especially when your schedule matched a vampire's—going out at 10 pm, getting home at 4 or 5 am, and sleeping long past noon in a dark cellar. My neurotic, pestering family made it nearly impossible. First thing in the morning my grandfather would try to wake me for breakfast: first, by stamping his feet on the floor above, then, by pounding down the stairs to the below sea level kitchen where he'd make breakfast while hollering, "Johnny, come on! Have some Rice Krispies with me!" When I didn't respond, he'd munch with such force, they snapped, crackled and exploded. If that didn't get a response, he'd hammer on my door with his cannon ball sized fist until I finally woke up. Even worse, my obsessive compulsive father, who woke at 6am for work, plodded into my room to make sure that not only were all the lights out, but that they still worked—by turning them on and off several times. Then he'd push furniture around (including my bed) to make sure nothing flammable was near any electric sockets. On his way out, he'd open and close the door repeatedly so it wouldn't stick in case of an emergency. Heaven forbid if I'd left my car unlocked. He'd bolt in grumbling about all the crooks living in the neighborhood, when the only one for miles actually lived with us. He'd rummage around my room tossing papers looking for my keys, making sure to wake me when he'd found them to tell me *where* he found them and *where* he'd leave them. My mother was the only sane one, although it took over a week to convince her you don't need hanging drapes and curtains in a windowless room. However, she somehow managed to convince me I needed a fresh bowl of artificial fruit on my elementary school desk every day.

This was the environment in which I taught myself how to write jokes on white-lined paper clamped in a ringed binder I'm sure I still have. Everyday I'd sit for over four hours trying to think of funny lines and after writing a few I thought might work, I'd dial a friend. Yes, I said and meant dial. The phone predated Prohibition and required nimble fingers to spin it clockwise ten times, connecting me with anyone lucky enough to have a modern push button phone. I'd badger Alan Zwiebel, Larry David, Bob Shaw, Bobby Kelton, David Sayh, Elayne Boosler and Richard Lewis, asking if any of the jokes were funny—and pleading with them not to hang up because I only had forty more to go.

As mentioned earlier, Elayne Boosler purchased the first joke I ever sold for fifty bucks. She was also my mentor on how to live the life of a comic, convincing me it was okay to go to movies alone during the day and more importantly, where to get the best food in New York City at 3 am. So as a result of her kindness, we quickly formed a friendship. A year into my cellar interment, Elayne said she was thinking of moving to L.A. Richard Lewis, Mark Lanow, and JoAnne Astrow (members of the Improvisation group Off the Wall and later, the co-owners of the L.A. Improv) had already moved out West. Ed Bluestone was also about to make L.A. his home, so as bad as I felt about losing friends, I knew spots would be opening in the NYC clubs. A true comic wouldn't hesitate trading a friend for a spot. The law of comic friendship = the better the spot, the better the friend.

By the time Elayne became a West Coast comic, I was getting better spots and was toying with the idea of moving into New York City. I put off the decision and decided to visit Elayne and a few friends in L.A. She suggested I stay at the Tropicana Motel, home of Duke's Coffee Shop, the best high cholesterol breakfast and lunch joint in town. Also the place where several hookers hung their wigs, not to mention the other needy people in L.A. that stayed out as late as comics—the junkies. So, being the obedient young comic I was, I followed Elayne's advice and booked a room for two weeks at the Tropicana, which at the time was one of the least expensive lodgings and unbeknownst to me at the time, home to Tom Waits. For all I knew, he could have been sitting beside me at the breakfast counter humming "Heart Attack And Vine." Coincidentally, the breakfasts at Duke's were guaranteed to provoke either a heart attack or a future stroke. Everything came pre-melted before it melted in your mouth— and the grease made it to slide down your throat so fast that it bypassed your stomach and skid through your intestines like a skier unable to slow his momentum.

The first night I met Elayne, Mark and JoAnne for dinner. The restaurant, as was typical for the time, put avocado on everything you ordered (including the check). Like all comics who hadn't seen each other in awhile, we didn't waste time on emotions or talking about trivial matters such as life—we immediately focused on comedy. We talked about all the New York comics now living in L.A., and how most of them worked at the Improv, which prevented them from working the Comedy Store. Mitzi Shore and Budd Friedman, the owners of The Comedy Store and The Improv, were very possessive of the acts they weren't paying. After dinner we went to the L.A. Improv, which hadn't burned down yet—and looked a hell of a lot less likely to burn down than the New York Improv, (which looked like it already had). There were two sections: the bar area through which you entered, mostly structural beams and plasterboard, and the show room, a huge vacuous space, where silence actually echoed—the perfect place for a joke to die. Ed Bluestone was on stage getting laughs as usual, but there was something different about his act. I couldn't pin it down until Elayne explained that when Ed first moved to L.A. his sets were, at best, mediocre. He couldn't figure out why, until one day he realized he had to talk slower. L.A. hadn't had the huge influx of New Yorkers yet and was still slower on the uptake, at least comedy wise.

Elayne did a set and just for some fun, tried out a few new lines for me. Of course, with Elayne's delivery they worked. In fact one of the lines, I ended up selling to her. Jay Leno was also on that night. He did his famous waking up and seeing that the ocean was on the wrong side joke. He was quicker on his feet than I realized. He had such command of the room that he worked the stage like it was built under him. After the show, Elayne, Jay and I joined Johnny Dark, Wil Shriner, Charlie Fleischer and several other comics at the West Coast version of the Green Kitchen, Theodore's—Canter's hadn't become the comic's late night hangout yet. Jay was incredibly friendly and quick-witted, capable of turning almost anything into a joke.

For the rest of the trip I spent almost every night at the Improv with Elayne, Mark and JoAnne, never getting the nerve to go on stage. When they were busy, I hung out at the Improv with Richard Lewis watching him search for the ingredient that eventually made him a star. I also made a call to Phil Foster, a New York comic from the 50's and 60's who helped out a lot of young comics, giving advice and even an additional place to work out. In New York he frequented a club called Al and Dick's (the Dick half being Dick Summerfield, known amongst the Broadway crowd for being a really nice guy). If the Improv was considered a nightclub than Al and Dick's was like a high-end lodge designed by Bugsy Segal. It was a singer's room, where people went expecting to hear trained voices performing jazz or show tunes, not jabbering young comics hoping to hit a punch line. Yet, Phil talked Dick into letting us do a few sets, as long as we didn't cause them to lose customers.

Phil was a semi-regular on "Laverne and Shirley," playing the father of either Laverne or Shirley, I forget which one. I guess I could look it up, but it wouldn't really change the story. Near the end of my L.A. trip he invited me to the show, which was the first time I'd been on the set of a sitcom. He introduced me to the producer, Garry Marshall (the brother of Penny Marshall, who either played Laverne or Shirley, or both) and the writing staff. Garry spent some time talking to me, asking questions about my work, which is not the norm in Hollywood. In Hollywood the only thing that would stop to give you the time of day was a broken clock. The rest of my trip to L.A. was educational and far less eventful then it would have been had I given Phil Foster my phone number. He spent the next several days looking for me; somehow he'd talked Garry Marshall into hiring me as a staff writer. By the time I made it home and found out about it, I was too late by a week or so. I probably wouldn't have taken it anyway. I wanted to be a standup comic and felt taking a TV job would have betrayed my art. Since then I have betrayed my art many, many times.

For some odd reason I was booked in first class on my return flight. I'd never flown anything but coach before, so prior to boarding, I called Joe Piscopo, who was picking me up at the airport, to boast. When the plane landed, the first class passengers of course exited first and as I walked beside upper echelon travelers, many dressed in expensive Italian suits, a real Italian from Jersey greeted me. Joe dressed up for the occasion in a torn guinea T-shirt splattered and stained with grease, ripped up work pants and sooty black galoshes three sizes too large. And for added effect, he emptied a whole bottle of Vitalis on his head and hadn't shaved. He wrapped his dirty arms around my shoulders and loudly talked about the washing machine he was fixing—and how his wife almost found out about the broad he was banging from the laundromat. I fought the urge to laugh and asked about the other broad he was screwing—the one who worked for the sanitation department. Continuing our gavone (or, cafone, depending on the part of Jersey you're from) act, we got into Joe's car and in less than ten minutes stopped in the middle of traffic, jumped out and started yelling at each other for not returning borrowed tools. After the honking horns reached an intensity that sounded like a flock of castrated migrating geese, we got back in the car and laughed all the way back to my parents' house. A place I wouldn't be calling home for much longer. The trip to L.A. made me realize I needed to slice and dice the apron strings and be where the standup world lay, and that meant moving to New York City.

A few weeks later, I signed a lease on a two-bedroom apartment on 75th and York with fellow comedian, Brant Von Hoffman. I officially became a New York standup comic.

Getting Better Most of The Time

"The shows had a lot of great comics, but it wasn't like we were major league players. It's a process where you get better. You can improve. We got better with age."

-ROBERT WUHL

In most cases, you can get better at anything you do long enough, except maybe breathing. For me being on stage and even bombing enough times built an inner toughness, which allowed me to relax when working a difficult room or being unmercifully heckled. A few years later, I worked a gig in Chicago, where I put a heckler down so bad that he charged the stage, flinging chairs, scattering tables until he was carried off—threatening to find and kill me. They wisely ended the show—and I wisely stayed in my room the whole weekend—unable to relax except on stage. The funniest retort ever came from Lenny Maxwell who was working a club in Texas when someone from the back of the room called him a prick. Lightning fast, Lenny replied, "Sir, someday you're going to eat those words."

In an unrelated story that somehow relates, my friend Bobby "King" Kelton was working a roast for Mickey Mantle, when one of the great ad libs of all time occurred. Mickey was getting back at all the guys who'd roasted him and turning to Kyle Rote (a Hall of Fame Giant receiver), called him a cocksucker to which Kyle immediately replied, "Just a lucky guess on your part."

Larry David had more than his share of hecklers, one time throwing gum at an audience member, another time calling five girls outside for a fight. Had it happened, I would have bet my cab fare on the girls. My all time favorite took place at the Improv. A drunken heckler shouted at Larry, "Your mother fucked my dog," and Larry turned it around in a way only he could, and replied, "And your dog probably didn't like it either."

Unlike today, the weekend shows were the only ones the clubs put acts in specific time slots. At the Improv, they booked the entire early show and the first five spots on the late show, while at Catch they slotted the entire weekend, which was great because if you had a date you could bring her to watch you perform, or you at least had a built-in excuse for not having a date. But if a heavyweight act showed up, booked or not, you got bumped!

I remember waiting for, what might have been, my first really good spot. I was nervously pacing like a confused pigeon, praying to any God, guru or goat I could think of that the MC might actually bring me up to a fresh, playfully drunk audience. Finally, I heard my introduction—only it went like this: "Please welcome, Robin Williams." I turned around and there was Robin running out from the light beneath the service bar, Chris pointing to him. For a split second I hoped he wouldn't make it to the stage—that a car would hit him, or an angry mobster would kill him or he'd simply internally combust. None of that happened. Instead, Chris walked over to me and said, "You're up next." Oh great, I thought. Robin will do his usual hour and I'll be left with a room resembling the aftermath of a necrophilia orgy.

A few years later, on New Year's Eve, I followed Robin Williams, who did his patented hour and destroyed the room. But in the interim, I'd learned a few tricks. I told the MC to bring me up while the audience was still applauding, before they had time to come down from the high. My plan worked and I had a great set.

All the nights of bombing and getting bumped and feeling like I was a bigger loser than my parents, my shrink, my guidance counselor ever predicted, had also turned me into a stronger, more confident comic.

"I judged how I was doing by how much I sweated. In the beginning my clothes were drenched. When I started to work regularly, the sweat moved up my body."

-BOBBY COLLINS

It was a Saturday night at the Improv and, due to a cancellation, I had just finished the first show. Despite having a very good set, I sat by myself at the bar pretending to look at my notes, so I wouldn't look so pathetically lonely, when I first met Ronnie Shakes. His coarse black hair stuck up as if each strand was doing the wave, but it wasn't half as thick as his moustache, which looked like a genetic mix of caterpillar and porcupine. It all somehow made him look taller, thinner and very funny. He walked towards me and timidly bent over like he was the host of a nature show trying to approach a skittish species. After doing the comedians' equivalent of a stare down, seeing who could avoid the other's eyes the longest, Ronnie broke the ice and told me he was thinking about being a standup comic and asked for advice.

I hadn't been doing standup very long, so asking me for advice made as much sense as a person purposely drowning to keep from feeling seasick—or a mob enforcer breaking the legs of a gambler in a wheelchair. But I didn't tell Ronnie any of this because his naiveté and his questions made me feel like a pro. Two months after, Ronnie became a regular at the Improv and then, at Catch—and eventually one of my best friends. Ronnie and I had similar styles, both one-liner guys from the Rodney Dangerfield and Woody Allen School of Comedy. And like them, he was brilliant. We often exchanged spots without asking permission knowing the MC's would approve since it wouldn't change the balance of the show.

I remember summer nights in the seventies being hot and humid; the kind of nights where you don't sweat, you flood. The power went off in New York City many times—the seventies was the decade of the Blackout—and to some it had nothing to do with electricity shortages. On one occasion, Shakes and I switched our second show spots so neither of us had to travel in the dark. Judy Orbach was Chris's second in command. If Chris was the soul of the Improv, Judy was its heart. Comics, out of their natural fear of life, tend to play hide and seek with themselves as well as with others. But once we entered the Improv, Judy would wave away acres of dirty blonde hair, to let her eyes pounce upon our hesitant presence, silently telling us that we'd reached the safety of home base. She was the welcome mat who slowed down our fears and drew us in. Her high-spirited personality steadied the nerves of the Improv and nourished its creative juices, that were hatched and cultivated by Budd Friedman and grew exponentially under Chris Albrecht. On that particular blackout Judy put candles on the piano, all around the stage and throughout the room, giving the place a World War II bomb shelter feel. When the power went out so did the microphone and the air-conditioning—which didn't do that great of a job when the power was on. That night, breathing in the Improv was like an asthmatic using a chimney as a bong.

For my kind of act, which is more deadpan and low key, compensating for not having a microphone is a difficult balance. If I shouted too much, the loser character became less believable; not enough and they couldn't hear all the words and I became soggy toast. Like Rodney used to say, "I don't wear funny hats," so I live and die by my words. Audience members yelling, "Can you repeat that?" screwed up my timing, but it was the heat that made the sets impossible. Heat and comedy is not a great combo. It's like being an agoraphobic and an arsonist. But as much dread as there was when doing a set, there was also a certain amount of excitement—a communal feeling. I was wearing one of those collarless hippie shirts made out of psychedelic hemp and had a full head of light brown hair I wish I had now, but not then, because it made me warmer. I kept thinking this could be disastrous, but even if it is, it'll be fun. Even if I failed, it was a win-win situation since no one with my kind of act could be expected to do well. Because I was both freed and boosted by those thoughts, I didn't bother trying to balance the level of my voice with my character; it just came naturally. I also got very lucky because before I went into my act, I came up with an ad lib that has become a standard. A waitress dropped a tray of glasses and I quickly said, "Some Polish guy just dropped his contact lens." My own ad lib caught me by surprise and actually cracked me up which gave the audience a subliminal message this was going to be a fun night. And it was. The more fun I had, the more the audience went with the flow.

I can still feel the heat and the smoke from the candles and cigarettes scouring my lungs. I can still see the audience, patches of dark sweating faces, swaying in the light that slow danced to the breeze from the open doors. The crowd, judging by the laughs that bounced off the walls, desired to contribute to the show. They were on my side. Both shows went well that night—and there wasn't a dry underarm in the house. The next night when asked how the show went at Catch, Shakes in his short crisp, almost Maxwell Smart delivery said,

"Uh…the audience loved me! It might have sounded like boos to the untrained ear."

One of the many lines of his I loved, was, "I signed up for a course in reincarnation. It was very expensive, but I figured, what the hell? You only live once." I remember when I told Ronnie I was getting married he looked at me in deadpan and said, "I didn't even know you were heterosexual." In his act he talked about how hot hell was and said, "I know that hell is hot, but is it humid? I can take the heat, but not the humidity."

Ronnie Shakes

Shaky, did four great Tonight Show spots and on his last, Johnny asked why he shaved his moustache. He ad libbed, "Tax purposes." If Johnny had always laughed that loud and hard, Ed McMahon would have found himself on the unemployment line. Shortly after, while jogging, he told his wife Susan he felt a pain in his chest and before his lips could form a punch line, his heart gave out and he died. He was 41.

I was in L.A. when I got the call. Too stunned to cry, I fell into a chair and sat quietly for a long time thinking of how only a few weeks before we'd played racquetball together for two hours, recalling our conversation on the court. He was going back East the next day and for some inexplicable reason, kept referring to the airport Sky Caps as wufftees. It found its way into conversations for the next week and kept cracking us up.

As much as I wanted to be at the funeral, I couldn't attend because of a work obligation. I don't know of a comic who didn't love Ronnie. At the funeral, the normally unsentimental Larry David, who played golf with him, collapsed in tears. To this very day, I often think about Shakes. Part of me wants to laugh and part of me wants to cry—another part mourns all the brilliant jokes that went unwritten. His tombstone reads: IT IS HUMID.

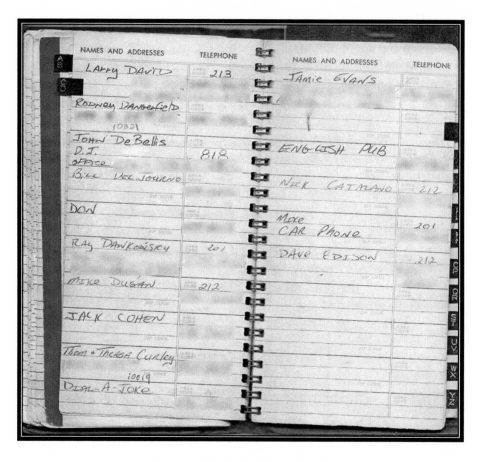

Ronnie Shake's phone book

Smart Minds Think Alike, Mediocre Minds Stink Alike

Sometimes in life, things besides a bald spot come full circle. I walked into Catch one Monday night, which is when auditions were held and the MC that night, Kelly Rodgers, said, "You've got to see this new comic; his stuff is really smart. I'm gonna make him a regular." Before Kelly could finish, I knew whom he was talking about. I'd briefly seen the guy a few weeks earlier when I was the MC and thought he was funny. The practice was to see if a comic could survive the audition crowd a few times without begging for the dreaded "your time is up" light or doubling their medication. Even for a pro, hosting the audition night crowd was like being an MC for a human sacrifice.

I was hanging out at the bar with the other comics as usual, talking about our problems as if they were the world's only problems, when Kelly called me over to see this brash, blond-haired comic, whose cocky attitude matched his smart material. He obviously had the potential to be very special and would probably never have to lie about his income on a dating site. Kelly passed him that night. Today, while this comic is no longer young, he's still brash, has even smarter material, dates girls that are younger than he was before he passed the auditions, and more importantly, has never forgotten the guys he started with. Kelly Rodgers was right. Bill Maher did become something very special. He became a unique voice: a mix of Will Rodgers, Lenny Bruce, Larry Flint and Viagra.

In this fickle business it's nearly impossible to pick who is going to become a star based on talent alone. There are many variables that control the unnatural selection of who attains stardom—or, star-dumb. A lot of it can be attributed to a popular breed of decision makers. Agents and managers who think not what they can do for their client, but what their client can do for them now dominate the comedy business. And there are others who are so worried about rocking the boat they can't see what's right in front of them.

Barry Farber was a radio host who, at one time either ran, or, considered running for mayor of New York. He seemed like a nice enough guy, with an inoffensive hairstyle and pleasant breath, but I don't think he understood young comics and our desire to be contrary—especially Larry's.

One night, he had a group of young comics on his show, but as my memory isn't so much selective as it is elective, I don't remember everyone who was there. I know Larry David and I were definitely present along with Barry's friend, the old-time comedian, Joey Adams. Barry talked about comedy with his pal Adams, who thought double entendre wife jokes were the epitome of comedy and then went around the table asking us to do a small portion of our acts. Of course, we all complied. The other comedians (whoever the hell they were) did their bits. I did a few of my parent jokes and then Larry offered his own unique slant. The conversation went something like this:

"This is comedian Larry David. Larry, will you perform a little of your act for our listeners?"

"I can't."

"What do you mean you *can't*?"

"I just can't," Larry replied.

"Why not?"

"Because my act is filthy"

"You don't have anything that's clean?"

"No, everything I do is filthy and disgusting."

"*Disgusting?*"

"Worse! It's all curses and garbage. Pure filth!"

"That's terrible!"

"I like filth! The more vulgar the better," Larry proudly proclaimed, heightening his fabrication.

"You think filth is funny?"

"I get laughs from filth. My whole act is repulsive. It's disgusting bile."

It continued to escalate, Larry insisting his entire act from beginning to end was nothing but stench and that he couldn't help being vulgar because it was who he was. Barry grew irate; offended that Larry had the audacity to come on his show. But LD didn't let up. He continued his ruse, talking about himself as a tasteless degenerate until a shouting match finally broke out. LD was kicked off the late night show that had few if any listeners not requiring hearing aids.

Meanwhile the rest of us did everything we could to keep from laughing. This was vintage LD and another example how everyone— except for us comics who couldn't get enough of it—misunderstood his sense of humor. For a long time, the system thought of Larry David as this weird, angry guy who was too off beat, too thin-skinned and far too volatile to ever become a household name—even in his own household. Giving a rowdy audience to Larry was like handing a bottle of nitroglycerin to a person during an earthquake. They saw Gilbert Gottfried as a late night comic who cleared out the audience by going on stage with drink trays as props. They often left so fast they'd tell the waitress to keep the change—even when he first morphed into his Murray, the overbearing talent agent. Keenan Wayans was said to be too good-looking, too middle of the road and not funny enough to become a big star. And Richard Belzer, Richard Lewis and Jay Leno had all been around way too long for anyone to take them as seriously funny guys. In the comedy business, unless you're a star it's not who you know but who knows you and for how long.

There's also a list of comics who were thought to be up-and-coming stars, sure shots, can't miss guys who somehow missed. I won't mention them by name because they may still make it. I hope they do and earn so much money they won't remember how much I owe them, or, make enough to pay me back. My point, is, back then comics were in it purely for the love of an art form—and okay, an occasional waitress, coat check girl or any female drunk enough to believe the ink-scrawled napkins and paper scraps they slept on were designer sheets.

What we saw as funny and talented was often very different from what show business execs and even the audience thought was funny. Heck, what comics saw as food most people saw as condiments or pest control bait. What was important to us wasn't how loud an audience laughed, but *why* they laughed and that they didn't get laughed out before you got on stage.

I remember one comic who did a bit with a small Christmas tree saying it was his brother who'd taken too much LSD. Another comic, Richard Morris, did a piece saying that slavery was okay—we just made slaves of the wrong people—we should have enslaved Canadians. About ten years ago I saw a hysterical and original comic who went on as a frightened magician, so self-conscious that he did his magic act behind the stage curtain, telling the audience, "Now, I'm pulling a rabbit out of the hat. Now, I'm making him disappear." I often wonder what happened to that extremely talented kid.

Of course there are times that luck, show business and talent all point to the same haunted soul. Woody Allen has said that if he hadn't been lucky, despite his talent, he may not have made it. He was given the opportunity to allow his genius to grow high enough to be seen from just about everywhere –except maybe the deep South and parts of Uzbekistan. Branch Rickey, the man responsible for breaking the color line in baseball by bringing Jackie Robinson to the major leagues, said that luck is the residue of design. I think in many cases he's right, but there are times when luck is absolutely clueless. Some gigantic stars deserve all of the adulation, but there are also those who shouldn't be able to afford the price of admission. When money is the goal, talent is often mistaken for the mediocrity needed to earn it. Smart minds think alike, mediocre minds stink alike.

Back then our wallets' egos were suppressed by the love of an art form and talent arrived in abundance. Most of the comics were saying something different, or the same thing, but differently. While there never was or ever will be room for everyone at the very top, those who don't let time or unfairness diminish their talent and motivation stand a chance to nab a slice of the fame pie—providing they don't starve to death first.

The New Kid on The Block: The Comic Strip

"The Improv was about learning your delivery, Catch was about delivering what you learned. The Comic Strip was about learning to take chances."

-JOHN DEBELLIS

"Richie Tienken and John McGowan wanted me to go see Tony Di Andria, a comic friend, perform at Catch A Rising Star's audition night. Catch was packing them in and we were treated rudely. Richie and John asked if I wanted to open up a comedy place. A few days later we went around the corner, found a place and bought it."

-BOB WACHS, OWNER OF THE COMIC STRIP

Sometime in the late summer of 1976 I heard through the comic grapevine that a first-rate, classy comedy club was opening. The club will have a real stage, a new microphone, a spacious showroom and, quite possibly, attractive waitresses. Best of all, it was just a short walk from Catch. No need for cab fare. The Comic Strip was coming to our neighborhood and the "life" was getting better! Glenn Hirsch called me early one morning— around the crack of sunset—to tell me they were holding auditions.

"Why should we audition?" I scoffed. "We're regulars at the Improv and Catch A Rising Star!" Glenn agreed, but after half an hour of whining, we decided that being we weren't heavyweights at the Improv or Catch yet, this could be the fast track to comedic success. My audition was a few hours earlier than Glenn's—perhaps because I lived closer, but more likely because he had a girlfriend, which meant he had a real reason to stay in bed longer.

The Comic Strip had three owners: John McGowan, Bob Wachs and Richie Tienken. Bob and Richie greeted me at the door—Bob, a sophisticated attorney, Richie, a straight-talking New York street guy with a full head of hair (now white) that even an Elvis impersonator would envy. They led me through the bar-in-progress to the showroom almost-in-progress. Something hit my shoulder. I thought it was an errant nail, but I looked up and saw a pigeon. There I was, about to start my audition, ankle deep in New York City dirt that was as close to quicksand as city ordinances would allow and ducking debris from a pigeon with irritable bowel syndrome I also had to force my vocal chords to shout my delicately crafted standup routine over a cacophony of carpenters, hammers and drills. Not only was I not getting any laughs, I was heckled by power tools, blinded by a setting sun seeping through the skeleton roof and — bombarded by a kamikaze pigeon. A wave of sweat poured off of my face with each line, dampening the mud, causing me to sink deeper and deeper. I was determined to finish my set before I had to yell for someone to toss me a rope. When it ended on the biggest non-laugh I'd ever gotten, Bob and Richie applauded wildly.

"Congratulations, you passed the audition," they said.

I snapped, "Audition? I thought this was an initiation," finally getting a laugh.

A few months later, when The Comic Strip opened, it was a state-of-the-art comedy club with a high, long stage that ran almost entirely across the back of the room. There was not only plenty of space for comics to strut, it had a nice in-tune piano and a drum set that could be struck without sticking an elbow into the ribs of a performer. At first, the Strip brought up the universal question: if a joke is told and there's no one there to laugh, is it still funny? In those early days, being a heavyweight at the Strip meant working prime time to one full table. When you told a joke, you didn't wait for the laugh, you waited for an echo. It didn't take nearly as long as I expected for people to realize there was another topnotch club to see comedy. At first it was just the weekends that had large audiences. In a matter of months the crowds grew until there were full houses on most weekdays and the entire weekend. The audiences were amazingly receptive; you'd have thought they got paid by the laugh. To this day I've had some of my best sets as the Strip. I've had several standing ovations there, the most memorable, was one that Eddie Murphy had a difficult time following.

"The comics (from the Improv and Catch) all came to the Strip to help us out. If they didn't we wouldn't have made it."

-RICHIE TIENKEN

As we regulars grew in stature at the Improv and Catch, we worked the Strip less and less. The two established clubs gave us more sets, better spots—and an increased flow of cab fare. It became more difficult to fit The Comic Strip into our performing schedules and the Strip started to develop their own acts that deservingly took up many of the spots. Even though they now had their own talent, no club treated us better than the Strip.

"I particularly remember Larry David coming into my office to complain that he couldn't get the mic out of the stand. Because Larry used to throw the mic down and break it. Lucien glued the mike into the stand so LD couldn't get it out. We even took the stand off the stage because he would break that."

-RICHIE TIENKEN

Richie Tienken said he originally got the idea of opening the club when he saw the long lines waiting outside Catch a Rising Star. In essence he was saying, "Build it and they will pay to come," and eventually they did. It's the only one of the three clubs that stayed in its original location and remained open through the 70's, 80s, 90's—to this present day.

Over the following years, I grew to really like the owners. John McGowan I knew the least. He seemed more of a silent partner. Bob Wachs, who was always accommodating, moved on as his entertainment law practice grew. To this day, almost every night about 9pm, Richie Tienken can be found sitting at The Comic Strip bar offering past and present standups free drinks.

Comedy club owners are unique and each owner of those original three showcase clubs is special in his own way. Budd Friedman was like a stepfather you loved but feared would abandon you. Chris Albrecht was the benevolent gang leader who sometimes got us into trouble, but also got us out of it. Rick Newman was the smooth and charmingly handsome guy all of us comics wanted to be, except for the females, who wanted to meet a guy like Rick. Richie Tienken was the guy we all wanted to hang out and get drunk with—not just because he paid for the drinks and laughed the loudest. Bob Wachs was the guy who took you to a swank restaurant and showed you how to act and to be more amused than embarrassed. And John McGowan was the guy who bought you an anonymous gift.

Although he wasn't a club owner, one can't mention The Comic Strip without talking about its first manager, Lucien Hold. Lucien didn't just put his stamp on the club, he made the mold that formed it. Lucien was a former actor/dancer/carpenter. You'd think it was the first two slashes that thrust him into the comedy world, but it was the latter. Richie Tienken had hired him to do carpentry work on the club and from there, a friendship grew, a bond, a trust and eventually, the spirit of the place. The early days were loose, hectic, creative and often laced with yogurt—Dennis Wolfberg closed his act by singing "American Pie" while smearing himself with various flavors of Dannon. That bit more than any other defined the club at the time. It was a comedy club finding itself, while discovering guys like Dennis Wolfberg, Jerry Seinfeld, Paul Reiser, Ray Romano, George Wallace, Carol Leifer, Larry Miller and Adam Sandler.

"Seinfeld was the first comedian to go to L.A. So that night a bunch of comics go down to M.C.Sorlies, Larry Miller, Seinfeld, me and Mark Schiff. We drank a lot. I left early because I was meeting a girl at The Strip. About an hour later the four of them come in the Strip and go into the bathroom. A few minutes later, they come out stark naked-- Seinfeld, Cain, Larry Miller and Mark Schiff... They walked onto Second Avenue to see who could walk the furthest. Believe it or not.... Seinfeld made it the furthest. They came back sat at the bar and spent the night drinking naked. That's how loose it was at the Strip."

-HIRAM KASTEN

Owners and management treated comics like equals. Equal, but not identical and I say that as a compliment. We were different and they permitted us to rejoice in it. Their minds were tilted just enough to understand us, appreciate us, manage us—and more importantly, organize a softball team—which Lucien did. He had a smile that was a display case for his soul. It stayed lit while he battled a deadly disease, fighting harder than a comic battles his own ego. A few years ago his body finally surrendered, but his legacy didn't die with the war. When Lucien passed away, he took a piece of us with him, but left his spirit at the Strip to watch over comics past, present and future.

The Comic Strip was the first comedy club to hold an annual Christmas party, although at the time they didn't know annual would add up to decades. Comics from every club were welcome to attend—sober, drunk or with doggie bags. Like the other clubs, The Comic Strip served food, hamburgers being the staple, which often went down like it was stapled to your stomach. Videotapes of those early parties exist thanks to comics like David Jay (who a few years later I spent six months looking for, while speaking to him weekly as David Edison), who owned video equipment. The rise of The Comic Strip was like adding another province to our small sovereign comic state. Before long most performers bounced back and forth, working the trifecta of clubs.

"It was more important to do the set to get the food than do the set, because if you didn't go on, you didn't get the hamburgers."
-BILL MAHER

"If you were really good, you got the shrimp."
-GEORGE WALLACE

"We used to say the minimum amount of chop meat to eat to be a good comic was 28 pounds a month."
-LARRY MILLER

"More than food or cab fare, I was into the free tee shirts I got from working the clubs. Some nights I got 5 or 6 tee shirts from doing 5 sets at the various clubs. I hoarded them for so many years that they actually shrunk in my storage boxes, and by then they were too small for me to wear."

-BOBBY KELTON

The Laugh Stops Here

For most young comics, performing during the first show on Saturday Night at Catch A Rising Star was like accepting an invite to heaven before you realized you first had to suffer a painful death. There wasn't a dry glass in the packed showroom and the bar was jammed with people thirsting for the second show. If you wanted a place to go over your act, you had to stand outside or in the entrance near the pay phones—or push your way to and through the coatroom to get to the basement. Then you had to pray you weren't interrupting a poker game or a mob hit—or both. The Catch bartenders, Al Weidan and Peter Perri, gave generous amounts of alcohol to the comics, knowing our fragile breed often needed some liquid spine. One night I was about to order my third when David Sayh, the MC, called me into the room, ran on stage, and without even hogging an extra second of stage time, introduced me.

The crowd had come to laugh and laugh they did. My attitude grew with each joke and the alcohol kept me from asking myself the question, "Can I keep getting big laughs like this the whole twenty minutes?" David must have flashed the *get off the stage light* a few times before I realized my twenty minutes had passed, so I wrapped up the set, ending with a giant laugh and applause I had only heard before for other comics.

It was the best set I'd ever had at Catch. I entered the bar and wiped off more sweat than should be possible for a guy my size, letting the waiting crowd know that I was the comic who had just killed. I needed another drink to stop myself from worrying, "Uh-oh, will they (the club managers) expect me to do this all the time?" I turned to Al to place my order when I heard a male voice ask, "Can I buy you a drink?"

The guy didn't look gay—his snug shirt was surrounded by a good-looking busty woman pressed against his chest.

"I get them for free," I said to Al the bartender's displeasure.

"Great set," the guy said.

"I messed the set up on the first shrink joke," I said, accepting praise like a true comic.

"No, you were hysterical. I just opened up a club in California: The Laff Stop. I'd love for you to work it."

"I should have ended on the virgin joke," I continued.

"We'll pay you, put you up in a condo and fly you out," the guy offered.

"Although the mirror over the bed joke got a big laugh...maybe I should have followed with the two women at the same time line?"

"You'll get plenty of stage time. It's three twenty-minute sets a night!"

"I forgot to do the Mutual of Sicily piece. It would have gotten a big laugh--"

Al interrupted my obsessive spiraling. "The guy wants to buy you a drink. Whaddaya want?"

"Oh, uh...I don't know, should I have a Bloody Mary or a beer? Beer's fattening. I could have a light beer. But I feel more like a real drink--"

I finally ordered a Screwdriver explaining that the orange juice had nutritious vitamin C, gulped it down and accepted the gig. So what if I had to work three sets a night? I was getting paid for stage time and I could visit some friends in L.A.. It was my first real professional gig: plane fare, plenty of stage time, a place to stay and actual money— maybe enough to get one or two of my teeth cleaned. But there was one small catch. There was more than just plenty of stage time. There were three different 20-minute sets a night to the same audience, which meant I needed an hour's worth of material! I figured I could look through my notes and find enough good jokes. The gig was over a month away, so I had time to break the material in.

If a comic sees a glass half full, it just means when he spills it there'll be more to clean up. Working out new material wasn't meant to be, thanks to the great set at Catch that got me the gig at the Laff Stop. I had started getting better spots and there was no way I could jeopardize my kingdom for one paying gig!

The month passed quicker than a comic's lifetime of positive thoughts. My sets, although not consistently on par with that Saturday night, actually improved. I was even able to break in a few new lines. I don't recall getting on the airplane or whom I threw up next to. I don't even remember how I got to Glenn Super's apartment. I just remember Glenn and I poring through jokes typed on paper so wrinkled the writing looked like hieroglyphics. We picked and categorized jokes and then, while Glenn worked on his act, I put them into routines. Next came the hard part: memorizing it all. As I've already mentioned, my memory is not the best. If I was pointing a gun at myself and reported it to the police, I wouldn't remember who the shooter was.

I figured if I could string together jokes into a loosely constructed story (ala Lenny Maxwell) with a time line, I had a better chance of remembering them. Then if I needed to fill in the blanks, I'd write a few new jokes and stretch out my act. If there was one thing in life I learned to have faith in, it was my ability to write jokes. I had gotten to the point where I could do one of the hardest things to do in writing standup comedy and that was to pull an inside straight. In layman's terms, that means finding the joke that fits in the middle and links the surrounding lines.

Just as we were about to take a break, George Wallace—the comedian, not the deceased racist senator from Alabama—stopped by. Although I'd been to L.A. before, most of my sightseeing was done at night on the way to clubs, so George offered me a guided tour of the city since it was one of the few smog-less days. He saved what he thought was the best part for last. He pulled off the road on Mulholland Drive overlooking the San Fernando Valley and jumped out of the car, walked to the edge of the overlook, spread his arms and proudly showed off his new hometown in all its expansive glory. I followed him to the ledge, unimpressed. What I saw were several small towns pretending to be one, patches of short flat odd colored houses with palm trees. It looked like a gigantic turtle condo!

A few days later during another work break we visited Larry Miller. Glenn told Larry about my reaction to seeing L.A. from Mulholland Drive. Larry related it to the time he was proudly showing his mother his spacious (compared to NYC) newly furnished L.A. apartment. He said, "She went from room to room inspecting the place, then returned to the living room shaking her head in utter disbelief." "Larry," she scolded. "I can't believe you don't have a garlic press!"

The day of reckoning had come. I had added as much as I could to my act and while Glenn drove to the club I kept trying to memorize the new material. Glenn promised to stay with me even if I was carried off by an angry patron and thrown into a truck full of nuclear waste headed for Mexico. I entered a large, dark room, which, like most comedy clubs of that era, was surrounded by walls covered with pictures of comics fictionally smiling. Either a bartender, a waitress or a bouncer, I can't remember which, said, "You must be the opening comic." I agreed with him or her in theory, so responded with a resounding understatement, "I guess I am." He or she, or both, shook my hand and then asked me for a head shot, which unlike most people from L.A., where sonograms of fetuses are 8 x 10s and have resumes stapled to the back, I didn't have one. I could have just admitted to my lack of show business etiquette. Instead I pulled out my Massachusetts driver's license, which had a picture of me because the law required it and justice was blind. I said, "I usually just have this blown up." The owner actually thought the idea was funny and said he wouldn't deduct the cost of the copies from my pay.

The club put me up in a small condo that hygienically left a lot to be inhaled. I spent as little time as possible in the room and to this day I'm not sure what I slept on, other than the fact that it wasn't a bed, but an object primarily meant for torture.

I found out that afternoon that the headliner was Gary Mule Deer and the middle act was Johnny Dark—comics I had heard of and felt I might dishonor by being on the same bill. Now the goal of most comedy club owners back then was to promote the art of drinking. Watching Gary's act could convince a teetotaler they were drunk. Imagine taking Jacques Cousteau out of water, giving him a bow and arrow and dressing him up like a thin Grizzly Adams. Combine that with three dizzy Steve Martins, each going in opposite directions, add zero gravity and then, give each audience watching him acid. Gary's Mule Deer's version of "Tell Laura I Love Her" was like a guitar bomb blowing up the Brill building and twisting the shreds of music into distorted chunks of comedy that kept exploding on stage.

Johnny Dark's act was saner, measured, laid out so that his best laughs came from uniquely delivered impressions. Despite being a new comic from back East, both guys treated me nicely and told me not to worry about getting laughs, as the noisy bar blender would cover any prolonged periods of silence. One of the worst things about being the opening act was that you were the opening act. Sure, the MC would warm up the audience by getting laughs from the usual "Where are you from?" questions and answers, but it was up to the opener to get them laughing with an actual act that didn't rely on the audience's zip codes, professions or mismatched clothing for material.

The showroom at the Laff Stop was not designed for comedy. The bar leaned from the right side into the audience, almost clipping the room in half so that you had to deliver your material from a corner stage, looking side to side rather than straight ahead. The constant droning chatter from the bar crowd was like a herd of hecklers that hummed their insults. As the MC warmed up the audience, I prayed that the alcohol would hit their systems as it touched their lips. Glenn Super kept patting me on the back with short quick slaps in an attempt to give me confidence, but stay within a comic's parameters—giving support without having to be challenged by the ambiguity of human affection.

When I heard my phony credits being given, I knew I was just a mispronunciation away from being on stage. My heart galloped unsteadily while my nervous system used every trick it knew to keep me from walking up to the microphone. I started with my usual opening line about the glass eye and got a decent laugh from both sides of the room, which gave my next line a jump-start. That line worked and so did the next and the next and so on. I didn't get any giant laughs during the act but at least I got several that could be heard over the blender. This first set was mainly old material, with about two minutes of new jokes weaved in, which in my case was about eight or nine lines. Most of them worked and the ones that didn't were sandwiched between two sure-fire jokes. I finished my first twenty-minute set with the audience consciously applauding. I had done my job.

Glenn was the first to greet me with a big manly handshake and smile. I was "comic happy" which meant that as soon as I felt a good feeling nudge its way to the surface I realized I had to do it all over again with new material—two more times that night! And three more times the next night! And three *more* times the night after that—and then hope I got paid. Yes, I was experiencing comic bliss.

Johnny Dark followed me and made my laughs look like they were in the first stages of evolution. Then it was Gary's turn. As soon as he hit the stage, The Laff Stop became his rubber room. The audience loved every lunatic moment and so did I, except for the fact he got much bigger laughs than me and made me realize I had a lot of room for improvement. Luckily, I wasn't as nervous going into my next set. Granted I had a few drinks between shows and was just shy of slurring, the fact that I had one successful set under my belt made 51% of my cells feel somewhat confident.

This set went even better than the first, mainly because I had saved most of my sex stuff for this one. If you work clean like I do, the best way to elevate your laughs is to go for sex or body function jokes, which I never used because I thought one's digestive track was too personal and thus, off limits. (Actually that's a lie. My mentor Lenny Maxwell drilled into me that doing body function jokes were infantile like a baby reaching into his diaper to play with his own secretions).

I've always felt that the third set of the night was always my best. By that time I was more confident and relaxed, but still had good energy having already received sixteen bucks cab fare. By the fourth set I'd not only be tired, I'd forget which material I had already done in the same set. There were nights when I'd perform two shows each at the Improv, Catch and The Comic Strip and by the fifth and sixth set, I'd mix up setups and punch lines from different jokes, but by then I didn't care. In fact, I could bomb and not think it was the end of the world until I went to sleep and ran every joke that didn't work over and over again in my head.

The entire gig went better than I expected. I didn't kill, but I got consistent laughs throughout the shows. And the club owner was happy because the audience didn't have to sober up to actually understand my jokes. When I was handed my pay, which was in cash without a deduction for head shot copies, I felt like a real comic.

Glenn Super had a gig, so I spent the remaining nights in L.A. at the Improv with Richard Lewis and his girlfriend, the beautiful actress Nina Van Pilante. In a ten-day period, I witnessed the metamorphosis of Richard's stage persona. His performance was always frenetic, shooting out in several directions at once, premises within premises within more premises, but something was subtly changing. Each night I watched Richard deliver his material, he grew more and more neurotic - slouching lower and lower until he looked like a bent water beetle, his arms flailing like he was trying to grab onto something to keep from drowning. Those physical moves put it all together, making the material a snug fit, becoming indistinguishable from his character. His laughs grew exponentially, which acted as a bonding agent solidifying his persona establishing the Richard Lewis brand.

That week he told me he was going to start doing the Letterman Show on a regular basis, hoping it would bolster his standup career. And it did. The perfect opportunity met the perfect opportunist at the perfect time and resulted in the perfect neurotic storm. If synergy really exists, this was it. Richard found the last piece of the puzzle, hidden in plain *fright* that put him on the list of the fifty greatest comics of all time.

When I returned to New York and performed for the first time, there was a slight letdown at first, but that quickly dissipated. I had reached a new level and was rewarded with bigger laughs and longer applause. Of course, I still only got money for cab fare.

The Proud, the Few: The Female Comics

Melanie Chartoff

"One night Dangerfield came to see us at Gertie's Folk City and sat right in front. I was doing a scene with an improv group and

noticed him nodding and nodding all through it. I was thrilled! Then I realized he was nodding out into his drink."

-MELANIE CHARTOFF

While standup comedy is often called a masculine art form, it's certainly not in the same sense that bronco busting, ultimate fighting and serial killing are. In fact, when the word "art" is used in anything, the percentage of testosterone is reduced by at least one testicle. I can understand why Neanderthal mind-sets consider standup masculine, given its aggressive nature and the fact that there are fewer women comics. When I started out there was only a handful--Elayne Boosler, Emily Levine, Nancy Parker, Melanie Chartoff, Abby Stein, Marjorie Gross and then shortly after, Rita Rudner, Adrianne Tolsch and Carol Leifer among others. Elayne Boosler was a heavyweight at Catch and the Improv—and I'm not referring to the physical space she occupied, but rather her seniority, power and ability. Her style was quick, smart, aggressive and eclectic, yet her sassy attitude and inclusiveness allowed her to maintain her own distinctive style and femininity. Although Phyllis Diller and Joan Rivers were her predecessors, she paved an entirely new and wider avenue of standup that rarely used femininity to get laughs. Without yet achieving fame, she was equal to any male comic in the showcase clubs. Her peers consider Elayne one of the best of her generation (male or female).

Back then there were so few women performing standup that they instantly were classified as a performing delicacy, an acquired taste. That wasn't the case with Elayne. She had a command of the stage and material that came off biting rather than bitchy. She was as adept as any male when it came to hecklers and considering the attitude of the times, it could be doubly embarrassing. Most of the time she'd deliver a knockout line with charm—like a teacher laying into a Second grade bully with his mother in the room.

We never felt any jealousy or prejudice towards women comics and certainly never felt superior. The only women I ever felt superior to were the ones who thought my baldness was a life choice. Male comics were our brothers, females, our sisters—ones we didn't have to take shopping. We were protective without being overbearing and never held them to a different set of morals, although we were envious of their lesser need to prowl for sexual partners. They were essentially our equals, except thanks to false assumptions that lingered in some club owners' brains, got less stage time. Female comics rarely were allowed to follow each other, even though identical quintuplet males could appear back to back to back to back to back in one show.

Like us, their acts were different from each other. As mentioned earlier, Elayne was a powerhouse on stage, her jokes crisp and her mind dangerously fast. Emily Levine was an offbeat storyteller who would twist her arms and legs in directions that only a zombie would attempt yet somehow the unsettling moves punctuated her odd ironic life. Marjorie Gross, with her nervous giggle and pauses of uncertainty like she couldn't decide what combinations of medications to overdose on, was the female Woody Allen. Nancy Parker did her own version of the Wizard of Oz, bobbing and weaving across the stage imitating the munchkins and witches almost simultaneously. She also did such a spot on Betty Davis, when she said, "Fasten your seat belts, it's going to be a bumpy night," a few inebriated audience members would occasionally oblige by falling out of their seats laughing.

Melanie Chartoff, was the first ingénue standup, her beauty an obstacle to the novice audiences of the time, still predisposed to thinking that comedy and sexy were mutually exclusive. To make her act successful she went against type portraying off beat characters with searing depth and ironic turns that were quite the opposite of her image. (In a few short years those comedic prejudices toward women would fade away. In fact, today, standup comedy is one of the few professions where women get paid equally for doing the same childish job as men. Back then they didn't get on as often as us males, but when they did, they would stuff their bank accounts with the same eight bucks in cab fare).

"I adored the dames. We were supportive of each other, and the guys were supportive of us; but I was beyond assistance. Most of them were doing set up, punch, and I never did that sort of joke stuff. My

comedy came primarily out of twisted characters, like Andy's, but he had a lot more audacity and weirdness than I did"

-MELANIE CHARTOFF

Rita Rudner was always softer and noticeably more feminine. Her smooth effortless delivery made it impossible to tell that she was performing. She could segue from subject to subject as seamless as the changing tide in the middle of the ocean and unlike most comics, male or female, there wasn't a trace of anger in her persona. She lit up the stage with innocence and charm as she delivered self–depreciating one-liners rich with wit and insight

Rita Rudner

Carol Leifer was nearer to Elayne in style only, forceful, less eclectic and at times more animated, using her eyes, facial expressions and body language to give her act its own special flavor. Adrianne Tolsch was quick-witted and more ethnic, a sarcastic complainer about the many dilemmas of her very tragic life. Abby Stein, although feminine and sexy both on and off stage, had a cheerful bawdiness emanating in a loud smile that could be seen through the challenge of her eyes, which helped make her one of the guys—in fact, she was one of the best poker players in our crew. That really wasn't saying much since most us didn't know the difference between a straight flush and a cheese omelet.

Elayne, Marjorie and Abby hung out the most with us after the shows. Carol Leifer was their equivalent at The Comic Strip and spent the nights hanging out with Jerry Seinfeld, Larry Miller and The Comic Strip crew. Rita, who usually was seen in the vicinity of Ronnie Shakes, would leave the clubs soon after her set to work on her act. I'll talk more about Rita's tireless work ethic later in the book.

In the seventies the West Side was still Hell's kitchen and East Side was the cool place to hang out—and where they wore gold chains instead of undershirts—so after the shows Elayne often led us down to the Village (closer to where she lived) for ice cream, or to Little Italy. Most of the time that meant Umberto's, Ronnie Shakes' favorite stop, which was also the start of my Barrett's esophagus (maximum strength acid reflux). We were either their last customers or in most cases their first customers of the day.

Melanie Chartoff's boyfriend, at the time, was a real romantic fellow. For her birthday he stole the picture of Woody Allen from the wall at Sardis and gave it to her for a present. She was appalled, not by the lack of wrapping, or the absence of a card, but by the fact that stolen-goods were not what she considered a loving gesture or even a poetic act. Considering the caricature's value, it was in fact grand larceny. She wanted to give it back, but was afraid of the consequences; jail time was not nearly as important to her as stage time. So she asked for my help. She didn't know that my grandfather had served 5 years for counterfeiting (proudly taking the rap for nine other guys) and if he'd gotten a hold of it he would have sold it to one of his fences.

Before he could even sniff that there was a crooked buck to be made I contacted Jack Rollins, Woody Allen's manager. Without saying who gave it to him, he returned the famous caricature to the legendary show business hang out, thus none of the parties involved had to rat anyone out in exchange for immunity. Shortly after that incident, Melanie wisely broke up with her light-fingered Romeo, loaded up a truck with furniture and moved her extra stuff into my parent's attic. It remained there for several decades, undetected by my grandfather, until my folks finally gave most of it to a neighbor (with Melanie's permission). My daughter, Alina, recently used one of the remaining pictures in a play she directed off-Broadway (also with Melanie's permission).

Towards the end of the seventies more female comics arrived on the scene, like Louis Bromfield, Nancy Redman and from the west coast, Judy Carter. I worked a gig in Arizona with Judy and from watching her work, learned how to play to out of town crowds that acted like there was a two dozen drink minimum vomiting zoo.

Then during the eighties there was an explosion of women to standup, Joy Behar, Cathy Ladman and Susie Essman to name just a few. Most of the migration across the standup frontier by females took place on the West Coast. Among the early Comedy Store pioneers were Lotis Weinstock and Shirley Hemphill.

Since I consider myself male based on self-evidence, I may not be the most qualified person to describe what it was like to be a female comic in the days when being a standup meant two things: you were a comic and it described the way you urinated.

Several things happened because of these female comics of the seventies and early eighties, the most important was breaking down barriers; woman can joke about subjects that only men had been allowed to talk about and can delve into areas that only their gender has experienced. Women can now be both funny and aggressive in their attitudes—plus they can be pretty. Not since Phyllis Diller and Joan Rivers had women gained so much comedic ground.

Naturally, there was some dating amongst male and female comics. Carol Leifer and Ritch Shydner got hitched and divorced. Adrianne Tolsch and Bill Sheft have been married over twenty years. But the one great romance of that time period was Elayne Boosler and Andy

Kaufman. If there is such a thing as puppy soul mates, they were it. Elayne told me dating Andy was like dating several different people. He would break into characters like his foreign man and his (the best ever) Elvis Presley. Elayne remained one of Andy's closest friends and was with him when he died. She has since married Bill Siddons who managed some of the best bands in the sixties and seventies (one of which was the Doors) and is very happy. We recently started hanging out again, even went to the new Yankee stadium for the first time together (where she kept me laughing so hard I didn't notice nor care that the Yankees were getting badly beaten). We frequently speak and it always brings me back to my early days at the club and that same comforting feeling.

Marjorie Gross who was close friends with Gilda Radner, Alan Zwiebel, Rita Rudner, Ron Zimmerman and Larry David died several years back. She was one of my late night buddies. We laughed, exchanged ideas and mostly bombed together. She borrowed several of my Kinks albums, which she never returned, but I suppose it's a little too late to ask for them back.

The Staff of the Life

The camaraderie between comics was also shared with the showcase staffs who, although not standup comics, were our brothers and sisters in *the life*. They made us feel special, took our drink and food orders, played along with our inside jokes and cleaned up the messes we made. They filled pie plates with whipped cream that we deftly carried through the audience. After displaying our perfect comic timing by shoving the plate into a comic's face, of course, the waitresses cleaned the stage, the mike, the front tables and our faces. During the late hours, when the few remaining audience members stared silently at us like a distant relative in a coffin, they were the only laughs we heard.

Their patience stabilized the chaotic atmosphere and their support encouraged us to take risks. As a result we grew as performers, despite the fact that we never showed our gratitude by ever leaving a gratuity and that our outrageous behavior and nasty heckler rebuffs often cost them several would-be tips. After the show they'd hang out at the bar, drinking with us, listening to our endless loop of complaints about our sets and station in life, laughed at our untried jokes and even participated in whatever childish endeavor we thought was sheer brilliance.

To many a comic (not counting women comics) the waitresses were the only continuous contact we had with females. As I've mentioned previously (and delve into more detail later), most comics were shy if not comatose when it came to talking to women. We chose the smoothness of silence over the charm of stuttering. We eventually gained enough confidence to talk to the waitresses because they had actually witnessed us being funny and saw us use our wit to make strong hunky hecklers and successful businessmen look like they couldn't spell IQ. So our fear of asking them out was not flagrant enough to be institutionalized, even though there was better than a ninety percent chance that we'd be rejected and would see the waitress every night for the next four or five years. Despite the waitresses rebukes there were few if any nervous breakdowns.

Marisa Tchornobai, Jamie Evans and Barbara Capelli

At the Improv any excursion, other than to play ball, was organized by either Judy Orbach with waitresses Debbie Rene, Pat Buckles and Marisa Tchornobai or by bartender Jamie Evans. The Catch picnics were arranged by bartender, Peter Perri, with the help of managers Terry Columbo, Billy Delgiorno and waiter Louis Feranda. They also brought the equipment and took the group pictures. The Comic Strip's outings were put together by its man for all seasons and reasons, the one and only, Lucien Hold. The showcase owners and top management, Howie Klein, Chris Albrecht, and (later) Silver Friedman (from the Improv), Rick Newman (from Catch), and Ritchie Tienken, Jim McGowan, and Bob Wachs (from Comic Strip) did their share of getting us together for photos and occasional meetings, but the bulk of the outings were planned by those who served the audience their drinks while never neglecting their job as our babysitters.

Many of the best pictures in this book only exist because waitresses like Debbie Rene, who owned and knew how to operate a camera (when buying film to match a camera was much harder for comics than figuring out what combination of clean shirts and dirty jeans to wear on stage). They were the visual chroniclers of our era and somehow managed to keep the pictures from being lost forever. If it were me who took the photos I'd have lost them two minutes after they were taken. I, like most of my brethren, could misplace anything. I could even lose a tattoo.

Debbie Rene Duperrieu and Larry David

Un-Sex Symbols

"The difference in a musician's groupie and a comedian's groupie...after a show, a Rock groupie will say to the musician, 'I think you're so talented , I want to screw your brains out.' The comedian's groupie will say to the comedian, 'I think you're so talented... this is my husband, Al.'"

-GLENN HIRSCH

John DeBellis Gilbert Gottfried and Joe Piscopo

Comics for the most part didn't have groupies—we had singers' rejects. We didn't score, we won by forfeit. If a comic were Adam in the Garden of Eden, even after he gave his rib to make Eve, he'd spend the night alone because he'd assume she had a boyfriend. I spent much of my after set time hanging out with Larry David, imagining new reasons and ways for girls to reject us.

It starts even deeper than just a horrific self-image. It evolves from our comic souls. Unlike the artistic soul, which is something to be nourished, the comic soul is something that we're stuck with—a deep feeling of not being one with the universe but being one *against* the universe. I'm not saying we didn't occasionally get lucky, but if looked upon from the proper prospective, it would really be a matter of how damn *unlucky* the woman was. It would beg the question: What atrocity did she commit in a previous life? Singers, musicians, actors—even jugglers—were the sex symbols, not comics. We were created to show them that there are a lot more horrible things to be than talentless, tasteless and unemployed. It was our job to make the girls laugh—it was our job to make them happy. Well, at least that's the way most of us felt about ourselves—at least the positive thinkers like me.

"Women would look at the comedian as the no-frills carnival that comes to town. It's not the circus, but it's all you've got."
-JEFF CESARIO

Dating was not natural to comics, because for most of us it required human contact and in extreme cases, affection. We'd also, at some point, have to carry on a conversation that doesn't start with, "Is this funny?" or end with "Can I use that?"

Comics like to be around other comics, not only for the laughs. We knew that whatever we felt about each other didn't have to be expressed in any form of physical contact other than an occasional pat on the back. Alan Lefkowitz, in an attempt for Glenn Hirsch and I to get over our aversion of physical affection between beings of a similar species and especially gender, suggested that whenever we left or greeted each other we should hug.

Both people pleasers and not wanting to disappoint the ultimate authority figure, Glenn and I grudgingly did as we were asked. At first the hugs were robotic and stiff, like two coat trees falling into each other, lasting as long as a blink. We'd exit a cab, pat each other before one of us dove back into the taxi and in our deepest voices spout manly phrases like, "Hurry, one of my girlfriends is waiting for me, lying naked on my coffee table that I personally constructed from giant empty steel cable spindles. I need to screw her before the ballgame starts."

After months of practice, our hugs became long enough to obsess over how long to hold it and who should break the hug first. We came to the conclusion that it was the responsibility of the person who initiated the hug to break it off before the other person felt uncomfortable. At first, these calculations made for false starts and stuttering break-offs, but after a few more months of trial and error, the parting time became instinctive, which in comic talk means self-conscious behavior without visible hesitation. The next phase was to transfer that skill to hugging other people, a phase that seems to be getting easier after twenty-five years. I figure that I'll be able to hug the priest who reads me my last rights.

Of course, as previously stated there was a small minority of comics who were very good with women, like Richard Lewis, Barry Diamond, David Sayh, Kelly Rogers, Richard Belzer and then there were the pheromone drenched Keenan Wayans, Brant Von Hoffman and Buddy Mantia (all three so handsome that women would make love to them shining a flashlight on their faces).

When I met David Sayh the first time, I realized almost immediately that he was one of the few comics who had a way with the ladies. When David spoke to a pretty girl, he would actually look in her eyes instead of completely avoiding her or her airspace by blinking and glancing around the room in spurts, as if following a wounded bee out for revenge. David would even hold her gaze and talk in complete sentences—not in long, disconnected phrases that collided and competed with each other.

I'm sad to say most comics don't see women as sexual objects, we see them as objects that get in the way of sex! When I was a very young comic, one woman actually said that she enjoyed having sex with me. She said I was so nervous that I was better than her vibrator. Okay, that's a line from my act. But it's probably not far from the truth. If we could, we'd slip a joke into a chemical formula. If Einstein were also a comic his Theory of Relativity would be called Einstein's Theory of My Cousin Is So Fat I Blame Her for the Expanding Universe and Relativity.

Glenn Hirsch was an abnormal breed for a comic. He was good looking, not handsome in the classic sense. He was also self-deprecating, displayed inappropriate behavior at comic appropriate times, and he had the standup's natural dread of affection, but he also could have had all the women *we* wanted. They chased after him, but he didn't want, nor need any. He was living with Sue Giosa, the beautiful woman he's still married to. If Glenn weren't so damn naturally funny, I'd doubt his comic credentials and think he was really a musician that had funny material written for him.

Imagine being with the same woman for over thirty years! Most comics couldn't look at the same Playboy centerfold for more than a month unless the other side had at least three pictures in different poses. Despite his ability to maintain a healthy long-term relationship, Glenn is still one of my comic idols. Glenn did two things that earned him that merit, that special place of honor amongst comics. Number one: Glenn was late for his own wedding because it was the first game Phil Simms started as the Giant's quarterback. Number two: he perpetrated what could possibly be the bravest, most manly act a comic ever committed, which spits in the frown of one of our biggest fears, the germ terrors. Glenn dropped his hairbrush in the toilet and started to comb his thick red locks with it. When Sue shouted at him for doing something so disgusting, Glenn told her that water from the toilet was clean because of the constant flushing, and then proceeded to scoop up a palm full of that good old toilet water and drink it. Need I say more?

"Throughout my entire showcase experience, I managed to keep my virginity." -**MARJORIE GROSS**
-

There were male comics who had steady girlfriends and some even had wives they would bring to the clubs. I don't remember a female comic bringing a non-comic boyfriend to any of the clubs. In fact I don't remember any of the female comics having non-comic boyfriends.

I would be headlining a comedy club, and after the show I couldn't even get a girl to talk to me. The opening act, a local guy, who maybe had been doing standup for six months and didn't get any laughs, got laid every night."

-GILBERT GOTTFRIED

One night Bobby Kelton actually brought a date along with Larry and I which, to say the least, was unusual. During the first year of standup the three of us were as conjoined as the Presidents on Mount Rushmore.

John DeBellis, Larry David and Bobby Kelton

I had found a parking space about a hundred yards from the diner. We exited my car and it took us almost a block before we realized we'd forgotten the girl. By the time we turned around she had fought her way through the mulching fast food and wrappers in my back seat to find the car door and figured out how to open it without a crow bar. I'm pretty sure she eventually caught up to us and I'm almost positive she paid for herself (probably because we forgot).

Oh, occasionally us "have-nots" would get lucky, which, in my case, often took other comics to recognize the opportunity for me. One night I was at the bar at Catch after having a few drinks with a girl from the audience. I didn't realize she was coming on to me, even though her legs were wrapped around me twice, we both were wearing her shirt and sharing a tongue. Buddy Mantia, got my cab fare from the bartender and thrust the eight bucks in my face and said, "John, take her home, now!"

One Sunday night at the Improv I had a great set and was standing at the bar, when a waitress brought a note to me that said, "Do you want to meet a sexy California girl?" Back then, when it came to meeting a girl, the only thing that really mattered was gender. I would have been willing to meet a girl from a land mass made from nuclear waste. Being a California girl brought up images from Beach Boy songs, which quickly faded when I saw my reflection in the mirror behind the bar and all I could think of was Alice Cooper. Of course, I handed the waitress back the note, on which I had nervously written, "Yes." It didn't occur to me to have the waitress point her out before I'd given her my reply.

I waited at the bar, trying out postures and expressions that would make me look like I wasn't counting the seconds until I'd be rejected, or overcome with fear that she might look like a girl every male in California rejected.

Before I had a chance to sweat out all the toxins in my body, she tapped me on the shoulder and said, "I'm the California girl." Much to my delight and near stroke, she was an Olivia Newton-John look-alike, but better because she wasn't Australian and was already feeling the two-drink minimum.

I don't remember much of our conversation, probably because most of what I said was either unintelligible or well worth forgetting. What I do recall is that she wanted to go out for real drinks and that she had a girlfriend. Yes, the dreaded girlfriend. And, of course, asked if I had a comic friend for her pal. Now, I figured since she hadn't introduced her friend as a California, Arizona, New Mexico, Rhode Island, District of

Columbia, or even an Area 51 girl, that she probably wasn't a looker. But I was really in luck that night. Sitting a few feet away in a booth was Peter Bales-- the same Peter Bales to whom Glenn Hirsch at a gig in the Jersey boondocks said his famous words, "Where are you going to take her to, your coat?" Back then Peter never met a woman or reasonable facsimile that he didn't lust after. Well, at least up until then.

Even guys like Peter knew the formula. It's simple math: the better looking the girl, the uglier the girlfriend. While my beach blanket beauty walked into the showroom, I pleaded, lied and offered to write an hour of new material for Peter if he stayed. Before I could offer to pay off his college loans, the California girl returned with a six-foot, knockout brunette. Peter was so happy I thought he might actually hug me.

We ended up at some bar on the Upper East Side, spending several months of cab fare on Tequila. The idea was for me to get drunk fast enough to not care about eventually getting the boot or to get her drunk enough that she couldn't find the boot. By the time we left the bar we were all drunk and before I could figure out where to go next, we found ourselves in an upscale NYC apartment. Me and the California girl, and Peter with his gorgeous Amazon woman.

It could have been a night that would be bragged about by comics at the Improv, Catch and the Comic Strip for centuries—one that I personally would brag about well into several of my next lives. But brag I would not. Embarrassed I would be. You see, shortly after our arrival, I started to throw up! Not, once, not twice, no, it marched out of me like an unending legend of Roman soldiers. I was the fat guy in Monty Python's vomit sketch, only sloppier. Since the apartment was a friend's sublet and it took us a while to find the bathroom, the place looked and smelled like an apartment that a bulimic Oscar Madison dwelled in for decades. Peter would have hated me for life if he hadn't been seen by several other comics leaving the club with Wonder Woman.

The next night, which was Monday and audition night at Catch, my stomach felt like it was being tortured for trying to escape, making me still sick enough to pass up the sixty bucks for emceeing.

Unfortunately, I had to show up in case my sub didn't. I was leaning against the bar with my back to the showroom entrance, nursing an orange juice and feeling relieved that my sub was on stage. I heard some comics stop talking and wondered what had put the brakes on their babble. I turned my head and not more than ten feet from me, as gorgeous as ever, was the California girl and her Paula Bunyan friend walking toward the showroom. I didn't know whether to say hello, wave, smile, frown, crack a vomit joke or throw the juice in my face and try to hide behind the pulp. It wouldn't have mattered if I had smiled thousand dollar bills, they glared at me like I had not only thrown up all over their friend's apartment but I suffocated their dog with my puke. Then they turned away, and any memory of me, current or future, disappeared forever—unless they're still telling stories about Vomit Guy.

I had one experience where a woman (a female comic) rejected me and while it turned out to be an embarrassing moment for her, became a humiliating one for me. I had asked out an attractive female comic, who turned me down politely by telling me she was gay. That kind of rejection is always easier on the ego unless you think that she turned gay the minute you asked her out, which I didn't. I had a good set that night, so there was no reason to feel that inadequate.

A few nights later, I entered my large, two bedroom apartment, which I shared with one of the "haves"—Brant Von Hoffman. Brant had left the door open to his room, not expecting me to come back between shows. Moaning loudly, with such pleasure it blocked out the self-mocking laughter in my head, was the female comic who turned me down by saying she was gay! Obviously, she was lying and didn't know Brant and I were roommates, or maybe she didn't care, or Brant was such a manly-man he turned her straight... Or worse yet, my asking her out (despite my great set in which I really killed) had indeed turned her gay and Brant in one evening had quickly turned her straight again.

One other experience I remember distinctly was a double date along with a comic buddy whose name I can't remember distinctly (most likely he was a singer who was mildly funny). We were bringing the girls back to my apartment for a special fish dinner, complete with a lobster. I have no idea how we had gotten the lobster. I'm sure whatever exchange took place, it wasn't a monetary one. Being a bachelor and according to the male rules, pots, pans and extra silverware were luxuries that had to be washed every once in a while. Larry David only had one spoon, one fork, one cup, one plate, one bowl, etc. Eating at his place was done in shifts. So, in order to make this feast we needed bachelor-unfriendly utensils.

Without money, there was only one place to get what we needed and that was the Improv. Chris Albrecht told us to take whatever we needed, just do it without the homicidal chef seeing. So late one night, after the chef had left, we took silverware and several large pots, not to mention a few round loaves of black bread. Amongst comedy clubs, the Improv had the best bread. It had a very thick outside crust and a soft solid inside that seemed to stay fresh for years. If you scooped it out, you could use it as a bank or a rat could use it as a bomb shelter.

The next night, the girls came over. My date, of course, was the shy one—the one that entered slowly, looking for an escape route. My friend's date, on the other hand, was looking for floor space. At first, we all sat in the living room, drinking beer. Wine was a decade away from being included in the comic's pallet—except for Ed Bluestone who waited to go on stage holding a goblet of Chardonnay. My pal took his date into my kitchenette, which was the size of a batter's box, to prepare the food, while I sat in the living room trying to think about what I could say to keep my date from running out.

I started to smell the food, which meant that there was a chance that I'd be able to use all four borrowed plates. And we had even gotten to the point where my date started to fill in the other half (okay, tenth) of the conversation. My pal and his girl were in still in the kitchenette, but by the sound of my creaking tiles and the kicking of cabinets his date had found almost enough floor space. Bothered by the noise in the kitchen, my date started talking more, faster and louder. Just as I was about to offer her a cleaner glass for her beer, the lights went out in the building. I couldn't see her, she couldn't see me and before she could scream, we heard loud banging of pots, pans and utensils, fish crashing, and shouts of either the greatest orgasm registered within ear shot of a comic, or two people and a lobster in pain. At that moment, the lights came on.

My date and I had circumvented my furniture and hopped our way to the kitchenette. On the floor with pots, pans, bouillabaisse and a dying lobster on top of them, were my friend and his date. Unconcerned about etiquette or the mixing of courses, they were determined to finish their own course. It was exactly like the beach scene in *From Here to Eternity*, only without the ocean, sand, the sun or swim suits; and here, the lovers weren't bathed in a romantic wave, they were littered with a smörgåsbord of fish, round bread and dented pots. With the lights on and only a few feet from the door, my date didn't wait to say, "Goodbye," "Thanks for the beer," or "Let's cover our friends with a blanket and still cook the lobster." She ran out the door and down the stairs, preferring not to wait for the elevator, its doors already opening. I left my friends, went into my room, closed and locked my door and ate a stale slice of pizza that I'd left on my night stand the day before, because as was my custom, I'd written a joke on the bottom of it.

My tragic love life has had its funny moments, but there were none funnier than Larry David's. The mishaps on Curb Your Enthusiasm and the neurosis rich Seinfeld are, for the most part, brilliant exaggerations of Larry David's life, or the thoughts that go on inside his cataclysmic mind. If Larry David had a date, it would become a major event of neurotic proportions, much like George Costanza on Seinfeld. He'd worry about how long ago he shaved, what t-shirt to wear, how wrinkled it was in case he had to take his shirt off, whether to tuck it in or leave it out, and all that, after deciding which jeans looked like date jeans. But his biggest concern was, and I'll use his exact words: "John, I didn't make yet. What happens if I have to make when I'm with her?"

In one of his Seinfeld episodes, George talks about being in bed with a girl and having to go to the bathroom—number 2. According to LD it actually happened to him, and the real problem was that it was a studio apartment and the bathroom was right next to the bed. Of course, LD didn't want the woman to hear anything, so he made up some excuse that he had to get something or other out of his pants and ran out of her apartment and never returned.

At one point, Larry was dating a girl for six months or so and was going to actually take her out to dinner, not at the club, but at a grown-up restaurant with pull out chairs, for her birthday. When he got to the restaurant, he feigned going to the men's room, took the waiter aside and gave him a two-for-one coupon and told the guy not to mention it when he brought the check. Well, the dinner went fine, other than the usual LD changing his mind on what to order several times, debating whether it was healthy or not, finally ordering and feeling guilty about it like he had broken an oath to a sacred dietician on his death bed. When his meal arrived he then became envious of what she was eating and complained that he should have ordered what she did the whole time he was eating everything on his plate. The meal, plus some additional self-consciousness about his eating form in a restaurant at night, must have stretched out longer than expected. LD signaled for the bill and a few minutes later a different waiter (because of shift change) presented Larry with the bill, and wanting to get a tip for the full price, not only specifically mentioned—but pointed out the two-for-one coupon. She was furious, left the restaurant and, of course, broke up with Larry.

It was a warm summer day and the girl Larry had a date with must have been very special, because LD put on his best pants, most likely his newest, or at least his cleanest jeans. He even wore shoes. Yes, shoes, not his treasured but worn-out black Chuck Taylor Converse All-Stars. The plan was for Larry to meet the girl in Central Park. LD, not wanting to give the woman any additional excuses to find him unacceptable arrived at their meeting spot very early. As he was sitting down on the park bench, he noticed something was different. What was it? His clothes looked fine, almost wrinkle-free. His hair was a loose afro and there wasn't even a breeze so there couldn't have been much wind damage done to it. And then it hit him. It was undeniable and way too familiar—the sweet fragrant smell of dog shit. He looked at his shoes—there was nothing on their soles. He sniffed some more as his nostrils closed in on the odor. It was all around him, but not in view. Yet there was nothing on the ground. And then it hit him harder than a Larry Holmes straight jab to the jaw. He was sitting in dog shit! Some dog didn't let nature take its normal course. Instead the beast jumped up onto the bench in that defining moment. Could it possibly have known Larry was coming? Maybe it was part of some citywide canine plot against him. There was no time to debate the neurotic possibilities, because LD had to either change his pants or somehow get them cleaned. He was too far from home to change and since no one had cell phones back then, it was too late to call her.

LD did the noble if not slightly insane thing. He ran to the closest place where there was running water, which happened to be Tavern on the Green. Now this was the seventies, the peak of the Tavern's popularity. He moved quickly, as not to arouse too many nostrils and made it to the men's room, which, luckily at the time, seemed empty. He took off his pants and standing in his underwear, started to wash them in the sink—a sink that sat in the men's room of the exclusive and swank Tavern on the Green! While he scrubbed the dog shit (not even thinking about how he was going to dry them), security guards who'd called the police exploded through the door. Before his date had even started, he was about to be arrested for indecent exposure. Somehow LD, who could out excuse just about anyone, talked his way out of being booked or even taken down to the precinct—but he did manage to stand up his date. Had he been standing up while waiting for his date, his whole future might have been different. Well, at least that night he wouldn't have been standing at the Improv bar telling me the story.

Years later, when I was living in L.A., and actually married at the time, Larry was single and living in Laurel Canyon. I think we were in our mid to late thirties. He called and asked me to come over to his house because he had something incredible to tell me. Well, when I got there, Larry's anxiety was not his normal everyday get-up-in-the-morning-and-hate-everything-about-myself panic. No, this was definitely heightened. His face had a washed-out pallor like a vampire who drank someone coming out of Starbucks and couldn't sleep from the caffeine. I figured either Larry had just read something about a new fatal disease and imagined he had contracted it and was about to die or it was a woman, which of course it was.

The night before, LD had gone to the movies and while at the refreshment stand fell head-over-sneakers for the popcorn girl. He kept saying, "John, I think I'm in love with the popcorn girl. And I think she might like me. I made her laugh and she gave me more popcorn. What should I do? I think she's in her twenties, is that too young?"

We decided that being a comic automatically took a few years off your appearance and a decade or more off your rate of maturity. So the fact that she was old enough to legally hold a job meant she was old enough to date a thirty-something comedian.

In our emotional life, there are people years and there are comic years. Psychologically, we're half-life regressive. For every decade a regular person matures, we mature five, until at some point we're physically old enough to either actually experience a partial life or just blame it on dementia.

Since LD did not ask the popcorn girl what her name was, or where she lived, and I knew Larry would never be able to just walk up to a strange woman, he'd have to approach her armed with his best weapon-- one that didn't require his standing before her stammering. It was far mightier than a sword or even a cocktail in his hand—the weapon was the written word. As previously mentioned, comics, especially Larry and I, were scared adolescents around a woman we fancied. If either of us were a Governor and a very pretty girl were in the electric chair and we could save her life, we'd be too insecure to pardon her, thinking she'd rather get toasted then talk to us.

He read the letter to me, and of course it was very funny. One line stood out. Larry had written, "If you go out with me, I'm prepared to give up meat for you."

He finished the letter and we decided to go to the movie theater that night so LD could hand-deliver it. LD had a brown Fiat (he purchased it when he worked on the TV show "Fridays") whose first engine he'd blown up because he'd forgotten to put oil in it since the day he bought it. So we drove there, parked nearby, walked into the theater and Larry asked for the popcorn girl. We were taken to a lanky guy, in his early twenties, with acne splattered across his cheeks like crumbs left on a comic's chair, wearing the exaggerated expression of a Broadway star belting out the lyrics, "I'm younger and better looking than both of you."

Larry feigned confidence that unfortunately toppled out of at his mouth and he stammered, "Uh… I'm looking for the popcorn girl."

"What popcorn girl?" the kid said, like the authority in his fiefdom was absolute.

"The one who was working here last night," Larry, trying to cover his disappointment, spoke like he had no authority anywhere on the planet.

"She's off tonight," he quickly cranked out, warning the universe the schedule he made was never ever to be broken.

Before His Honor could dismiss us, LD squeezed in, "Can you give her this?" Not giving the Sheriff of Nottingham the time to say no, Larry handed the guy the envelope.

The multiplex mogul, no longer feeling threatened by us thirty-something, alfalfa males, actually smiled nicely at us and said, "Sure, I'll give it to her when she comes in tomorrow."

LD and I turned and walked back to his car, discussing how long he should wait for a reply before knowing whether he'd been rejected or not.

We circled the block and were about to go home, when I thought I saw the guy open up the letter. I told LD, and Larry, never being one to back down from the opportunity to confront his own embarrassment, decided to go back and find out.

When we approached the ticket booth, the guy was indeed reading the letter, not just to himself, but to three or four other members of the acne brother and sisterhood.

LD walked up to the guy and asked as impolitely and impotently as he could, "Are you reading my note?"

The kid smiled and said, "Yes," after which he and his crew of pimple people began laughing.

"That was personal… That wasn't to you… That was personal."

"I got permission," he said, like he was shoving a dirty newspaper in a dog's face.

"From the popcorn girl?" LD asked more surprised than curious.

The guy shot back. "Yeah, she's my girlfriend."

"She's your girlfriend!" LD repeated like bad Mexican food that hung onto your esophagus, dangling awhile, before it did a nosedive into your gut.

Their laughter was Miracle Grow for pimples, as thousands of pink mounds leaned toward us cackling. LD didn't have his usual temper tantrum. No, this time he didn't have a stage to walk off of, or a bum to fight to the death over a tuna sandwich. He just shouted from the top, bottom and middle of his lungs. "You shouldn't read other people's letters!" as he steamed toward the car. When we were driving away, I saw the letter being passed around, the ticket booth bursting with knives of laughter, looking at us until LD and his humiliation passed out of sight.

One Day a Year at a Time

As you must know by now, the comic's day starts as close to sundown as possible. We don't awaken as much as we just get bored of sleeping—even our subconscious suffers from ADD. The first thing I usually did was to try to find the telephone and quickly ruin another comic's sleep. We'd both hold on to consciousness by asking each other if we had anything planned for the day, which we both knew we didn't. Our time was usually spent trying to figure out what to do until we met at the clubs. Usually this meant a couple of us meeting for breakfast at Poachers or the Green Kitchen; on other days, several of us came out, which made leaving a tip possible.

After breakfast, which could last an hour or two at least, I'd go back to my apartment and call one of the comics I'd just left, to discuss something else about ourselves. We never talked about the world's problems, or how to make a contribution to society, unless it could be turned into a line or a bit. When I finished that call, I made a few more calls to other comics and talked about the same stuff, unless we included sports, which was considered a serious socially relevant conversation. Almost as important as talking about weekend spots.

The week the Jonestown Massacre occurred, where over 400 hundred people took their own lives drinking Kool Aid, I bought three newspapers: The New York Daily News, The New York Post and The New York Times. After reading all three, I still didn't know about the mass suicide because on the same day, the Yankees signed Tommy John. I skipped all of the billboard-sized Jonestown headlines and went straight to the sports section. Joe Piscopo called and said that he couldn't believe what had happened. My reply was in complete agreement, and I added that Tommy John, being a left-handed ground ball pitcher would be perfect for Yankee stadium. Joe, of course, had been talking about the events in Jonestown, but quickly changed subjects when he found out the Yankees acquired Tommy John.

For me, the rest of the day was devoted to writing, or avoiding writing until it was dark. Most of the time I'd write jokes for myself, but in order to pay the bills I'd spend at least a couple of days a month writing jokes for Catskills comics, all of which wound up in piles of papers that some would call a dog-eared shuffle. After deducting several phone calls, trips to the bathroom, opening and closing drawers, sitting and lying in several positions, reading the sports, or talking to my roommate Brant about how I should be writing, I spent between two and four hours actually writing. Out of the pages of doodles and scribbles that looked like something found in the trash bin of a psych ward, I usually found one or two jokes to try out.

After writing I'd call around to see which clubs everyone would be at so I could decide where my best opportunity to get on was and who I could split a cab with. We'd also discuss who the MCs were at each club, which was an important factor in deciding where to spend your night, since each MC had his or her own favorite comics. We'd also try to figure out which clubs might have the largest crowds, how long they'd last and if we had a chance to get on that night. Once dressed, I spent my usual fifteen or twenty minutes trying to locate my keys, wallet and the jokes I had just written—and then, I was ready to go out.

We hardly ever ate dinner at home or had dinner plans, because, until the club cut out the kitchen to put in more seats, we'd eat there. If my plan was to go to the Improv first, I'd drive Brant across town (since he worked the Improv almost exclusively), otherwise I'd walk the four blocks to Catch, or the six blocks to the Strip and later, I'd get my car and go to the Improv.

As mentioned earlier, for the first year and a half in NYC I shared a huge two-bedroom apartment with Brant Von Hoffman. Back then, you could live a month in the city for less than it costs to survive a day now. We didn't have many extravagant needs other than a few things that had to eventually be refrigerated. We each had large, almost loft-size, bedrooms that ran next to each other divided by a common wall. The bedrooms opened into a hallway, where the bathroom and a closet with a Nerf basketball hoop was, widening to room size as it neared the kitchen. In the fat end of the foyer, we placed a table and several chairs that became ground zero for our poker parlor. Zero being the amount I usually had at the end of the night.

Brant and I, like most comics, were not known for our housekeeping. To us, trash was something that eventually disintegrated, thus, the roaches found ample crumbs and nourishment. In fact, they were so well fed, I imagined them moving furniture to make room for their own gym. One night, while scrounging for an evening snack, Brant and I turned on the kitchen light to find a brigade of roaches munching on floor tiles. They didn't even bother to turn away or run. They just stood there flexing their antennas at us while their leader, a cucumber-sized roach clinging to the wall, flipped the light switch off. Brant and I were standing in the dark kitchen surrounded by a band of militant insects. We finally had had enough. We came up with an idea: instead of insecticide, which we might confuse with a condiment, we went to a pet store and bought gecko lizards, whose diet consisted of mostly roaches. Black and about four or five inches long. If it weren't for the large mouths, big eyes, long tails and four legs, the geckos could have been mistaken for a decent cigar. Like us, they only came out at night, but unlike us, it was only in pitch darkness, and the roaches were not their competition, they were their health food.

For the first few weeks, Brant and I would turn the lights off, wait about an hour and then rush into the kitchen with a flashlight only to find our geckos, on the wall, burping. After six months or so, the roaches were gone and so were the geckos, which we were told by the pet shop owner would find their way to another roach-infested apartment.

The bugs and lizards disappeared, but comics continued to fill the apartment during our off-duty hours. With the Nerf basketball hoop we'd hung in the hallway, Buddy Manita, Kelly Rodgers, Robert Wuhl, Joe Piscopo, Mark Schiff, Glenn Hirsch, Larry David, Bobby Kelton, Steve Mittleman, Brant and myself played one-man games, usually H.O.R.S.E. or out. Sometimes we'd just shoot baskets. I established the record of making 25 straight shots from the foul line (a piece of tape on the floor). One night, after losing in the bottom of the ninth to Buddy in our APBA baseball league, I scolded the dice and decided that life was just too taxing to be lived on a conscious level, so I closed my door and went to sleep. About six hours later, Brant and I woke to the sound of wood being smashed, objects breaking and maniacal screams loud enough to knock the earth off its axis and start global warming. We rushed out of our rooms, both carrying baseball bats, ready to beat the intruder senseless. It turned out Buddy had been outside my room shooting baskets for six hours. He'd made 25 straight baskets and missed what would have been the record-breaking shot, the Nerf ball riding the rim for a few seconds. So naturally this led to his demolishing everything in sight.

Joe Piscopo and John DeBellis

Birthday parties were another activity that regularly took place at our apartment. We held one for Kelly Rodgers, a combined party for Rodney Dangerfield and Pat Benatar, as well as several other birthday-bashes. It was during one of these birthday parties, probably mine, that Joe Piscopo, Brant Von Hoffman, Kelly Rodgers, Buddy Mantia, Steve Mittleman, Mark Schiff and I started throwing around the football. We'd run across my room, someone would toss the ball and we'd try to make circus catches as we dove onto my bed, which had ancient springs that had long lost their bounce. We even played a little tackle football in the foyer. This all went on hours after the clubs had closed. Finally, my downstairs neighbor called and Piscopo answered the phone. The neighbor shouted, "It's 4 am, for Christ's sake!" Joe offered a logical rebuttal, "We work at night!" and we kept playing.

On the weekends the shows could go on to 4 am. After the paying customers had cleared out, one of our comic brothers would occasionally enter the building and for two hours become the king of rock and roll, Elvis. And when Andy Kaufman was Elvis, you thought the King had risen from the dead to show all his impersonators how far from the real deal they were. Every gyration, sneer, karate stance and bead of sweat made for the perfect Elvis. And then Andy/Elvis would leave the building and we'd go to the Green Kitchen.

At the Green Kitchen, Sid Rosenbloom, a comic who had polio as a child, would climb out of his wheelchair, crawl around the floor and under people's tables (sometimes reaching up to take a French fry). Kelly Rodgers and I would send chicken dinners to the table of a couple of cute girls, or send an attractive woman twelve, or thirteen beers at once.

I'd often stand in front of Catch or the Green Kitchen and get strange people (by supplying them with the money) to walk up to Gilbert Gottfried (proud to be the cheapest person alive or dead) and hand him a dollar, which he gladly stuffed in his pocket without asking why. After he finally caught on, when people would walk toward him, he'd just hold his hand out. A few times people who weren't involved in our dumb jokes would think he was begging and hand him money

There were other nights where we took our activities outside. Buddy and I would play Wiffle ball on 75th Street at 3 am. Warren Bloom and Kelly Rodgers would play frisbee in the middle of First Avenue at 4 a.m., like it was noon on an empty sandlot.

Brant and I lived in that apartment for a year or so, until he and his girlfriend decided to get married. I volunteered to move out, so they could stay. I found a place on 60th Street and Ninth Avenue: Apartment 4X, which had no relation to my love life, but was more of a cruel joke. It was a large, one bedroom in a building with a doorman and a private park that ran between 60th and 58th street. I got the place through Lenny Maxwell's girlfriend, Joan Levi, who was a bartender at the Improv and now my next door neighbor. She had told me how to blatantly bribe the building manager.

One of my last nights at the East Side apartment, I was packing boxes with Larry David's help and telling him that by moving to the West Side, we could hang out more. Larry, as neurotic as he was, helped me pack even though he had to leave for an important audition…an audition that turned out to be very successful. That night he landed a job as a regular performer on the new competition of "SNL" in the late night sketch comedy wars, called "Fridays," which, of course was on Friday night. LD wrote and performed on Fridays. It was also where he met Michael Richards and Larry Charles, a writer/producer on "Seinfeld." He also was reunited with comic's Bruce Mahler and Melanie Chartoff.

"I was glad Larry and Bruce were there--they felt like my cousins and had similar taste. ABC wanted to clone SNL and we were mortified. That made for a tense atmosphere. Also, our writers, producers and director were high most of the time, which made crazy working conditions for us straight people."

-MELANIE CHARTOFF

I moved to the West Side and my comic routine changed. Gone were the long breakfasts at Poacher's. At first, I ate breakfast alone at the Flame Diner, reading only the sports. About that time, LD's older brother, Ken, had divorced his wife and started to hang out at the Improv with Larry.

Ken, or KD as some of us called him, is the exact opposite of his brother. He's louder, naturally confident, gregarious—and can talk to anyone, including women. Ken and I quickly became friends and he spent weekends sleeping on the couch Larry sold me, until he eventually, found his own apartment a few blocks away. Two of the things we had in common were that we were both Yankees and New York Giants fans, which was far more important that belonging to the same political party or being a member of a local, communist sleeper cell. All my life I had wanted season tickets to the Giants games, but there was always one tiny obstacle--a waiting list of over a hundred thousand. I had asked Robert Klein if he could get me tickets. He tried, but couldn't. Then I asked Rodney Dangerfield. In spite of his loser image, he successfully got me two Giants season tickets. I couldn't afford both, so Ken used the other ticket (which he handed down to Glenn Hirsch).

Shortly before I moved to the West Side, Larry David moved to Manhattan Plaza, a building which was subsidized by the city for people in the arts. I'm amazed that some bureaucrat actually realized that standup comedy was an art form. Kenny Kramer, who was a former comic and the model for the Kramer character on "Seinfeld," lived right down the hall from LD.

For "Seinfeld," Larry borrowed the essence of Kenny Kramer—his crazy schemes, his odd friends and his ability to seduce woman. The one thing that didn't transfer, were Kenny's physical traits: his grand mal smile and eyes that amplified the fortuitousness of life (his mostly).

Glenn Hirsch and Kenny Kramer

At one point in the late seventies, little red neon lights you could attach to your shirt became a craze, and people thought these psychedelic pinpricks made them look cool instead of like a radioactive hemophiliac. Kenny bought, traded or conned someone out of the parts and paid starving comics, musicians and actors to assemble them. He opened a concession at Bonds, one of the hottest nightclubs at the time. I think it was Kenny himself who told me he made 100 grand on those little red illuminating dots. As on "Seinfeld," Kenny and Larry left their doors open and could barge in on each other at any moment, not that Kenny would be interrupting anything risqué at Larry's place. A few months later, Barry Diamond moved into Manhattan Plaza and Chris Albrecht moved to an apartment across the street. Manhattan Plaza, with Kenny's assistance or persistence, became a wild social scene with stories of sordid sexual escapades, which I'm sure Larry, like me, had no part in. If LD did, he never told me about it, which is unlike him, since back then it would be more of an accomplishment that an escapade.

LD and I often went to the movies between shows at the Improv. Larry didn't like to stand in lines and came up with a brilliant way to avoid them. We'd stand in the street in the back of a newsstand, and as the line moved into the movie, we'd easily slip in. We saw *Star Wars* between shows using that method. The times when we went to movies that we couldn't sneak into lines, like at the Ziegfield, I'd do the waiting and LD somehow always managed to show up just before the line was let into the theater.

One New Year's Eve, after the first show, LD and I decided to walk the two blocks to Times Square to see the ball drop. Larry and I didn't normally like crowds that we aren't standing above, nor enjoyed seeing a ball that wasn't meant to be caught. We fought the discomfort and boredom and stayed long enough to see the ball slide down on the first moment of the New Year. Standing next to me the whole time, totally by accident, was a guy I knew fairly well from high school. But the thing that really made this coincidental reunion memorable was watching him pick the pocket of the guy next to him. In the great New Jersey tradition, my thieving hometown friend went on to become a police officer.

My apartment on the West Side also became a hangout after shows. In fact, we held what might have been the first post-1960s " 60s party" in my apartment. Somewhere downtown I bought a strobe light for the living room. We removed all the furniture from the bedroom and stored it in the basement, because Kenny Kramer, who had previously owned a head shop, filled the room with black lights and dozens of psychedelic posters.

Steve Mittleman, Brant Von Hoffman, and John DeBellis

And much to my amazement, many of the comics including Kelly Rodgers, Steve Mittleman, Brant Von Hoffman, Glenn Hirsch, Kramer, Mark Schiff, Adrianne Tolsch and Larry Ragland actually went out of their way and dressed like hippies with fake beards and mustaches. I don't recall if LD came, but if he had, I'm sure he didn't dress for the occasion. I know his brother Ken was there and did dress up—I have the pictures to prove it.

My upstairs neighbor was actor and singer Tony Darrow (later of "The Sopranos"), who helped Brant Von Hoffman and Bobby Kelton's brother, Michael, get an apartment in the attached building across our private park. I have no idea how he managed that feat but I imagine it would have worked well as an audition for "The Sopranos." A few years later, after Brant and his wife moved to L.A., another comic, Kenny Block, took over his apartment and as far as I know never found any body parts hidden in the walls.

When Brant got married, for a wedding present, Joe Piscopo, Keenan Wayans, Steven Mittleman, Paul Provenza, Buddy Mantia, Chris Albrecht, Glenn Hirsch and I chipped in and bought him a dachshund he named Flash. Flash lived for well over a decade past Brant's divorce; in fact, he lasted an incredible eighteen years, some of that time sitting on a specially designed seat on Brant's ultra light airplane.

Larry David on drums, Mark Schiff on keyboards
and Paul Provenza on saxophone

Keenan Wayans didn't have an infectious laugh—he had a pandemic laugh that broke out easily. He was a comic whose only problem with women was tearing them off of his limbs without losing a few layers a skin. At Brant's (very WASP) wedding, women would, of course, approach Keenan and start conversations he might have found engaging if it weren't for the lewd gestures that Joe Piscopo, Steve

Mittleman and I would be doing behind the women's backs. After a while, Keenan, who was the only Afro-American at the wedding (or ever in the county), finally got frustrated trying to hold back his monster laugh and decided to get even. While Joe and I were talking to a woman, Keenan got behind her and starting doing even lewder gestures. Of course we didn't laugh, not at first, not until she turned and caught him *blue-handed.* Now we were all laughing hysterically except for the fifty or so white (mostly blonde Aryan) people that saw Keenan's filthy hand jive.

Thanksgiving Dinner; John DeBellis, Larry David, Richard Morris's girlfriend, Richard Morris, Steve Mittleman and Lenny Maxwell

Since the majority of my brethren were Jewish, holidays, especially Christmas and Easter, were spent at my parents' house in New Jersey. Gilbert Gottfried, Joe Piscopo, Larry David, Bobby Kelton, Richard Morris, Steve Mittleman and Lenny Maxwell sat at a long dining room table eating delicious free food, smoking my neighbor Lou Caporaso's free cigars, spreading good cheer and slander packed insults while having deep philosophical discussions about issues like, "Would living forever make it appropriate to date a woman half your age?" At one Christmas dinner Lenny Maxwell gave Larry a wig and told him it was made from LD's hair that they swept off the Improv floor. We never questioned whether or not Lenny was telling the truth, we just laughed. LD loved my mother's roasted potatoes so much so that in an episode of Seinfeld he gave that specialty to George Costanza's mother.

I don't remember if it was Bobby Alto or Buddy Mantia (both members of the amazing comedy team "The Untouchables") that came into possession of a mechanical horse racing game, which turned Catch A Rising Star into an after-hours track for comedians. For a few months one summer, about twenty comics and a half dozen musicians and singers would scream and yell at plastic horses, the size of guitar picks, as most of us lost our hard-earned cab fare.

And if we were lucky enough to win, we'd most likely lose it all on our all-night poker games (to Buddy Mantia), where disputes were encouraged because there's nothing funnier (other than comics at a funeral—especially a comic's funeral) than two comics, usually Mark Schiff and Buddy, threatening to beat each other up within an inch of their egos. Brant Von Hoffman would jump in between them, which would only encourage Schiff to fire his lunatic remarks like a fuel injected Woody Woodpecker. No matter how heated the situation became, we all knew that the only punches ever thrown in a comic's fight were, of course, punch lines. Some of us even had pet poker names for each other, Steve Mittleman was Jersey Slow (for very obvious painstaking reasons), I was Johnny Deck (named by Bobby Kelton for my absent-mindedness), Buddy Mantia the Cincinnati Kid (because he was from Dayton, which makes a lot of sense), and Brant Von Hoffman was Mad Dog, for no reason other than he liked calling himself that.

We were such a tight group that one evening, while leaving Central Park, Chris Albrecht, without warning us, ran behind a tree and pretended to throw a hand grenade. There wasn't a split second's hesitation, we all dropped to the ground and started to play soldiers like a seasoned squad on patrol. This same sort of episode got carried away just a wee bit more at Glenn Hirsch's wedding when we again followed Chris's lead, only this time we were throwing carrots, tomatoes, broccoli, and hunks of cheese. Glenn even joined our brigade, which ended when I dislocated my shoulder (which I did often) and Buddy Mantia (as he did often—twice at a Catch picnic) put it back in its socket. Instead of me lying over a park bench and Buddy pulling my arm down, I leaned over a railing, and being slightly drunk, almost fell over it as he yanked on my arm.

During the day, if we weren't playing softball or touch football, we'd go to ball games, the Yankees in particular. Larry Miller and I would be watching a game at home and then decide to go to the game as late as the fourth inning. Most of the time it was group trips. One game, about eight of us went, including Larry David, Glenn Hirsch, Marjorie Gross, Chris Albrecht, Brant Von Hoffman, Bob Wuhl, a few others and myself. Larry ended up sitting next to Bob Wuhl, who would run a loud account of what was happening at every moment of the game. LD said it was like sitting next to a disco. Bob is a really nice guy and knows baseball, but he can be loud. We tried everything. We even bought him a bag of peanuts to shut him up. Finally, one by one, starting with Larry, we snuck back a few rows. Bob didn't even notice. We watched him sitting three rows below us, running moment-by-moment commentary and sharing his peanuts with the stranger sitting next to him. I guess one of things I really like about Bob is that he's got a blue collar heart and will give everyone the time of the day, sometimes louder than a noon time whistle.

One afternoon, I'd gone to a game with LD and Kelton, and towards the end of it, we snuck down to seats a few rows from the field. LD, who possesses strong vocal chords, got angry about a bad call or something and put them into action to shout relentlessly. He was such an annoyance to the people around us that they called the stadium cops, who forcibly removed him from the section. There, thirty or so rows from us, LD continued to yell. And he yelled even louder (than Wuhl), so it was just as hard on the ears of the people in the section he'd been forced to vacate.

Did I mention LD hated waiting on lines? On another afternoon, Brant, Larry and I went to Yankee stadium. The ticket line was far longer than Larry could tolerate. He suddenly started to walk and act like Quasimodo. One by one the frightened people on line moved aside, until Larry got to the ticket booth and in his regular voice and posture, bought our seats. On the way into the stadium he turned to us and said, "God is going to punish me." I think on that day God was either looking the other way or found LD quite amusing.

Two decades later, we were watching a playoff game at my apartment in L.A. with comic Bill Rutkoski. It was a hot day and the air conditioning hadn't been working, and LD wanted to take off his shirt. He turned to us, his body language asking us permission and said, "Hey, we're all guys here. I can take off my shirt, right? You don't mind. I mean we're all heterosexual guys! Uh…it's just my shirt. It's okay for guys to do that, right?" This went on for about ten minutes before LD decided to take off his shirt.

Larry, Bobby Kelton and I had a philosophy. If you thought and/or expressed anything positive about an outcome during a Yankees game, it would turn disastrous. Would-be star players might prematurely end their careers. So LD and I were being our usual, proudly negative selves. Bill Rukoski, even though he was a comic—a profession best described by the word negative—finally had to leave, because he couldn't handle our negativity.

That day, LD asked me if I wanted to fly to Baltimore for the rest of the playoffs. Of course, I told him I couldn't even afford to split a cab. He told me for his birthday they had given him a free trip on the NBC (although he'd quit Seinfeld two years earlier) jet so the flight wouldn't cost anything and that he'd pay for hotels, tickets, etc.

LD put me up in the same hotel as he was in (but a different floor, of course—a heterosexual comic can never be too homophobic) and, as stated, paid for everything, including not only the original tickets he'd gotten, but for better ones he doled out a hefty scalper's fee for the next game. The morning of the day game, LD had something to do, so he gave me my ticket and said he'd meet me at the game. Through a call to Buddy Mantia, I found out Bob Wuhl was in town and left a message for him on his L.A. answering machine. Cell phones were just figments of the imaginations of the telecommunication companies' wallets then. A few minutes later, Wuhl called and said he was down the block from my hotel and he'd be over in five minutes. He insisted I go to the game with him, since he could get us press passes and he had Steinbrenner's seats. Like I said, we didn't have cell phones, so all I could do was leave a message at the hotel for Larry.

The seats we had were not only the best seats I'd ever sat in, but we had passes that allowed us to go on to the field or any other place we wanted. At one point, we were even in the announcing booth with Joe Morgan, Bob Uecker and Bob Costas. Not to mention all the free food! After a few innings, I went to the seats LD had spent over $400 bucks each for and they were nowhere near as good as ours. LD paid for my entire stay, flew me to Baltimore, got a second set of tickets in order to have better seats and I wound up with the best seats in the Stadium for free, and a pass to go anywhere in the ball park. Not being ungrateful, I gave LD my pass and the tickets to the other seats. We wound up switching back and forth the entire game. The seats were so good Bob Wuhl could have shouted his head off--neither of us would have cared. I left the park, walking through the underground corridors with Bob Costas, who couldn't be nicer if he had been Ghandi's feminine side in a previous life. We talked about the game and LD and Costas said, "that guy Larry David—he's a genius." I wouldn't disagree with him, even if I hadn't wound up with better seats than Larry.

My favorite LD baseball story happened a few years later. He'd gotten seats from someone in the American League commissioner's office (a position that no longer exists). Larry told me to meet him under the giant bat outside Yankee stadium, which I did, and to my surprise or shock, there was LD under the Giant Bat, smiling. Yes, I said, smiling—mouth open wide, ends tilted upward, and teeth front and center. LD, instead of getting just two tickets, was given four. By then he was already wealthy, just coming off of "Seinfeld" and the airing of the pilot for "Curb Your Enthusiasm" on HBO. Larry, to this day, has never forgotten the value of a buck. That's not to say he's cheap by any means. It's just that he became rich later in life and still understands the reality of money. He was uncharacteristically grinning, because he had decided he was going to scalp the tickets and give me the loot. I told LD that I didn't need it, but he'd made up his mind (and Larry's mind is not easily changed without a cranial transplant or his head being shrunk and eaten by cannibals). Finally, I convinced him that we would use the money for food. So there's LD, unashamedly trying to scalp tickets (for me) while he's being recognized from "Curb Your Enthusiasm." He finally sold two at face value and shoved the money in my pocket (my jacket pocket, not pants pockets, just so you don't get any rich guy, homoerotic, comics-scalping-tickets fantasies).

We arrived at our seats, which were in the commissioner's box, just two rows from the field, by the Texas Rangers' on deck circle. Juan Gonzalez, who was at the peak of his career and was one of the best hitters in baseball, was standing a few feet away. A guy one row in front of us in a suit started to call him every name in the foulest book written (and I'm talking the unabridged version), while insulting every member of his family, nationality and blood type. LD, of course, took it personally, and felt the barrage of insults aimed at Juan Gonzales was cruel and started screaming at the loud, foul-mouth in front of us. We were in the commissioner's box and LD was close to having a fistfight with a guy who could have been the commissioner's brother for all we knew. They were nose to nose, and started shoving each other when I stepped in between them. LD, whose temper was stretching every facial muscle to its limits, cooled off enough to not require restraints, when the guy, now in fear of his life, backed away and shut up. After about the fifth inning, LD turned to me and said in the exasperated manner only he could do properly, "The guy ruined the first four innings for me. I think I'm calming down. I can finally enjoy the game." Color, that no longer indicated a possible heart attack, came back to his face. We watched the Yankees win and that was the end of it. Oh, it turned out the food was free and despite my objections, LD made me keep the money.

Neither Larry David nor I ever put our head shot up at Catch or the Improv. I always felt my face was my worst feature. Larry had own his neurotic reasons I'm sure. So we decided to do something different. There's a famous photo of Mickey Mantle, who was our idol, and Roger Maris in their batting stances on opposite sides of home plate. Larry and I decided to get our heads superimposed on each of their shoulders. Well, it didn't work out as we intended. During a crowded Thursday night at Catch in the middle of the bar, Larry and I got in a huge argument over whose head was going to be on Mickey Mantle's shoulders. Larry decided since he was right handed he should be Mantle and because I was left handed I should be Maris. I, of course, didn't agree with his logic.

I can picture comics, bartenders and customers watching as two people they were about to pay to watch on stage, stood red face to red face yelling at each other. Larry and I were tugging on separate ends of the photo almost tearing the picture of Mantle and Maris apart (we didn't have the picture with us: added it because it makes the moment more dramatic). As immature as we were, I think we'd still do the same damn thing today. At least I would.

During the shows, at the bar we'd joke around with our comic pals on a nightly basis, but sometimes, after the show, what spontaneously occurred on stage was just plain magical. On this particular spring night it was like the musical segment of an early Marx Brother's film. It was at least four am at the Improv, if not closer to five, when we paid tribute to the 1961 Yankees. There were at least forty of us in the showroom, comprised of comics, singers, musicians, waitresses, bartenders and their friends. One of our regular piano players was playing a sort of gospel-inspired melody when a comic, who'd rather remain anonymous, started to make up and shout lyrics to a song that we now call the '61 Yankees.

That night, we sang about Whitey Ford winning 25 games and losing only four, Louis Arroyo saving many of his games a decade before the term "save" entered into baseball lingo, three Yankee catchers combining for over 60 homers, and, of course, the amazing home run race between Roger Maris and our messiah Mickey Mantle. We oohed and ahhed, and repeated the chorus "The Sixty-One Yankees;" the lyrics grew more specific and intense as our faces and extremities tilted upward in adulation, almost tearing our heads from out of our necks whenever he spoke the name of our God, Mickey Mantle.

We swayed, swooned and cheered for what seemed like hours. Waves of hair, arms, beer bottles, hats and dust circled the room, every movement becoming more grandiose with each verse. Supposedly, below the speed of light, time is finite—measured by clocks and calendars. But I think time gives up its boundaries to the measure of youth, especially at moments like these.

By the time the tribute ended, the sun had risen. We were ready to argue over breakfast. Before we could even order our food that moment had found a spot in my memory, where it would be seen forever as the gospel according to the Improv and the '61 Yankees. Sure, there are better ways to finish off a day, but to me this was special because it was a spiritual moment celebrated with my flock in the great church of the Improvisation.

In the mid-seventies there were only thirty or forty comics in New York. One night, Richard Belzer and a few friends tried to count all the comics in the United States and they couldn't even get to two hundred. Now there are thousands on Match.com alone. Politicians are beginning to appeal to the comedian vote. We were a weird group of guys and girls who rather than living life to the fullest, saw it as a source of material. We had no money, maintained diets that had the nutritional value of carbon monoxide poisoning, but we had each other—an amazing camaraderie with funny, egocentric, self-centered, neurotic guys and girls like ourselves, who understood us. It was like group solitary confinement.

It was the best of times, it was the worst of times, but more importantly is was our time and we damn well made the most of it.

Softball

"Howie Klein [the manager of the Improv] said to me, "Do you want to get on quicker? Do you play softball?" I said, "Yeah." And it worked. I started getting spots. "

–JOHN MENDOZA

Glenn Hirsch (Gleeb) stood on the ball field in Central Park each year and announced, "Guys, for the next two months we're going to be men again," as if we were ever men in the first place.

Several members of our team were good athletes, but none of us would be considered jocks. By my definition, a jock is someone whose body works perfectly without the use of his mind. A comic's body works despite the use of his mind.

The Improvisation played in the Broadway Show League where the only spikes used were five-inch heels and most had taps on them. For a few years, our collection of comic odd balls was a very good team— except for the first year in which we were so bad that when we went into the batting cage the pitching machine would throw underhanded.

One night after a spring training Yankee win, Chris suggested we start a softball team and join the Broadway Show League. Since he said the club would pay for equipment and uniforms (which was just a T-shirt), there was no reason to snub the offer. We held tryouts that Sunday at the Central Park diamonds. Anyone who had a glove and could figure out which hand to put it on made the team. The Improv bought the bats, balls, catcher's equipment and a duffle bag at Pyramid Sports downtown. I suggested we get the uniforms in my New Jersey hometown because I could get them cheaper. So Bobby Kelton, Larry David and I went to Bauer's Sports store in Dumont and picked out royal blue softball shirts with gold short sleeves, letters and numbers. Of course, a week later I went back to the store alone and had Mickey Mantle's number 7 printed on the back of my shirt.

In celebration of getting our new shirts at a discount, we invited the owner of Bauer's Sports to the second show on a Saturday night. We sat him at the best table—the one that wobbled directly in front of the microphone. Chris waived the cover charge and gave him free drinks the entire night. Mr. Bauer seemed to be enjoying the show. And several of us who went on early loved his hearty laughter. About a third of the way through, after several rounds of drinks, his bubonic laugh started drowning out the comics' jokes, erupting erratically, before or after punch lines. Nothing throws a comic's timing off more than getting laughs that don't coincide with punch lines. After a dozen free drinks Mr. Bauer stood up and started screaming insults at the comics. Hecklers are easy prey for most seasoned comics, except when they tower over us like inebriated grizzlies, howl in tongues, charge the stage and throw punches. The surrounding tables, loaded with drinks, exploded like a dozen volcanic gin mills. A herd of comics and bouncers ran into the room, dove across a few booths and wrestled the creature from Bergen County to the ground. They lifted him and carried him across the stage to the side door and catapulted him onto the street. Between the broken glasses and customers' drinks that had to be replaced, the discounted shirts turned out costing Chris seventy-five bucks apiece. Luckily, they fit well and "Improvisation" was spelled correctly. I felt like an idiot who was in charge at NASA and put an astronaut on the moon only to discover he was a werewolf. Bauer's Sports is still in business. I never set foot in the store again but can only hope Mr. Bauer discovered the Dumont chapter of AA.

Larry David playing shortstop

As one would expect, our softball team was full of idiosyncrasies such as Robert Wuhl playing first base in a sports jacket; Joe Piscopo having to be taught which leg to throw off of each season; Larry David, our afro-haired shortstop, who, after making an error, would accuse his own outfielders of talking about him; Buddy Mantia hitting himself in the head with his bat because he made an out with men on base. But the oddity that stood out amongst the others was that our team was sixty-percent left handers (way past the ten percent in normal society).

I batted lead-off and then came, in this exact order or close to it, Glenn Hirsch, Larry David, Bobby Kelton, Robert Wuhl, Joe Rock (a singer—no comic worth his neuroses would be named that), Tony Darrow, Buddy Mantia, Joe Piscopo, Brant Von Hoffman and Chris Albrecht. On our bench was John Mendoza, Richard Morris, Mark

Lonow, Richie Cantor, Kelly Rodgers, Warren Bloom, Glenn Super, Marjorie Gross, Aaron Jack, David Sayh, Howie Klein, Richard T. Bear and for a few games, Keenan Wayans. Not a fearsome bunch.

Just when you thought you'd never find a less intimidating group of guys, came our arch rivals, The Comic Strip—the menches of Second Avenue—where Jerry Seinfeld, Paul Reiser, Larry Miller, Fred Raker, Hiram Kasten, Joe Bolster, Mark Schiff, George Wallace, Dennis Wolfberg and Ron Richards. In all my years in softball, I've never played in games with so many arguments and disagreements, most of which were from our own teammates. Of course, there were almost as many laughs as there were screaming matches. We had a few close contests, one where I made a running catch in the outfield with the bases loaded and threw a bullet to second for a double play, ending the inning and my left arm (which, at its peak, had difficulty getting a ball off the ground). To this day, I'm very proud to say we always beat The Comic Strip and I saved a game.

In the first year or two, the Improv team played horribly and we blamed other forces for our poor performances—like too much space between galaxies made us drop the ball or the grass was mowed in the wrong direction for the type of sneakers we wore. Despite our eccentricity, there were moments when teamwork was needed. We devised our own hit and run plays. When the pitcher released the ball, the runner would break for the next base and it was up to the batter to hit the ball. The signal for the hit and run was a verbal one. The third base coach would yell out, "Peanut butter and jelly." Not exactly a term that brings athletic prowess to mind, but it was possible for a starving comic to request food during a game, thus deceiving the opposing team.

In the latter innings of a very tight game, Mark Lonow was the third base coach and called for a hit and run play. He kept yelling out, "Grilled cheese, Grilled cheese!" to the confused runners on base and hitter (me), who thought he might be having a Velveeta hallucination. Of course, during the first pitch or two, I didn't swing and the runners didn't try to advance. He ran halfway to home shouting at me "Grilled cheese!" I dumbly checked my pockets. Finally he got so frustrated he streaked to the middle of the diamond and yelled, "Hit and Run!"

The games were played loosely, friends who visited from out of town and even my cousin Butch, a fireman from Jersey City, occasionally played. The other teams didn't care, because we lost. We even had a female comic, Marjorie Gross, on our team who we played in a few games. In the middle of one game, Larry stormed off the field screaming, "I can't play shortstop with a girl at second base!" After his screaming match with the world, the usual realization that he was acting like an idiot hit him and he burst out laughing at himself. He wasn't so much embarrassed by his behavior as he was amused by it. His skin would redden and a prideful smile would crisscross his face before blasting a series of inside out laughs. No matter how maniacal LD could get he possessed the ability to suddenly observe himself and crack up at his own childish behavior (much like we do when we watch Curb Your Enthusiasm).

That first year, the selfish comic side of us was far more dominant than the teamwork aspect of the game. Bobby Kelton, was a natural athlete and had played baseball for Syracuse University. He was in center field, brooding because of a horrible injustice done to him. On a pop up the short fielder (an actual position in softball) stepped in front of him to catch it. None of us noticed the horrible slight because we were too busy brooding over less consequential things ourselves. Bobby decided that the short fielder's audacity to catch a fly ball meant solely for him, was too big of a wound to continue on and ran off the field. Our team came out of its stupor when saw Bobby running in the wrong direction. When he was in the stands tossing his glove on the ground, we realized that he was quitting. The only player left on our bench was David Sayh, who brought his son along to watch the game, never thinking he'd actually play. David, whose athleticism peeks when he puts a microphone back in the stand, reluctantly ran out to his position. Now, being supportive teammates, we immediately ran off the field begging Bobby to stay. "We'll have to use David! He's a horrible ball player!" we said right in front of David's son. Bobby was not to be persuaded. As fate would have it, the very first ball was hit to David, who completely missed an easy play, three runs scored and the Improv lost the game. We ran off the field stomping our feet like a runaway herd of cattle, insensitively blaming the loss on David, while his son looked on.

The game I remember the most from those early softball seasons, was one in which the rain halted play right before the last inning when we were trailing by eight runs. Bobby "King" Kelton (we called him "King" just because it sounded good) and I, Johnny "Deck" DeBellis, thought the game was going to be rained out and went to his aunt's apartment for lunch. We had finished our second or third sandwiches when we saw our dessert come out of the fridge. Unfortunately, the rain suddenly stopped. King and I raced back to the field with our mouth's bleeding chocolate cake, but arrived too late to play. It was the last inning; in that inning our team had miraculously scored five runs without us. Now there were two outs, the bases were loaded, we were still down by three runs and Larry David was up. Larry was our last hope and that didn't give us much hope, after all, as good a hitter as LD was, a home run would be too much to ask. Well, he hit a blast into the gap clearing the bases and as he jumped on home plate, he was mobbed, yes, actually physically touched (and he allowed it) by his fellow comics who piled on their hero who just won the game. Well, sort of. The umpire had somehow miscounted the runs and announced the game was only tied. I think Larry would have killed the umpire but I don't think he wanted to touch another human being that day. And so the game and the ump's life continued, but I'm sad to say we lost the game in the next inning. Larry was living the unlucky life of George Costanza years before he created the character.

We played against our share of celebrities in the Broadway show league. The most VIP celebrity, I remember, was Al Pacino. Even though I didn't talk to him, I liked him immediately. He was shorter than me for starters. He was also a very good athlete who played third base not in sneakers, spikes, or even high heels, but in street shoes. His hitting style was old school. He batted from the right side and would literally run up in the batter's box a few steps to hit the pitch and belt the hell out of it. He didn't say much because he must have realized he'd have to strain his voice in order to be heard over us yelling at each other—but he was competitive, encouraging to his teammates and really into the game.

In our freshman and sophomore seasons, Meat Loaf's team would look forward to politely beating the hell out of us without getting a spot on their real softball uniforms with matching stretch baseball pants, shirts, hats and even socks. I think they enjoyed watching a team self-destruct. One thing I remember about Meat Loaf was how little ego he had on the field. He was usually their starting pitcher, but would take himself out in order to put other players in the game that weren't even bitching at him—not like us Improv guys.

Meat Loaf, though extremely competitive, was always a gracious winner and loser. When we started to beat them regularly he didn't blame everyone else in the world like one of us was bred to do. The last time we beat them, it was by at least ten runs, and by then we had gotten used to winning. He was supportive of his teammates and even complimentary to us, almost enough for me to erase my bootleg tape of his "Bat Out Of Hell" album, and go out and buy one.

That year, we were undefeated and on our way to a division win. Chris's ex-girlfriend was managing our rival, an undefeated team with the most feared hitter of the Broadway Show league. We called him "The Great White Slugger." He was six and half feet tall and had an arm the size of Big Richie's waist (the bouncer at Catch A Rising Star whose waist actually had a horizon). He held his back straight up perpendicular to his head, which was so large that even a stage actor's ego couldn't fill it. His swing was swift, smooth, effortless and powerful. When he hit the ball squarely, it would travel onto the infield of the baseball diamond behind our field. Before the game we decided to walk him every time he got up no matter how many men were on base. During a key at-bat near the end of a game, when we were only ahead by two runs, he came up with the bases loaded and two out. Chris, without hesitating, walked him for the fourth time forcing in a run. With a one-run lead on a three-and-two pitch, Chris got the next batter to pop out. I thought for sure that the big guy was going to charge the mound and kill Chris, thus I had my escape route planned. In the top half of the last inning, I was on first base with another runner on second and Joe Rock at bat. I remember Mark Lonow yelling out, "peanut butter crackers," which was close enough to "peanut butter and jelly" and I took off for second, the runner on second for third, and then

I heard it, not just a crack of a bat, but a sonic boom. I slowed down and turned to the outfield and watched the ball sail over the trees past the next diamond. Joe Rock, of the "girls look at me and try to resist my skimpy shorts and muscle T," hit the farthest shot I had ever seen and secured the first division championship for the Improv team. Several of us actually hugged and held it for a few seconds. It was a moment of group humanity.

In the last game on my last at bat, I hit a ball that was trapped (caught on a bounce) by the outfielder and mistakenly called an out by the umpire, so I came up one hit short of batting .700. Of course, I didn't let an umpire's bad call stop me from bragging that I hit seven hundred.

"It was the greatest display of hitting I've ever seen."
–GLENN HIRSCH

Around that time, Catch had formed a team and joined the Tuesday fast pitch Broadway Show league. Buddy Mantia, Tony Darrow, Larry David, Glenn Hirsch, Richie Cantor, Bobby Kelton, Brant Von Hoffman, Joe Rock and I played on both the Improv team and the Catch A Rising Star team. Catch, always a rung up on the Improv, had much nicer two-tone blue uniform shirts. The rest of the team was made up of ringers (great players who never heard of Broadway; the closest they ever came to seeing a musical was watching a woman strip to *Y.M.C.A.*) The Catch games were played harder than the Improv's. Players actually dove for balls without doing a pirouette and caught them, and the league was loaded with much bigger and meaner guys, who were on steroids as opposed to antidepressants.

On an overcast Tuesday morning, we were playing a team sponsored by either a locksmith company or a bail bondsman. In fact, most of the guys looked like they escaped from prison and were playing for their own bail money. Tony Darrow was a real bona fide tough guy; so tough that he kicked a heckler's teeth out. Another time, a standup bass player disrespected Tony's musical charts by stepping on them, so Tony kicked a hole in his bass. And on another occasion, he worked a club where they didn't allow the performers to eat the same food as the manager. That didn't please Tony's palette, so he threw a table full of food on the manager and the owner. Don't get me wrong, when Tony is your friend, he's you friend for life and there's not much he wouldn't do for you, with or without your permission. We lived in the same building and he'd get the maintenance crew to fix things before I finished breaking them. Tony could put fear into you with a sneeze. I, on the other hand, was a victim-in-waiting. I was the guy who gets shot to prove a point.

Most of the games in that league were very competitive, especially this one. We were tied for first place and it was the bottom of the last inning. They were two out with the bases empty. Tony was standing next to me on the sidelines, pointing to the opposing pitcher, who just happened to be the largest guy in the park, an irritated genie who looked like he just popped out of the Superdome because of the tight fit. Tony started yelling insults about the pitcher's immediate family and his ancestors. He kept questioning the monster's manhood, which couldn't be doubted even if the guy was wearing a strapless evening gown. Tony, of course, was just trying to get the mound monster so angry that he'd lose his concentration and walk a couple of guys (which he did), and maybe even throw a few fat pitches. He didn't care that I was now on deck and one of those pitches might not just be fat, but very fast and knock my head into the next diamond. Well, he did his best to ignore Tony, which wasn't easy and threw a pitch—a very fat pitch—that crossed the middle of the plate thigh high. The batter, who at birth was much bigger and far braver than I was, tagged the ball that split the outfielders and seemed to roll forever. I don't know who ran faster, the base runners the batter or me. As soon as I realized that we were going to score the winning run, I got as far from Tony as possible. He and the pitcher wound up going at it, face to steaming face, but something in Tony's eyes must have scared the genie back into his bottle, because he backed down and walked away with Tony grinning from ear to ear and me walking back to the field behind every tree, bush and grandstand.

The year of the Improv's division championship team, we were asked to play a few games against a Puerto Rican team from uptown.

That next night at Catch I told a few of the comics about the upcoming game. Larry David's friend from college, Stan, was there and joined the conversation. An hour later Larry arrived at Catch and I told him I'd invited Stan to play. I should have known better. LD had what many shrinks would call a temper tantrum—or the beginning of a psychotic episode. As always, he had the look of a mass murderer whose gun had jammed. Before it got to the point where Larry's insanity could peak, I split a cab across town with another comic.

The next day, most of us had showed up at the park early. Two of those people were me and Larry. After about five minutes, LD and I found ourselves in the outfield, yelling at each other—LD screaming that by me asking Stan, who was his friend first, before Larry did, it made Larry look like he didn't want him to play. I shouted back that Stan had stumbled into a conversation and it would have been rude for me not to ask him to play. We debated whose point was more important for a while. LD, of course, shouted the loudest and the most absurd stuff. At the peak of his tirade (which put his anger between a rabid drill sergeant and a jilted Incredible Hulk), mid-word he realized how truly ridiculous his argument was and started to laugh at himself and then we both cracked up. That was the most laughing we did that day, since we got trounced by the Puerto Rican team.

Those summers and autumns we played softball, we even loaded up cars and drove to my hometown, Dumont, New Jersey (avoiding Bauer's Sports) to play touch football. Running along the unimpressed grass of Memorial park were Glenn Hirsch, Barry Diamond, LD, Chris Albrecht, Robert Wuhl, Keenan Wayans, Brant Von Hoffman, Joe Piscopo, Jay Thomas, Buddy Mantia, Richie Cantor, Howie Klein, Bobby Kelton, and me. One Sunday (I don't know what the occasion was), Richard Lewis, Larry David and myself played stickball in the playground behind Lincoln School, in Dumont. LD and Richard were much better stickball players than I was, since in Dumont, we played mostly Wiffle ball. I quickly dropped out of the game to watch Richard and LD argue about everything that could even minutely be disagreed upon, both of them accusing the other of cheating, while both of them were doing their best to cheat. This time, I was the only one laughing.

Not once did I offer an impartial ruling. I just shut my mouth and enjoyed the show.

We Were What We Delivered

"When you have a piece of material and it gets a laugh, it's like going from earth to heaven."

-JERRY SEINFELD

For a comic, no matter how old, successful or how long you've been in therapy, there's almost no bigger thrill than writing and delivering a new joke that actually works. You've created something that caused the audience to have a strong reaction and physically show their enjoyment. Comics are forever searching their minds, conversations, rejections, crumpled scraps of paper, thousands of ink-scrawled napkins and smeared blue palms looking for that new joke. Once, while falling asleep, I thought of a joke, woke myself up from my sexual fantasy (one in which I die in the end), reached onto my night table, felt around for a pen and wrote a joke on a stale turkey sandwich, which I unsuccessfully tried to eat the next morning.

There was many a night when I'd return home in the usual disappointing company of myself to hear ten minutes of Rodney Dangerfield trying out jokes on my answering machine. He was so conditioned by his craft that he'd even leave spaces for laughs. The next day I'd return his call with my opinions and an occasional helpful thought. To see Rodney develop his six minute Carson spot was the ultimate comedy learning experience. He worked on material he'd written then added jokes people sent him. If they or any part of them worked, he'd always pay them for the entire joke.

"I remember David Brenner told me this: 'One six minute appearance on The Tonight Show or Letterman that reaches millions of people was like being at the Improv every night for a hundred and fifty thousand years.'"

-RICHARD LEWIS

Most of the time I'd ride with Rodney to the clubs. We'd alternate, one night I'd drive and the next he drove. Even though my car was a generation older than his, when I drove it was far safer than Rodney trying to control one of his newer faster vehicles. Being a passenger with Rodney at the wheel was the equivalent of riding a wild bronco through a slaughterhouse. If there was traffic, Rodney didn't hesitate to drive onto the sidewalk or make his own private swerving lane. It's a well-known fact that Rodney would alter his consciousness with alcohol, which didn't improve his driving or help contain my fear, but it did slow him down enough so pedestrians could leap out of the way—and give a thumb's up to their hero. Rodney told me whenever he got stopped by a cop, they'd recognize him and let him go with only his autograph on the back of their ticket book.

After we survived our journey to the clubs, Rodney would go on stage and do a shortened version of his regular show. Halfway through, he'd try his new jokes and gauge the audience's reaction. He usually gave a joke a few tries before tossing it away. Sometimes, he'd just use the setup and write a new punch line, or vice versa. Every night he'd do two or three sets, trying all or parts of the same material. He'd eliminate, move or even add a word. So much of standup comedy is rhythm. Although his delivery was short and quick, each joke had a certain meter that fit Rodney. In a week or so, he'd have a handful of jokes that worked. He'd string them together by subject matter, making up segues in line with the Dangerfield persona, giving him as much leeway as a lawyer with the truth. He's the only comic I've ever witnessed who during his six minutes, would be married, single, divorced, have girlfriends, no girlfriends, no children, several children; was sick, dying, healthy and ugly. The one Dangerfield constant, besides his hand pulling on his shirt collar and twist of his neck, was that he was always the loser and always, always, always funny. In two weeks he'd have three minutes or so of jokes working and getting the kinds of laughs that the easier, primed TV audience saluted with applause.

Rodney was the most economical of one-liner comics. He probably used fewer words to get from the set-up to the punch line than anyone who has ever told a joke. At a rate of five or six jokes a minute, he'd have to have over thirty new jokes and then, another ten or more when he sat down on the couch next to Johnny Carson. At the height of his fame he was doing a Tonight Show shot every six weeks. At age 67 he was working harder then us 25 year old diner studs.

From the Improv bar, we'd watch Rodney on The Tonight Show kill with jokes that sounded like he'd been doing them longer than all the time the Catch mobsters spent in prison combined, even counting time spent on parole. A few days after he'd arrive back in New York he'd be in the clubs working on his next set.

One night, Rodney, hanging at the bar at Catch, waiting to try out new material, turned to a bunch of us comics and said, "Do you know what the worst thing about oral sex is?" No one gave him an answer, and he replied, "The view!" Everyone laughed and Rodney smiled just for an instant. Several years back, I had spoken to Rodney, who, for the first time in his life, at eighty seemed genuinely happy. I heard he was on antidepressants, or maybe it was his beautiful new wife. I was complaining about a difficult situation and in a cheerful voice he said, "John, you're talented, you're funny and you're still young. You got plenty of time. You'll be okay!" That was the last time I spoke to him. It's a good way to remember a very good man.

Standup is one of the most difficult forms of comedy to write sober, drunk, high or even with a new magic marker on a clean napkin. Woody Allen said that in a year, he could only write 25 minutes of material and that was after he had been a TV writer for several years. For most comics, twenty new minutes of material usually took two or three years and very little of it matched the quality of Woody Allen and Rodney Dangerfield.

It took the combination of desire, discipline and a vacuous social life to drive me to write from two to six hours a day. I usually wrote from late afternoon right up until the time I sniffed out a clean shirt to wear to the club. By instinct (accent on the "stink"), I wrote down just about anything I thought was a joke or a set-up. And believe me, most of it was not worth the effort to decipher my handwriting. Sometimes jokes are written in one quick burst and other times they have to be hunted down and assembled, some missing a piece that takes years to find. Paul Reiser told me about a joke where he had written one part and then eight years later wrote another part of the line that made it funny. I've had a joke or an idea that I couldn't figure out. Years later, looking over my notes with fresh eyes, I suddenly saw how if I approached it from another angle, added a word, or subtracted a phrase, I could make it funny.

Years ago, Rodney and I were bouncing around a punch line about a girl being ugly and seeing her image in a bowl of oatmeal, but neither of us could ever get it to work. Then, a few years later I figured it out. It was so simple: "She had such bad skin she could see her reflection in a bowl of oatmeal."

At first, the amount of jokes I wrote compared to what actually worked was about one in fifty or worse. But the more I wrote, the better I got and now on a good day I could get at least one real good joke for every ten. I may have to write fifty jokes to get to that one in ten percentage, since I usually have to fight my way through the comic's inner voice, which in most normal people is their inner child. In a comic (for me at least), it's their inner evil step-parent, or drill sergeant shouting, "You're not funny. You can't write! You're a piece of shit!" Once I quiet that voice, I usually begin to sense where the funny is, or where the approach to funny might be. Then, somewhere in the next hour or so, ideas, possible set-ups and punch lines start to emerge. Some days it happens almost immediately; other days it can take three hours before I found a groove. Of course, there also are days that everything I write sounds like it was written by the voice on my digital answering machine.

I had been writing and performing standup for a year or so when I became friends with Rita Rudner, who was just starting out. She is not only one of the brightest comics around, she may be the hardest worker I've ever seen. Everywhere she went, she brought her writing pads. The guys would start feeling guilty, not because they may have thought about hitting on her, but because they wanted to tear up her pads and stop her from writing. She'd work all day and call me up, many times leaving long messages on my answering machine asking, "Is this a joke?" I'd finally say, "No, but I think you might have a set-up." By sheer determination and belief in her talent, or the ability to alter her perspective on reality (female comics were considered a novelty act then), she shunned any thoughts of discouragement and became one hell of a great writer.

There were comics who never actually sat down at all with pen, pencil, typewriter or tape recorder. All their new material came from conversations or ad libs on stage. Richard Belzer, Barry Diamond, Robin Williams, Gilbert Gottfried, Andy Kauffman (his character's dialogue) and to a much lesser degree, Larry David and Richard Lewis (they would elaborate on material they'd written at home), who did some of their writing on stage. The two L's would go up with an idea, or premise and then as they felt the piece, their instincts would lead them to the laughs and those laughs would encourage them to go deeper into the premise or character. Many times, magic would happen—new lines, character traits and even a whole other premise would emerge.

Much of Richard Belzer's act, like Don Rickles, Pat Cooper and Jackie Leonard before him, came from diving mouth-first into the audience—preemptive comedy attacks, assaulting those closest to the stage and training them to respond like an idiot on command. On the other hand, Jimmy Brogan (former Jay Leno producer) would sneak up on an audience with a gentler style and make fun of the enemy by sticking them with a blade sheathed in kindness. Most times he'd start off asking the audience member questions, the most typical were, of course, the MC standby's, "Where are you from?" and "What do you do for a living?" It would get to the point where there wasn't a place or an occupation that Jimmy didn't have a ready-made ad lib for, or, if need be, a resume and application already prepared.

I mentioned earlier that comics often get material from conversations, especially with each other. And no two comics argued more about the rights to a gag or a bit than Larry David and Richard Lewis, although Larry David and Bobby Kelton came close. There is a vague comic's rule: It's never been written anywhere, probably never even said out loud or even whispered on a deathbed, but I will be the first to put the rule in black and white, so it can be read, memorized and passed down verbatim from generation to generation of standups. The comic's conversation rule is:

"The first comic who mentions the subject matter gets any joke derived from that conversation unless the amount of that contribution out-weighs the first-say, first-keep rule."

Sounds simple, except for the fact that to comics, rules are not made to be broken as much as they are to be argued over until one of the comics gives in; they get a second, third, fourth and fifth opinion, which they might ignore completely; one quits the business; one pays the other (or for the check and cab fare); one does the piece on The Tonight Show (which would end a friendship); or they find out that someone else is doing a piece like it.

Even though there was the occasional nightly comic's argument over material, if you looked around the bar for a few guys avoiding each other's eyes and listened, you'd hear the regurgitation of comics working on each other's act. Whenever I finished a set, I was usually greeted by a hyper-zealous comedian friend with advice on my delivery, a piece of material, or asking me if I wanted to share a cab.

David Sayh, a very funny observational comic, was working on a piece about a cop stopping someone driving too slowly, but he lacked one punch line. He told me the set-up, which was the cop saying, "Do you realize how slow you were going?" As soon as he said it, the punch line seemed to come to me out of nowhere, like mildew on my toothbrush. I just changed a word and added a little question, which made the premise work. So the joke now went: "Do you realize how slow you were driving? Where are you going, to the dentist?"

I had a joke, which I mentioned earlier about how I always came last with my mother. "She wouldn't breast feed me; she said she needed the milk for the cats," which got a big laugh. After a set, someone gave me the tag—a tag is usually a short phrase, said a few beats after the original joke gets a laugh. So the joke became: "She wouldn't breast feed me, she said she needed the milk for the cats." Wait a beat for the tag: "And they were my neighbor's cats." On the heels of the other joke, a good tag would not only add a laugh, sometimes it would make it grow into applause.

By watching our comic friends' acts and bouncing jokes off of each other, it not only made us less egocentric in a way we could rationalize away by saying it was only business, it made us better comics and better writers. An old comic friend, Phil Foster (the father on *Laverne and Shirley*), God rest his funny soul, put it best. He said, with a voice that sounded like he was talking with a Jersey landfill in his mouth,

"When you see someone who stole your material doing one of your jokes, it's like seeing someone hit your kids."

Most of us grew up during the time of the singer/songwriters, like Dylan, The Beatles, Joni Mitchell, Neil Young and later Bruce Springsteen, just to name a few. The comics from that same period, Woody Allen, Bill Cosby, Lenny Bruce, George Carlin, Richard Pryor, Bob Newhart, Jonathon Winters, Shelley Berman, Robert Klein, Rodney Dangerfield, David Brenner and a dozen or so others, wrote their own jokes, so it was only natural for us to write our own material. But there were those who stole whole or parts of jokes, or switched subjects or actions slightly to make it seem like a different gag. We were protective of each other's material, which wasn't very difficult to do. When you hear a comic's act two or three times a night for five years, their jokes seep into permanent crevices in your brain. During an audition, a guest spot, or anywhere we saw someone doing a joke that had either the same premise or punch line as one of our crew, they were told in no uncertain terms not to do it again if they ever wanted to get on stage in the showcase clubs. If they were much bigger than us, we'd say it standing next to one of the bouncers or managers. If we spotted someone doing jokes from more than one of our crew in the same set, or the comedian didn't listen to our first warning, they were told they couldn't go on stage. Besides doing everything on our part to ruin the thief's reputation (especially if he brought a girlfriend with him), we didn't allow those guys back on stage at any of the New York showcase clubs. Cab fare, dinner banter, late night poker games, endless hours spent debating the most trivial of subjects and dating the girl he brought would never be any part of that comic's future.

Sure, there would be conflicts with certain premises, especially observation humor, which is derived from without, concerning society's truths and idiosyncrasies. We settled that by figuring out who performed it or said it first. Since any one of us had seen just about every set another member of our crew had done, a bit's genesis wasn't hard to pin down.

There were certain premises comics had that were similar, and if they were from a general area but had completely different punch lines, we'd work out a system where the guy who went on earlier that night did the premise. That became difficult on weekends, when we ran from club to club trying to get three or four sets in. And if the take on the premise was different enough, it didn't matter who worked earlier in a show and both comics were permitted to do the premise during the show.

And it wasn't just stealing jokes, bits, set-ups and premises that we protected. No, we even guarded over each other's persona or attitude, which often led to some long-heated battles that some comics thrived on. It was kind of funny to hear another comic accusing the other of stealing their personality, as if anyone would want one of our personalities. But those disputes were amongst our own guys. If it were a slimy outsider, we didn't approach them, they were usually left wondering why they never got a spot at the Improv, Catch, or the Comic Strip, and why most of the comics didn't talk to them or let them share a cab across town even if they offered to pay. Okay, Gilly would definitely share the cab, even if it were guy trying to escape because he just murdered Gilbert's family and as long as he didn't take his wallet.

Sometimes, especially if two comics came from different parts of the country, they could have conceivably written a similar joke or bit at about the same time. This happened once to me in L.A. and luckily with one of the classiest comics, Wil Shriner. We were at the Improv and someone told us about the joke. In less than two minutes we came up with a solution. If we were working the same club whoever went up first that night would use that joke.

I remember on one of my earlier trips to L.A., I was coming off stage at the Improv and a comic who was notorious for stealing jokes said to me, "I like your material." I pulled him aside and a little up the wall until we were face-to-face (he was smaller than me) and told him not to memorize it. The next day, a comic friend told me that the joke thief carried a gun, which probably explained why he was allowed on stage. A decade or so later, he was working cruise ships and phoned me, trying to con me into revealing the punch line of a joke in my act. He told me that he was just thinking about that line and started laughing and wanted to tell me how funny it was. Of course, the punch line, which supposedly left him in hysterics, had inexplicably slipped his mind and he wanted me to refresh his memory. I pretended not to know which line he was talking about and hung up.

"I was standing with Ed Bluestone and John DeBellis in front of the World Trade Center, looking at the 300 foot King Kong replica they had just used in shooting the movie. Bluestone, in a classic non sequitur, turned to John and me and said, "If I died, how long do you think it would take before someone starting doing my material?"

-BOBBY KELTON

There were other kinds of joke thieves. I won't reveal the name of one of the big ones because he's somewhat well known, is larger than me, and I'd rather not face a lawsuit since I can't afford a lawyer, much less a suit. This unnamed comic would call me up pretty stoned on grass and ramble on and on about how he wanted me to write jokes for him. He'd either try to bounce ideas off me, or get me to write stuff with the promise of payment. Luckily, he had a reputation for stealing, using the old sit-in-the-audience-and-record-your-jokes heist, or, by the, more subtle, buy a line and give you the "check is on the way" technique.

There were a few very big name comics who got away with stealing material. They were too big to outright accuse or even suggest there was a conflict, so whenever any of these comics came into the club, it was a fight to see which one of us had to go on. Usually that was one of the times the new guys got to go up early.

Most of us were very ethical, some more that others—Richard Morris, Glenn Hirsch, Larry David, Elayne Boosler, Rita Rudner, Jerry Seinfeld, Bobby Kelton, Paul Reiser, Larry Miller and Bill Maher for instance. But no one was more of a purist than Richard Lewis. If he even heard another comic use a premise even remotely similar, he would stop doing his own bit.

"Once I started doing fairly well, I didn't want to hear anybody's jokes or premises. I didn't want to hear anyone doing a routine on a sweater, because I'm really ethical about this and my brain would shut down and not think about sweaters for a long time."

-RICHARD LEWIS

Nowadays it's changed. Comics have as much bond as Post-It notes and don't care if they're doing another comic's material, even if he was the comic that got him the gig. We used to give each other punch lines. Today, they just take them from each other, along with the set-ups. I'm not saying that all the comics are stealing each other's material but the prevailing attitude is definitely less supportive and far more adversarial.

To us comics who believed that no subject matter was too out-of-bounds to be reduced to ridicule, there was nothing more sacred than our material. Our jokes were an extension of whom we were and what we had to offer. During even the worst circumstances with the most hostile audiences, our integrity would rise above it all. And no thief could ever take that away from us.

The Day the Showcase Died

I remember the moment I realized the creative days were about to go the way of the clean act. Robin Williams had worked the clubs throughout the years and killed based on his performance rather than the fame he was soon to achieve. One night, I recall seeing the new usual, a full house and the nervous comic on deck vibrating like he was caught between dimensions—when Robin showed up. The MC saw him standing under the light by the bar and immediately introduced him. Robin ran past the disintegrating comic's ego and onto the stage, the audience chanting "Mork! Mork! Mork!" As I looked around the room, I noticed for the first time that the crowd had changed. Gone were the sophisticated Broadway show people-- run out of the clubs by a generation of sitcom-watching kids who quoted lines from the TV Guide.

The show case clubs had become mainstream, so it was only a matter of time before us starving comics realized that we were an undervalued commodity. On a fall afternoon at The Comic Strip, following our brethren in L.A., who endured a lengthy strike (and a comic's suicide), we decided to strike. The clubs in the city were thriving—full houses all week long. The comics, whose popularity had grown to outrageous proportions, were still only getting paid eight dollars a night for cab fare. So at a meeting in The Comic Strip showroom, where there was no food, which really tested the comic's patience, the performers and club owners voiced their subjective views. Comic selfish and club owner selfish are two separate beasts. If a comic is in a plane crash and has no food, he will eat himself before any passengers can eat him. If a club owner is in a plane crash he will eat all the passengers and then ask, "What's for dessert?"

When it became clear we were at a stalemate and no one was close to suggesting we send out for pizza, something had to be done. I don't know how many, if any, of the comics know this or care. The strike was settled that day in I guess what you can call a secret meeting (although we only moved a few feet away) between Chris Albrecht and me, I'm not bragging. I'm just coming clean.

Unlike the other club owners, Chris was, at one time, part of a comedy team with Bob Zamuda (the creator of Comic Relief), so he lived our plight and knew the eight bucks a day could only be stretched so far. I told him what we wanted in terms of money, not career goals or our love lives. He told me what the clubs owners could pay for each set, not in terms of a fair wage or how they'd keep their profit margin. We managed to find a middle ground (which they would soon own) that I could feel myself sinking in as we shook hands. The strike was settled, I went and got a slice of pizza, ironically the smallest of the pie, and that day marked the beginning of the end of freewheeling, improvisational, loosely coordinated shows that were incubators of creativity. As soon as the owners started paying the performers, (as was their right) the show became theirs and it ended a system where creativity was king. The emcee, who ran the show like a benevolent dictator, had become slave to the almighty buck. Just as importantly, they would soon stop serving many of the comics "free meals." And to a comic, "free" is considered a food group.

The clubs didn't change immediately. It was gradual. Catch first, the Improv next and finally The Comic Strip to a much lesser degree. To this day they give the current comics and the alumni free drinks at the Strip. If you're lucky enough to arrive there on a night Richie Tienken is sitting at the bar, the drinking and laughter could last until closing.

Within a few years, when my generation of comics moved on to *bitter and better* things, the difference in the quality of the shows became evident. The next group of comics had the talent, but the clubs now derived their energy from money instead of creativity and the shows reflected it.

The combination of paying and the popularity of comedy made singers less and less a part of the show. Where it used to be an *"Aren't I wonderful?"* singer, then a comic, then another *"I should be a star"* singer, a comic or two, and then another *"no one else has ever done these same old tired standards the way I do"* singer, it became almost entirely comic after comic after comic. It made the comics work harder for laughs, which didn't make comics better—it just made them reach lower. Since you were now getting paid, bombing was no longer a learning experience; it was a losing proposition.

Judy Orbach singing at the Improv

There were, in fact, several incredibly talented singers like Pat Benatar, Sara Krieger, Joanie Peltz, Bobby Scott, Ann Silver, Judy Orbach, Jake Holmes, Mike Sergio and Patty Smyth, to name a few, who deserved a lot more than the comedy frenzied audience would normally give them, so it got more artistically challenging for them.

"The first "real" singing job I had was at Catch. Meaning, I didn't also have to wait on tables in between sets. They actually paid a small stipend (cab money, basically) if you performed. That was huge! Being chosen to be one of the few singers that "made it" on to the bill on any given night was actually quite an honor... Even more so when some of

the comedians would come in to hear the music. It was a tough crowd... but a good one."

-SARA KRIEGER (jazz singer)

"Richard Pryor never compromised. That's what good comedians should do—be themselves and not sell out. Richard Pryor was like the sun, and we were like the planets around him."

-RICHARD BELZER

When Lenny Bruce used profanity it was to make a point, and at the time it made getting laughs more difficult. He disarmed our preconceptions and our prejudices, taking away the damaging effects of certain words, freeing them and us, thus giving those words a new power. Richard Pryor, to many of us a genius, used more four letter words than a New York Cab driver with Tourette's Syndrome, but those words were authentic, growing out of a childhood spent in a brothel, not an amplification to get a laugh from a weak punch line. Unfortunately, under the pressure of *precious paying* stage time, comics wrote jokes starting with the word "fuck" and worked around it.

Don't get me wrong, I have nothing against using the word "fuck" (or doing it every decade or so), especially to accentuate an attitude. I just don't think it should be used as a timing device, or to replace wit, or to camouflage the lack of it. Back then, most of us felt you could talk about anything and use any *fucking* curse word you wanted as long as the cleverness of the joke transcended the subject matter and the language (unlike my above use of it). It was a simple formula that had its hysterical exceptions, but, for the most part, it kept the *young hack*s at bay, but not for long.

The Powerful MC

Arguably the most important position in sports is the quarterback. In the showcase clubs, it was arguably the MC, the Master of Ceremonies—the ruler of our docile domain. They were not only the glue that kept the show together, they were responsible for assembling it and on weeknights, making up the lineup on the fly. For the most part, the MC had absolute power, which corrupted almost absolutely, especially if the MC needed the extra time to work on material—the audience was so great it would be a shame to waste them on another act. When an audience became so burnt out at the end of the night the MC usually just wanted the show to end. In that case, they would put on a house-clearing act or appoint a young comic to MC and let them rule over garbage time.

In the early days of the Improv, Budd Friedman was both owner and MC. His power was God-like, and his equally commanding voice could make a comic's natural twitch tremble. When I arrived on the scene, Budd spent most his time in his new L.A. club and was only the MC during short visits to New York. He wasn't as funny as the comic MCs, but legend gave him a dimension that added importance and credibility to a show that didn't have one paid act!

"When I became an MC, on audition night, it was a REAL RESPONSIBILITY because I knew how important it was to the people auditioning, like Keenan Wayans, Robert Wuhl, Joe Piscopo, Paul Reiser and Paul Provenza, whom I chose. I felt real resentment and anger from some people who blamed me for never becoming a regular. Besides the normal everyday death threats, I once received a picture of someone shooting at me from a roof."

-GLENN HIRSCH

The route to becoming an MC at the Improv was quicker than at Catch. Audition night at the Improv was held on Sunday nights. It was also sort of an audition night for the new MCs, although, by then, they'd probably done enough late night emceeing that Chris and Judy Orbach would know they could handle the job.

I don't know what Judy's official title was at the Improv, but as I mentioned earlier, it's nearly impossible to think of the Improv without thinking of Judy or vice versa. She was a terrific singer/songwriter but more importantly she had a laugh that was in perfect tune with the comic's ears. She, along with the MC, ran the Improv's audition night. Most of the time, you'd bring up the acts, but other times Judy would sit in the middle of the room, in the dark, and call out an auditioner's number over a microphone that had its own echo chamber. When a regular came in to do a guest spot, which was one of the few nights a non-heavyweight could get to work to a full house, the MC would introduce the act.

When I first started to perform guest spots on audition night, I always felt the additional pressure of having to do better than the auditioners. When I did do better, I got a slight taste of what I thought being a heavyweight might feel like. I pranced around the room, hoping every audience member saw me, and watched the auditioners part as I strutted through them slowly. If I did worse, I'd practically run out of the room, hiding as much of myself as possible, avoiding all auditioners and, if I had any self-esteem left, get my cab fare and race across town hoping to do another set that might halt my fantasies of failure.

Audition night at the Improv was less frequent than at Catch and less deadly. The Catch auditions were held Monday nights and were a big draw-- a carnival atmosphere for the carnivorous; jammed with sadistic New Yorkers like a pack of Son of Sams looking for victims. Thirty or more amateurs would come with the hope of fame, and most would leave with the hope that their humiliation would fade and a microbe of hope would return within a fortnight.

The top MC in New York was Richard Belzer, who only emceed at Catch A Rising Star, and, besides Budd Friedman, was the most intimidating person in the clubs. Whenever he moved through the bar or showroom, he left a trail of young comics that looked like chum floating in his wake.

I recently ran into Budd at Elaine's in NYC with his lovely wife Alex. He had spotted me at my table, and called my name with that voice—one God could have used to kick Adam and Eve out of the Garden of Eden When I nervously turned toward him, his smile was the kind I'd imagined a loving father would have given to a son who just came back from the Crusades. He invited me and my musician pal, Joe Passaro, whose birthday we were celebrating, to his table. The intimidation that was once a trademark had morphed into warmth and all out generosity putting me completely at ease (okay, maybe in a little shock). Budd was finally happy with his life. Through most of the night he held Alex's hand and told us stories and I laughed (not to please him, but because I was pleased). I was sorry to see the night end, but I knew his transformation was complete when Budd picked up the check.

As was the custom, the first MC spots I did were late night garbage time. Even ruling over the half a dozen acts and the remaining audience members—who either hoped to spot a gem at a comic garage sale or were too tired or drunk to leave—gave me a sense of power equivalent to a kid learning to control his nocturnal emissions.

The first real test for a new MC was starting the show and warming up the audience. For me, that occurred at the Improv on a weeknight (rather than audition night). I stood at the back of the room, near the hallway leading to the bar, just a short puke from the bathroom (which, at the Improv, would work as a room deodorizer) and looked at the ragged circle of stage lights that surrounded the mic stand. In a few minutes, it would be 10:20 and I'd walk on stage and try and make the audience laugh without relying on my act, but instead on imaginative questions like, "Where are you from?" or, "What do you do for a living?" I didn't write any lines designed for the MC spot, figuring that if I wanted to be a regular MC, I would have to learn to live or die by the ad lib. I wasn't particularly known for being quick on my feet, but I wasn't known for being slow-witted either. I just had the kind of act that was structured and worked best when left to live or die on its own.

I took the mic off the stand with my left hand since I'm left-handed, and why not start off with your strength? I looked out into the audience, waited for my eyes to adjust to the darkness below the trim of the spots and said my first words as an official MC, "Welcome to the Improv." Okay, so I had one rehearsed line, not exactly a killer.

Then I went into the standard audience questions, hoping that something funny would emerge or that I'd be rescued by a statewide blackout, a fire evacuation, or the audience would miraculously have their vocal chords replaced with a laugh track. Somehow, something funny did gather in my head and survived the warm up. I did have a plan for the rest of the show, however, that was based on my philosophy (or deeply rationalized excuse) that an MC's primary job is to set up the audience for the acts, and that being funny (except for the warm-up) was just a tool more than a goal.

After relieving myself of the initial pressure of getting constant laughs, I loosened up enough to be relatively funny. Still, I felt that at any moment I might be spit on. As the night drove forward, the moments of silence felt heightened and the search for funny answers deepened as I competed with my own remarkable ad libs from earlier in the evening. Towards the middle of the show, I stemmed the mounting stress level by sneaking in my own material, as I instinctively blended my loser MC persona with my regular persona. Once free to use my act, I found ways to segue whole chunks of material and, with the aid of well placed stuttering, made the material sound ad libbed. I finally relaxed thanks to the extra stage time and the realization that the audience didn't hate me (or at least weren't drunk enough to express it with airborne debris).

I did well enough the first night to start emceeing on a regular basis. I never took up much time between acts and made sure that all my intros amplified the comic's credits and talent. One night I actually got a little carried away trying to give a great intro (although looking back, it was more prophetic), where I introduced Larry David as a comic genius ahead of his time. LD didn't have a very good set, even if he didn't challenge anyone to a fight, and blamed it on my introduction because he felt he couldn't live up to it. Only LD could become intimidated by an introduction. A few nights later, when he was emceeing, he got back at me. He introduced me with, "If you like shit, you'll really like this guy." I either thought it was funny or felt it was something I could live up to and it didn't affect my set. I bombed on my own merits.

The next challenge was being the MC at Catch. It wasn't that the MC was more important at Catch, but the more Vegas-style show business atmosphere added an additional layer of pressure. The silent partners of questionable backgrounds didn't help either. My first regular MC spot at Catch wasn't as terrifying as it might have been because I had already succeeded in warming-up and taming an audience at the Improv a few times.

Being the MC at Catch, in the beginning, felt like I was standing in the shadow of Richard Belzer's mouth, where he might bite the microphone out of my hand at any moment. Another reason Catch was more daunting was that you could actually see most of the audience, especially the first few rows. The problem here is that when I can see individual members of the audience and any movement, expression, or discharge they might make, I start to imagine the terrible things they might be thinking.

My first MC night at Catch was on a Tuesday, which is usually the deadest night in the club. When I lifted the microphone off the stand and looked down at the faces smacked with light and waiting for me to speak it was like each one of them was a Nazi commandant shouting, "Go ahead, say something funny! Now!" The worst thing you can say to a comic besides telling them how funny the other comics were, or saying things like, "I got a joke you can use," or "I thought your act was cute," is telling a comic to "say something funny."

I started my warm-up by giving the crowd my sincerest of disingenuous welcomes and jumped right into asking where they were from and what did they do for a living. I managed to find a few funny comebacks every time and the night ran smoothly, which meant I drank enough to feel like I was funny, but didn't get too drunk to think I deserved to get paid.

When Larry David was the MC, he had his own very unique system. He'd elect an audience president, and much of the banter would be directed at the new Head of Hate. He didn't do it all the time, but the times he did, it worked and made the audience seem less like a lynch mob and more like a domestic terrorist group forced to check in their

explosives. Actually, if the audience went with LD, Larry could be as funny and kind as the meekest of comics, but one "nay" could turn things quickly into the
Inquisition.

As I emceed more, dealing with the audience became the easiest part of the job. The hardest part became choosing which acts to put on-- the singers being the most difficult. Not that the singers were more insistent, but by then we were using so few singers they had to wait while comic after comic would go on stage. I felt sorry for them. Also, very few singers really loved being the opening act, which is what we comics thought God designed them for. The first act to make it big from the clubs was Pat Benatar. It was an example of synchronicity when her voice, persona and vision were matched perfectly with the musical mastermind of her husband, songwriter and guitar player, Neil Geraldo. When I started at the clubs she was a cabaret singer. Even then we all could tell that she had something special (her four-octave range was a clue). When she ventured in to rock and roll she exploited her powerful voice in a distinctive style that was electric. Pat did a riveting version of "Stairway to Heaven" and a blazingly hot "Fever" that had the audience salivating and the comics hoping they didn't have to follow her.

My first steady MC gig was being the host at Monday night's Catch a Rising Star's audition night. I had succeeded Kelly Rogers, who had succeeded David Sayh, who had succeeded Bob Shaw and Elayne Boosler, who succeeded the king of MC's, the Belz-- Richard Belzer. Bill Maher, Adrienne Tolsch and her future husband Bill Scheft followed us.

As mentioned earlier, audition night at Catch was a big hit and drew a raucous crowd with the kind of people who'd go to a relative's execution and call it a family outing. The job of the MC was to keep the show moving into the growling stomach of the insatiable bridge-and-tunnel crowd that steamed the room. Every so often, I'd bring up a regular to break the feeding frenzy before they tore into me.

We usually had about thirty to forty acts doing some kind of performance for five or six minutes. One of the crowd-favorites was Jane D. (her first name was changed and her last name has been shortened to the wrong initial to protect the guilty), a cute singer, if you like the insane what-is-wrong-with-this-pretty-picture type. She wore a white cowboy hat and a fringed skirt. Jane, or was it Joan (that I purposely used to mislead those who know her) didn't carry a melody; she dropped it down several flights of stairs. For some strange reason unbeknownst to me, the audience loved her. They'd yell encore repeatedly and Jackie (or Joan or Jane or Jeffrey to confuse myself and those who thought they were in the know more), who believed with all her heart—which had broken off its relationship with her ears—thought she was a diva. The first few times we saw her we laughed. It was the one time I believed freedom of expression should be declared illegal. We had other crazy acts, like a magician who filled his mouth with razor blades and then cleverly bled. Needless to say, he didn't go over very well, especially in the first few rows.

Paul Provenza

I don't remember whom I passed on audition night, but I do remember seeing comics who I knew would become regulars like Freddy Stoller, Rita Rudner, Bill Maher, Robert Townsend, Paul Provenza, Bill Scheft, Rich Shydner and John Mendoza. Most of the comics that passed had some spark—something that told you their time would come.

Being a regular MC gave me my first taste and sometimes, distaste, of power. I tried to be fair, but it was nearly impossible given how many close comic friends I had and the degree of irritability the now stage starved singers displayed.

For years, the opening act at the Improv was Wieden and Finkle, an odd-looking duo, who would only look normal in the outtakes of a Fellini film. They wrote, performed and sang funny songs, like "Trenton, New Jersey," where they smoked, coughed and blew smoke at the audience. Wieden (or was it Finkel) was tall and thin, and Finkel (or was it Wieden) was short and stocky. I can still hear them singing their signature opening song, "A Couple of Guys with Class." If you got a couple of Improv comics together today, we could probably harmonize most of their act and even do an encore.

During the week, we'd tell a few comics and singers to come in early so we'd be sure to have someone (usually a first or second year regular) cover the first few slots until all the regulars arrived. Sometimes that didn't work out. I was emceeing one night, in fact it was a Wednesday, and I'd been doing the warm up. At around the ten minute mark, I looked towards the bar for acts. I didn't see any, so I stayed on another ten minutes and still no acts. At around 45 minutes, a singer—a very good singer—one of the best I'd ever heard arrived. I motioned for her to come on stage. She refused. I rebutted with my most earnest request face and she returned with her meanest refusal. She obviously felt it was beneath her to open the show. At the time, she was overweight, so, to her, there was a lot of beneath. I must have been on close to an hour and was into my weaker material. Fortunately, the audience had either a long attention span, or such a short attention span that they thought I was several different acts and kept laughing. I finally spotted a couple of comics in the bar and immediately brought one on.

I ran offstage and into the bar ready to rip the singer a new mouth—only one a little further south that leads to a more toxic environment. By now, Rick Newman, Kelly Rodgers and couple of comics had arrived and gone down to Rick's office, which was slightly larger than this paragraph. Shortly after, the singer, who must have been in the ladies room freshening her ego, entered the bar. Now, I don't have much of a temper to lose, but that night I completely lost sight of it. As I mentioned, the singer happened to be slightly smaller than a fat farm and I started in on how fat she was. On the spot, I made up at least half a dozen lines about her abundance of self. For good old mean spirited fun, I added harsher insults philosophically (if crudely) comparing her mouth to a part of a female's anatomy. The comics and the bartenders were in shock at my tirade, but as soon as the singer ran downstairs to tell Rick, they all burst out laughing. It was one of those rare moments where you say the things that everyone else was thinking. The singer barged into Rick's office and started repeating the fat lines (verbatim and with perfect timing, all the lines I wish I could remember). Rick and the crew tried to act concerned, but as she repeated the jokes they lost control over their laughter-restraining mechanism. She ran out of the office, up the stairs and exited the club, either enraged or trying to lose the excess poundage.

I eventually made up with the singer and we sorted out our differences. I apologized for my tirade and of course asked her if she remembered any of the jokes. After that, we never had any problems and she always went on when I asked. She also lost the excess weight and her looks closely matched her amazing voice making me wonder if I shouldn't sign up at Jenny Craig to be a weight loss coach.

I don't recall whether or not I was ever the MC at The Comic Strip. I probably was a few times. Their main guys were Larry Miller, Jerry Seinfeld, Paul Reiser, Dennis Wolfberg, George Wallace, Hiram Kasten, D.F. Sweedler, Larry Cobb and several others you probably never heard of. One thing I do remember vividly was that it was a great room to work, the audience was often far more appreciative than we deserved.

You weren't really a powerful MC until you emceed on the weekend at the Improv, The Comic Strip and especially at Catch. At the Improv and the Strip, even though the first and most of the second shows were booked on the weekends, the rooms remained loose, and the audiences for the first shows were almost always great. The second show was open-ended, but you could appoint a younger guy to finish the last hour or so. The second show at Catch went on until 3:00 or 3:30 and the MC was required to be there for the entire show. Catch was much more tightly organized and run more like the Marines, while the Improv ran like the Boy Scouts and the Strip like an amusement park. The first shows in all clubs usually had great audiences and always ended near a particular time. There were nights that the clubs used split MCs (different ones for each show), but they were rare.

When I emceed, especially at Catch on the weekends, I always felt like I had to prove myself since my regular act was considered low energy and required the audience to actually think (at least that's what I told myself when they didn't laugh). I wasn't as flashy or as aggressive as most MCs, but my shows always ran smoothly—except for Joe Piscopo getting his nose broken, Jerry Seinfeld having a beer mug thrown at him, Jack Graiman almost being choked to death by Rich Newman, and Larry David walking off, threatening the audience, which happened no matter who the MC was.

Being the MC whenever Lenny Schultz went on was never a simple process. You'd have to stay on stage and try to keep the audience's attention while the debris (which consisted of cereal, parts of fruit, puddles of water, whipped cream, small people and anything else that could splatter) was cleaned up. I pictured a police forensic team examining the scene trying to discover which bits Lenny performed. It's not easy following a guy who ends up standing in his bikini underwear with a banana stuffed up his butt. I usually didn't even attempt to be funny. It would be like following the atom bomb with a water balloon. I mostly talked about Lenny's performance, almost like a question and answer session with the audience, until they could digest what they had just witnessed.

Being an MC trained me to work different kinds of crowds and to adapt, without changing who I was on stage. Through ad libs I gained new lines and I even formed some jokes that were designed for hosting a show. Today, the MC spot is usually given to a younger comic to basically introduce the acts, which I think shortchanges the show. I believe a good MC can make the show last longer and be 20-40% funnier for the comics. I always felt that back then you earned the position of MC and, in a way, it was a rite of passage (and the first taste of power) on your way to being a club heavyweight.

Becoming a Heavyweight

A heavyweight bumping a comic, who has paid his dues as a regular, and is finally getting an opportunity to work to a full house is almost as bad as waiting to be introduced while an MC works on enlarging his ego. I once waited for nearly an hour. Your anxiety reaches a dangerous level when the MC starts into your intro and then stops abruptly, like a stripper who suddenly finds Jesus under her G-string, to do another long winded ad lib.

Then, just when the MC truly starts your intro, Elayne Boosler, Richard Lewis, Bob Shaw, Ed Bluestone, Robert Klein or Rodney Dangerfield walks through the door and the club manager quickly drags the heavyweight into the spotlight. The MC, who seconds earlier acted like he was the only comic in existence, instantly brings up the heavyweight. In those BYH days (Before You're a Heavyweight), this can happen a few times a night. Getting bumped at the last second is one of the worst things a comic can experience and one I couldn't wait to do to someone as a heavyweight myself.

For me, becoming a heavyweight took about three years. It wasn't something that I suddenly realized. It came on gradually much like going bald.

"To see a comic make it to the next level was the greatest thing to me. It meant there was a crack in the wall."

-JOHN MENDOZA

Being a heavyweight meant getting the best spots, the most spots, being able to MC just about any time you needed dough, being in demand at all three clubs on weekends, and best of all, was getting to bump almost all the other comics. You received the ultimate respect of being rushed into the club, wasting a young comic's anxiety attack and getting monster laughs from a primed audience meant for the kid lying in a booth in the fetal position.

As a heavyweight, you got perks—free T-shirts (well, one or two), free drinks for all your friends, better food (steak at Catch, shrimp at

The Comic Strip or stolen black bread at the Improv), the ability to book spots when requested, and at Catch, being invited down to hang out in Rick's office. You also got to promise spots to comic friends and more importantly, got prime spots for when celebrities showed up or for auditions. Besides being a bumper, one of the best privileges at Catch was being able to hang out behind the rope in the small area that divided the bar from the showroom. If you had a serious girlfriend or one that was just using you, you could spend time with her in that five by four foot VIP area, until Terry Columbo's boom box vocal chords (the Catch manager) would yell, "Everybody, on the other side of the rope now."

As a heavyweight, you were not only always included on the after-show trips to Chinatown, the Village or Little Italy, but also involved in deciding and re-deciding where we went. Young comics would ask you for advice, which was gladly given, because that kind of giving was also receiving where you needed it most—your ego. With other comics—some of them famous—you had the power to give them spots on the show and then introduce them. If the phone rang and it was a club calling for a comic and you hadn't gone up yet, you'd be haggled over; and if you had gone up, you'd be one of the first to be asked for, which is much better than being stared at while the manager says, "There aren't any comics here."

As a heavyweight, it was much easier to find another eager comic to share a cab with, and sometimes even pay for it. You became showcase royalty, almost on equal footing with Elayne, Lewis, Bluestone, Lenny Shultz, Belzer, Kaufman and Shaw, etc. I remember enjoying, more so than the power, the feeling of being recognized for my work by both my peers and the club owners. And with that came a feeling of belonging because I really deserved it (like the 36% I got in geometry), which gave me a sense of freedom (unlike the 36% in geometry, which gave me a real feeling of being in summer school).

Sure, I'd never feel the star power of Belzer, or the Untouchables, who built Catch, or Richard Lewis, Freddie Prinze, and Robert Klein who helped establish the birth place of showcase comedy, the Improv, but I did feel like one of the guys that was carrying on the tradition. For me, it has never gotten better than that, nor would I want it to, unless it meant financial security and a divine promise to live forever. I've been a head writer, a producer and even written and directed a movie, but none of that ever gave me the sense of oneness that being a heavyweight did. Being a heavyweight, I felt like, at last, I was one with the universe of my peers...except for the comic I just bumped, that is.

All The Roads Lead Through Jerry Stanley's New Jersey

In the late Travolta-seventies, when even dogs walked around with their collars open, Jerry Stanley, a friend of one of the comics started booking clubs in New Jersey, where we could actually make fifty bucks—or as much as Rodney paid for a single joke.

Jerry like many of us at the time had a full-bodied mustache, stood several inches over me, his eyes had more confidence than my entire heritage and unlike most bookers, acted like someone you could trust— and was actually trustable. He prided himself in being fair to the comics, which in reality meant being unfair to his own self. Comics, for the most part, always feel like they're getting the short end of the stick while at the same time subconsciously feel like they deserve even less.

Mark Schiff and Jerry Stanley

"In 1979 I went to the Improv to see Brant Von Hoffman. Brant told me the comedians were only paid $5.00 a set, which gave me the idea

to start 'comedy nights' where comics would get paid decently. My friend who owned a popular club in northern New Jersey called Freddie's gave me Sunday nights. Our first show on August 3ʳᵈ 1979 was sold out and was the first of over 400 shows at that venue. It featured, John DeBellis, Peter Bales, and Glenn Hirsch. .

-JERRY STANLEY

Jerry Stanley was one of the primary ingredients for the comedy boom that was soon to come. To us 16-buck-a-night-comics, those 55 buck Stanley gigs were a Jersey gold rush. The early Stanley gigs were in areas where most of us city guys never knew existed—guys who saw grass as a threat to nature's cement.

"I worked one place, and we drove for hours and hours. I remember we got out of the car—it was always a bad sign if there were chickens in the parking lot. So this was going to be a rough night. We went into the place and it was Hell's Angels night in this particular club. It was them and their mommas. So I was standing there, and at that point, all my material was about being a ballerina."

-RITA RUDNER

The entertainment consisted of three comics, the newest of which would open the show, MC, get paid the least and take the abuse of drunken locals who thought funny was anything with the word "fuck" in it.

"John was working for me at a club in Greenburg NY, and Larry David came along for the ride sort of last minute. The whole time in the car he completely ignored me and complained to John about doing a gig for $55.00. He had no concern that I may be offended, which I wasn't. Larry was very much the character that he now plays on Curb Your Enthusiasm...and that was 29 years ago!"

-JERRY STANLEY

Just to show you where my priorities were at the time, the first Jerry Stanley gig was on a Sunday night, the very same Sunday night that Lenny Maxwell bought me a third row, middle aisle ticket to see Frank Sinatra. Not Joe Piscopo doing Sinatra, not Frank Sinatra, Jr. doing Frank Sinatra, the real and only Frances Albert Sinatra. I received $75, which started a row between Jerry and my pal Glenn Hirsch, who was only getting $55, until Glenn found out that the other $20 was tossed in because I was driving.

Shortly after the Stanley gigs, Stars Comedy Club in Philadelphia opened and was one of my first regular, almost grown up paying gigs. You could actually take a train there, stay for the weekend, eat a meal or two, drink for free, possibly make out with a waitress and return home with a hundred bucks or so. Most guys fantasize about a girl in a French maid's outfit. A comic's dream girl is wearing a black T-shirt with a club logo, a stained white apron hastily tied at the waist and sneakers that match nothing she's wearing except maybe the food and drink stains.

Larry David and Bobby Kelton were working at Grandma Minnie's in Philadelphia and decided to visit Constitution Hall. The museum had roped off the podium where many of our founding fathers spoke. LD climbed over the ropes and stood behind the podium, and became Ben Franklin loudly giving a speech to the other founding fathers. After about 3 minutes into his moving discourse he was caught by security and thrown out of the museum like he was a red coat spy.

Six months or so after Stars in Philly, Garvin's Grill in Washington D.C. started standup on weekends and we had the beginnings of a real comedy circuit. You could do this circuit three or four times a year and clear close to five hundred dollars, without including transportation costs, meals, taxes and tipping the waitress in the hope she'd do more than make out with you wearing her sexy urban waitress gear.

The Garvin's Grill gig was started by Sandy Kaleneck, a very pretty blonde with an IQ that was higher than all her fetching measurements added together, multiplied by all the comics she rejected. Every comic who worked there dreamed they'd have such a great set that she'd let them touch hers, but none of us, not even the best, got close, even in our best dreams.

There were nights at the clubs when I, Gilbert and Larry David would kill—destroy the room, get a standing ovation—and who got the girl? Not me, nor Gilbert and certainly not Larry. Although he came closest than any of us, if you consider that the man who got the woman—any woman—was KD, Larry's older, non-show business, computer programmer brother, Ken David. Don't get me wrong LD was never envious of his brother. In fact, as hard as it might be to comprehend, especially if you believe his character on "Curb," LD was actually happy for Ken. And it was in Washington D.C. almost some twenty odd years ago that sexy Sandy Kaleneck made a choice that I'm sure today she doesn't regret (or doesn't even remember *was* a choice) when she chose Ken David, over the rest of us. Today Larry is one of the richest, most successful funniest comedians in the world, but Ken has the memory of being with the elusive Sandy Kaleneck.

My roommate Brant Von Hoffman and I were booked to work a weekend at Garvin's Grill in Washington DC. For some reason, we decided to fly down instead of taking a train. Staying consistent with my karma, there was an airline strike that eliminated most flights and first class seating. Our plane was packed with wealthy business types and as Brant and I took our seats, I noticed two startling eyes that looked familiar, though a color I'd not seen on a human before. A wave of black hair swept past like a veil that was hiding something meant to be displayed. She turned and gave me a warm, inclusive smile that indicated I might actually be a member of the same species, which disarmed me of all my misconceptions about her. One row behind us— so close that the space denied her lovely legs room to stretch out—was Elizabeth Taylor. We listened as she spoke freely to the stranger sitting next to her, but neither Brant nor I turned to speak to her. Instead, we talked at a volume that would have qualified as bragging, even for a young Mohammed Ali, about our being comedians and our gig in Washington D.C.

Call it youthful stupidity, or having unrealistic views of our own importance, but we actually thought it would impress her enough to jump up, squeeze her head between our seats and join our conversation, becoming entranced in the careers of two trail-blazing young comedians dressed for recess. Of course, she probably never heard a word we were yelling, or if she did, and she was having a charitable, delusional day, she might have thought it was cute. She certainly never gave a single hint that we were either of any interest or even too loud. During the whole flight not a word was exchanged between us. But I did manage to find reasons to look at her a few more times, not out of curiosity or sexual lust, but to admire her eyes like two rare jewels that might have originated in another galaxy—as distant as the chance that she'd come to our shows and snatch us up. Well, we were at least part of her jet set crowd for that one-hour—one row in front of her, screaming to each other like one of us was still on the ground.

Upon landing, I grabbed my luggage from the overhead compartment, trying to find a muscle to flex, she looked up and softly said, "That's my bag, can you hand it to me please?" I was so nervous I almost dropped it on her head. I handed it to her, not shaking quite enough to sway the plane as I nearly touched her hand; and as I looked into her eyes a little too long, waiting to be sucked up into them, she smiled, probably having seen this a million times before, and said, "Thank you." Then she moved on, as the uninformed crowd pushed her forward.

When we worked those early gigs, since we had to share a room, we tried to book it with a comic friend who was as much a slob as we were, which didn't eliminate many of our peers and allowed each other's roaches to meet, thus varying their gene pools. I often worked with Kelly Rogers, who once washed his pants with a paperback book in his back pocket, could smoke a cigarette in his eyelid and dated a girl who threw him out of his own apartment. We used towels and blankets to keep the light out of the hotel room, smeared green and red toothpaste on the TV to make it seem like color, and when the maid tried to enter, we tossed our sneakers at her. Oh, and we once started a bulldozer parked outside and almost drove it into the hotel. Maybe it was Glenn Hirsch—or Glenn and Kelly.

During those years, practical jokes ran more rampant than the comic's mouths. One winter night, Jerry Seinfeld and Larry Miller went on stage in their underwear, which of course got huge laughs from the sophisticated crowd and assured me I wasn't gay. Of course, someone from the club took their pants to the bar down the street and had the bouncer hide them. At first, Jerry and Larry Miller laughed, and then, when no one would get their pants, they froze trying to retrieve them.

Standup comedy was becoming more and more popular, so in the late 70's, Catch A Rising Star ran a comedy tour that ventured into the deep south, which at the time was just *a wee bit* backward in the racist department. You could see bumper stickers on cars that said, "We brake for blacks," but not in those exact words. I once worked a club in Mississippi and the next day was invited to the owner's bachelor party and they had sheep jump out of the cake (the marriage didn't last, but the wife got a nice wool coat in the settlement). Comics are probably the least prejudiced people in the world. We believe that no matter what race, creed, sex or religion a person is, we are inferior to them. Actually, I think it's because, to us, racism is a set up with a punch line designed solely to kill the spirit of an audience it can no longer keep captive.

That southern tour featured Pat Benatar, her black piano player Raymond Johnson and comics Richard Belzer and Barry Diamond. Barry once performed a gig where a member of the hosting organization was killed in a car accident on the way to the venue. The MC tearfully informed the audience, who began to collectively weep, about the fatal accident and ended a moment of silence with, "And now for the comedy portion of our show, Barry Diamond."

As I mentioned earlier, comics love practical jokes and we will do almost anything for a laugh, including dropping napalm on ourselves, and we are very good at convincing others to join in. Ray Johnson had gone to sleep early, so Richard Belzer and Barry Diamond talked Pat into sneaking into Ray's room and to lying down next to him in bed (not undressed). Then they pounded on the door screaming in Southern accents, "I heard you have a white girl in there!" Ray woke and was shocked to see Pat next to him as the door burst open and Richard and Barry stormed in wearing sheets on their heads ala the Ku Klux Klan. I hate to use the cliché, but it applies here. Ray nearly turned as white as a 1950's kissing contest at the University of Alabama, until he realized what was happening and burst out laughing. Love may make the world go round, but laughter keeps us from taking the gravity of life too seriously.

Standup comedy crawled from the pot holes of New York City into the woods of New Jersey and found its way to a more fertile ground.

"Within a year I was booking approximately 65 comedians in twelve clubs a week in the New York/New Jersey area. Within two years I was booking over 150 comics in seventeen cities in the US and Canada. In 1981 I opened "The Comedy Stop" at the Tropicana Hotel and Casino in Atlantic City. "

-JERRY STANLEY

The Real Road

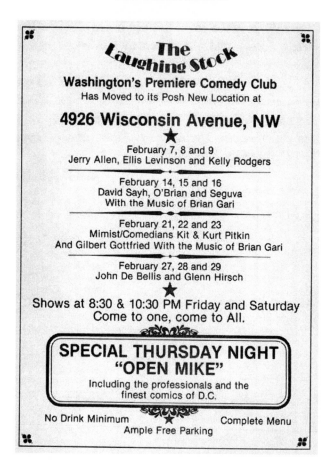

Jerry Stanley's gigs, Stars in Philadelphia and Garvin's Grill in Washington, which were the seeds that sprouted the real comedy road that shot across the country like a bumbling brush fire out of control, which almost burnt itself out. Overnight, hundreds of clubs popped up—sometimes two or three in the same city. Cab fare was no longer our staple. Our main food source became comedy clubs, which sprouted any place they could set up folding chairs in front of a wooden platform that supported most of our weight, a bare patch of floor with a microphone. We were no longer at the bottom of the entertainment food chain. We were complaining our way toward the top.

During the 70s, there was still a college circuit left over from the sixties, which managed to avoid most of us. In fact, the only acts I can remember working colleges on a steady basis were a comedy team, Edmonds and Curly, and Uncle Dirty. The rest of us were living off of cab fare and working Pips and Jerry Stanley gigs. We did get some other odd low-paying jobs like working NIT, New Jersey Institute of Technology. They were the kids who, after graduation, washed the cars of the kids who graduated from MIT. We performed at lunch hour, standing on a table while kids passed their macaroni and cheese and peas through our legs. When a comic hears the word "daytime" in regards to a gig, we knew the pay was going to be just about enough to buy lunch, though we would be working an audience that wanted us for lunch.

It was either in the late 70's or early 80s that we jumped from the possibility of working the two or three paying jobs at Improv, Catch and The Strip, to dozens and then hundreds. Club owners saw money instead of talent. If a comic could get laughs by killing every waitress and someone would pay to see it, that comic would get steady work and the club owners would hire a new wait staff, taking his deceased employees' tips of course. You were only as good as the audiences told the club owner you were. The somewhat sophisticated audiences that once supported comedians were now the minority.

It used to be that we'd see a terrific comic and think, *I wish I were as funny as him.* It got so the new breed would see a comic and think, *God, I'm much funnier that that guy, and would be even funnier if I used his jokes.* It was like instant evolution. Men and women, who took thousands of years to finally stand erect, were now hunching over, trying to get laughs. Guidance counselors now added being a standup comedian to career choices. What was once an art form was now a form to be filled out by your employee.

The most difficult part of producing a comedy show was finding a place for the comics to sleep. Where there's money, there's always a way, and the club owners found it in comic condominiums. They'd find an apartment with a bedroom for the headliner, a couch for the middle act, and the opener was usually someone local who lived at home with his parents. I even worked one gig where the headliner slept in a spare bedroom in the opener's parents' house and the middle act on their couch.

At this point in the story of standup guys, we were sprouting our wings. I started writing for TV and didn't work the road as much as my comic brothers and sisters. Working on the road was like a family drifting apart in order to make their way in life, or as a comic would have it, it was more like getting out of the way of life.

Comics crisscrossed the country forming other friendships with comics from all parts of our great land, which seemed much larger when driving through Texas. We didn't work in the South very much. Down there, they thought Jewish was what someone said after they blew out birthday candles. We had to learn to work crowds that spoke the same language, but only understood what they were saying to each other.

I once worked a gig for the Pipe Fitters Local 101 in Pittsburgh, where it was bad enough that the first three rows were angry nuns, but they gave out awards behind me on stage during my set. I adjusted to my audience, of course, and started my set with a string of abortion jokes. I might not have gotten any laughs, but at least they stopped the awards ceremony. By then, bombing was easy, but not being paid attention to still hurt.

One of my first road gigs was the Great Gorge Playboy Club, which I worked with Brant Von Hoffman. They put us up in the hotel, and of course we had to share a room. The gig started off on the wrong foot, or possibly on the right foot pointing in the wrong direction. The Great Gorge Club was huge and had a long hallway and led to two stages—each one on the opposite side of the room. When they announced my name, I entered the room to a nice round of applause, which in this case really indicated that they were going to be a great audience, since there was no one at the microphone. I had entered on the wrong stage, behind them. I made it out to be part of my act and got a big laugh, long enough for me to run down the hall and enter on the right stage.

It turned out to be a wonderful gig, not because we got paid a great amount of money or we met any Playboy Bunnies. They let us turn the lights on in their gigantic Howard Hughes' Grey Goose-size indoor tennis courts. Brant and I, as always, had our baseball gloves, balls and bats in my trunk, so we spent most of the night at the Playboy Club, not getting shagged, but shagging fly balls.

My First Real Job

What I mean by "real job," is a job that pays enough money for one to be considered making a living, unlike a standup gig, where you make barely enough to keep you alive. My first real making-a-living job was writing for "Saturday Night Live."

I didn't even consider myself a contender for SNL, since they were primarily looking for performers. As I had done before, on an important audition for my comic pals, I opened the show. I did that for two reasons. Reason one (and least important from my perspective) was that I'm one of the easier acts to follow, because of the thinking nature of my material. It's easier for an audience to go from reacting with their brains to reacting from their groins. To go from groin to brain would be like going from having sex with a gorgeous girl to spending the rest of the night with an ugly mathematician reciting algorithms. The other, more important, reason was that by opening the show at the Improv and having most of the acts waiting to audition, I could run across town and do another set at Catch, and possibly a third at The Comic Strip.

I found out the next day, from Chris Albrecht, my manager, that the producers were interested in me for a writing job. A meeting was set up, which I thought I might have blown when they asked what my goal as a writer was and I told them, "To make enough money that I'd never have to work during a Yankee game." Despite that remark I was offered the job. Gilbert Gottfried literally was almost thrown out of the room during his interview when they asked him, "Under what conditions would you consider performing on 'SNL'?" and he told the producer, "Only if they fired you." Luckily, I had already been hired and convinced the powers that be that Gillie was a comic, and comedians are like soldiers walking through a field of land mines hoping to find one by stepping on it.

Chris Albrecht told me in the Improv bar, the day after my interview, that I had the job and would make nearly 70 grand. I wasn't accustomed to making 70 of anything all at once. I immediately had several drinks but I don't have any memory of how I ended my night of celebration. I do know I arrived at the evening's finish line alone but feeling liked I was sleeping with someone special.

I'm not going to spend much time talking about the inner workings of SNL because there were so many personalities and events that had very little to do with the Standup Guys. But there is one anecdote that fits perfectly. While I was writing for SNL, Larry David was writing and performing on "Fridays." Each week, usually several times, we'd call each other up complaining about some irritating personality on the show or how the Yankees never should have fired Dick Howser as their manager. I made no secret about my friendship with LD. On one episode of Fridays they did a similar sketch to one we did on SNL the following day, which should have simply proved the shows had similar bad taste. Of course, at SNL they thought the bit was stolen, and there were rumors that I was telling Larry our sketches and he was clandestinely feeding them to their writers. I was too self-absorbed in what I was writing to pay close attention to another writer's bit or even waste my time trying to recall it to LD. The rumor died quickly when Joe Piscopo, and possibly Gilbert and Eddie Murphy, came to my defense. Or maybe they realized that Larry and I had no interest in what anyone else in the world was doing.

For the next several months I lived high off a hog I should have left alone. I was able to pay the rent on my new apartment, pay off my bills, run up larger bills fixing up my new apartment; but most importantly, the job allowed me to take many of my starving comic friends out to dinner.

SNL was the first time any of us still left on the east coast had a high-paying job with a steady paycheck. Kelly Rodgers, who had money from stocks, and I would do crazy things like buy other comics like Steve Mittleman ugly suits or weird useless gifts, and would even go out to real restaurants to eat full a la carte meals with wine, dessert, coffee, drinks and we left a tip we didn't have to hide under the table cloth.

On one of his trips back east, on the recommendation of one of the producers of SNL, I took LD (who had money from Fridays) and a few friends to Pearls, a Chinese restaurant frequented by the rich and famous. We wound up sitting at the table next to Andy Warhol and his clan. I never would have dreamed that LD would wind up being wealthier than Andy Warhol. Of course, Andy is now dead, which limits his earning power.

The hours on SNL were long and I never found time to do laundry, which wouldn't have taken much effort since there was a fluff and fold cleaning crew in our basement. In one of the shops near 30 Rock, there was a clothes store that sold very expensive Mac Keen jeans, which were made more appealing by the knockout salesgirl, who I never made a pass at. I just kept buying jeans until I had thirty pairs and she moved on to another career or bought her own store from commissions made off of me. In order to avoid doing laundry, I wound up purchasing 130 pairs of socks and underwear from different stores throughout Manhattan, most without attractive salespeople. I had two whole coffin-size draws filled with them. Good thing the style back then didn't include wearing undershirts.

For a brief period in NYC, it suddenly became stylish to wear cowboy hats. I hate to admit this, but I fell prey to the allure of looking like a NYC broncobuster. Kelly and I went to the best, Billy Martin's Western shop, and bought expensive, Stetson cowboy hats. Mine was a colorful grey hat with a brown leather brim. Of course, we both also wore cowboy boots. Neither of us ever wore chaps, spoke with a Western accent or even once said, "Howdy." We knew that we looked stupid, but we didn't care. We were Catch A Rising Star and Improv heavyweight comics and this was merely a disguise so no one would recognize us. At one point, we discussed starting a new trend; it was a tossup between wearing fireman's hats and boots, or dressing in a bee keeper's outfit. We did neither, but what we did manage to do for several months was spend close to a thousand dollars a week.

I never had any disposable income besides bad checks before and I did my best to assure that I wouldn't have it for very long. I should have saved and planned for a rainy day, but I also should have had therapy upon leaving the womb. It was a brief taste of having money, and although it was fun, it also put me on a road that would soon end those innocent wonderful days.

Billy Ball

John DeBellis and Joe Piscopo

During a hiatus at SNL, I was about to work a new club on the West Side that used mostly singers. Even though I knew it wasn't going to be a great room, I needed to get rid of my comic rust, which for me results in bad timing, not remembering my act and dealing with hecklers like I was a bulimic on an empty stomach. Right before I went on, the manager told me that the Yankee catcher, Rich Cerone was in the audience.

Most comics were more impressed by athletes than movie stars, so we tend to be more anxious when performing in front of them. But I was actually so confident that I didn't even consider the possibility of bombing in front of a Yankee (one Yankee to me is the equivalent of the entire Mets organization, or every Red Sox player who ever lived). Prior to working on SNL, my sets had grown such that I was getting frequent standing ovations. I had turned a corner: my material and I were indistinguishable; and yet the audience didn't see me as the loser I portrayed. Rodney was the best example of that. He was the ultimate loser on stage and you really believed he got no respect, while at the same time he commanded your total respect.

Before I went on stage, I could see Rick Cerone standing near the bar. I had made up my mind to talk to him after my set, and all I needed was to get my nervous system's approval. The room was wide and dimly lit, with a crescent of bright light illuminating a prodigious bar, which can make it difficult for comics to do their act, since the bar patrons often don't feel like they're really in the audience and carry on loud conversations. I was determined to have a good set. After all, a real live ball player—the man who succeeded Thurman Munson as the Yankee catcher—was less than sixty feet, six inches away, which is the distance between the pitching rubber and home plate. Considering the circumstances I had a pretty good set. After an inner debate, I found my nerve and walked up to Rick and told him I was a writer for SNL. I gave him my card, which was another person's business card with their name crossed off and my info written on the back, and told him to come to the show.

As the showcase clubs started to gain notoriety it wasn't uncommon to find celebrities, even famous athletes, like the great New York Knick's guard, Walt Frazier, or the Met's Rusty Staub, or lightweight boxing champion, Roberto Duran, in the audience or in the bar. Roberto Duran was nice enough to take his picture with all of us, but must have been a little punch and or alcohol drunk that night. He sat in the showroom eating a steak and, not realizing where he was, spit the fat out on the floor.

One rainy weeknight at the Improv I performed a set while John Madden, who I consider the greatest football color-commentator ever and Super Bowl-winning coach of the Raiders, was in the audience. Back then, the Giants were one of the worst teams in the NFL and were known for terrible personnel decisions. I walked on stage slowly, my shoulders slumped like I was trying to squeeze through a porthole, picked up the mic and with the best defeatist expression on my face, turned toward the area where John Madden was sitting and said, "You may not realize this, but I was the Giants number one draft choice this year." I heard his indisputable laugh and that alone made my evening.

One night, around that same time period, LD actually seemed pleased. He entered the club almost smiling. That day he'd done his first voice over for a radio commercial promoting Elvis Costello's new album, not that LD cared about or had heard of Elvis Costello. I always thought LD's taste in music leaned toward show tunes and the minuet (actually he liked classical music and played a decent piano). Well, Larry went on for his usual late night set and before he could finish his first few jokes he started to get heckled. LD fought back with some clever lines that hadn't been inspired by his temper, but the heckler had several drinks past a twelve-drink minimum and his crude heckles expanded to monstrous insults. Larry started shouting at him, and just before it turned into a fistfight, LD walked off-stage and was out of the room and away from Elvis Costello.

A week after meeting Rick Cerone, SNL was back in production and I had brought my parents to see the show for the first time. While I was visiting them in the guest room, I got a call from Cerone who informed me that he was taking me up on my invite and was coming to the show. It turned out to be especially great night for my parents who were rabid Yankee fans. It also ended up being a fun night for me. Rick Cerone wound up coming to the after party with me and Joe Piscopo. It only took Rick telling a couple of Yankee stories for us to become friends. Rick came to the Improv several times, but, more importantly, he got me into several Yankee games for free.

After one game we planned on meeting Rick and Bucky Dent (or, as he's known in Boston, Bucky-Fucking-Dent) at a bar in Jersey. As we waited for Rick, I went to talk to Joe, who was with baseball legend, Mr. Cub Ernie Banks. Ernie is famous for walking on to the field on a Saturday afternoon and saying, "Let's play two." As I stutter-stepped towards Joe, two security guards saw me and began, not so gently, moving me away. Joe had his back to me, but Ernie saw me being escorted away. He had no idea who I was, or whom I was with; all he knew was that I was wearing a Yankee t-shirt. He quickly left Joe and politely, but firmly, told the security guards that I was obviously a baseball fan and that he would be happy to talk to me. He must have repeated that phrase, "He is a baseball fan," several times, like it was a sacred station in life and it was not only his duty but his pleasure to spend time with a fan. We spoke for quite a while and he gave me an autographed ball and some other memorabilia. If all human beings were like Ernie Banks, there'd never be any wars, torture or proprietary loans. The only problem would be that there would be nothing but baseball, which, considering the alternative is not all that bad.

All of this would turn out to be a set-up to what was to occur in L.A. a year or so later. By then, I had become friends with Billy Crystal, who was also a Yankee fan. "Fan" comes from the word "fanatic," which is someone who's obsessive enough about something to be kept locked up in an attic. So whenever the Yankees came into Anaheim to play the Angels, I'd call Rick, who'd get us into the game. Afterwards, we'd hang out with Rick, Bucky Dent and other Yankees. So in a way, I and Rick Cerone were the original guys who introduced Billy to the Yankees. Of course, that Yankee team is long gone and in subsequent years Billy became friends with the newer players.

I was at a game in New York with LD a few years back, when we ran into Billy. I told him he owed me and he should take me to some games. He said, "Sure, give me a call." Well, I gave his production office a call, since I lost his phone number, and I'm still waiting for the favor to be returned. Don't misunderstand me. I love Billy. He'd gone out of his way to be kind to me at a time when I knew very few people in L.A. and that will always have a special meaning to me. But Billy, if you read this book, or someone tears out this page and reads it to you, LD has my phone number. Call him and he'll give you mine. Right now I want to see some games at the new Yankee stadium, in those incredibly expensive seats I want someone else to pay for.

Eddie Murphy's Twenty-First Birthday and Studio 54

If it hadn't been mentioned on TV because of the sensational scandals and talked about in every newspaper and magazine, most of the comics at the clubs would not have heard of Studio 54. As I've inferred, comics were on the bottom of the night people scale—we were the zombies to the jet-set vampires. There were a few exceptions like Kelly Rodgers, David Sayh and possibly Bill Maher, who spent a lot of time in the city's hip bars and clubs. It wasn't until Eddy Murphy's 21st birthday party that I saw the inside of Studio 54 for the first and only time.

To see a few hundred comics in Studio 54 was like watching the cast of *Night of the Living Dead* in the House of Dracula. It wasn't exactly an easy fit. In fact, it was more of a lost cause. Imagine trying to put an earring on a burning Monk.

I'm not sure if a live band or disco eight tracks tried to break my eardrums with an incessantly repeating beat like a stuttering echo. For me it's difficult enough to keep a beat with music, let alone music I resent. Lucky for me, drinks were plentiful and free. So after a while, I was too busy trying to keep my balance to worry about being in synch with the never ending drum roll.

I remember seeing Richie Tienken and Bob Wachs, owners of The Comic Strip and Eddie Murphy's managers, but I can't recall seeing Eddie. I'm pretty sure he was there though, unlike a few years later when he didn't show up for the filming of Joe Piscopo's second HBO special. We were shooting a "Miami Vice" sketch on a crumbling dock in Jersey, which politicians called long-range urban renewal. The rest of the cast, Joe and the whole crew patiently waited for a couple of shivering hours. Waiting for anything on a dock in New Jersey in the winter is the equivalent of trying to hold your breath with a jaw full of ice while someone vacuums out your mouth.

Luckily, Richie Tienken lost his patience before we lost anyone to frostbite and decided to go to Eddie's house. Richie and I drove to Eddie's mansion in Englewood Cliffs, which was surrounded by a ten-foot red brick wall that hid his house from view. When one of Eddie's entourage told Richie the master was in his bedroom, he didn't wait to be announced. We got as far as Eddie's door, which Eddie wouldn't open, even after we explained our situation. I thought the next words should just be between manager and client. I left the house and waited in the car, which was a civilization away from waiting on a Jersey dock in wind that tore the top layer off of anything not coated in lead.

As I sat there, I thought about something a nineteen-year-old Eddie Murphy had said, I believe with more confidence than malice, to a comic who had long paid his dues. (I'm paraphrasing). "Look at us working together. I'm on my way up, and you're on your way down." I was hoping that this incident was as far down as Eddie would ever get.

About ten minutes later, Richie got in the car. I could tell by the rising blood pressure that had sun-burned his face that things didn't end in a satisfactory compromise.

"He talked to me through a door!" he yelled. "I've known the kid since he was eighteen. I don't need this bullshit anymore. I just quit as his manager! I was rich before I met him. I don't need to be treated like this!"

Eddie showed up on the set the next day, but Richie hadn't changed his mind. He was now one client shorter and his face had lost its hemorrhaging tan. They eventually made up enough to become friendly, but not enough to be manager and client again. Shortly after he arrived, I went to Eddie's trailer and he apologized for being a no-show the day before. It was a disturbing apology—not at all insincere—just so softly solemn, his eyes drifting inward, looking at me and past me, emotions confused by fame and its ramifications.

I was once with Rodney in his dressing room at Dangerfield's at the height of his popularity. He turned to me, surrounded in his red, terry cloth robe, eyes swollen in the false promise of his ego. He said, "John, I've never been so depressed. I finally have everything I've ever wanted. I've never been more popular—commercials, Carson, movies. I thought it would make me happy. It just makes me more miserable knowing it didn't make me happy." I think Eddie was just learning that same lesson, only at a much younger age.

Several years later, I testified in court for Eddie in a dispute over a former manager who claimed to be representing Eddie on SNL. I was working at SNL then and witnessed Richie Tienken and Bob Wachs representing him. I turned out to be the key witness. I'd flown in from L.A., and after the hearing, Eddie invited me out with his friends, which I think included Keenan Wayans, who is, like his brother Damon, one of the truly nice guys in the business. I was working on a show and had to get back to L.A. that same night. Eddie said that if there was anything I wanted to just ask. I did ask him for one small thing: for him to write a blurb for a book I was working on. He said, "Sure, no problem." I have yet to receive that blurb. I should have asked for a million bucks. At least then I could understand him not keeping his promise.

This doesn't mean Eddie's a bad guy or had particularly good taste. In fact, I still really like him. I think people who become huge stars when they're so young go through periods where they have to adjust their egos so they don't block their view of other people. It could have also been because there are so many people asking for pieces of you it's impossible to remember who you gave them to. One thing I saw that day, after I had testified, was his magic smile aimed at me, so genuine, so rich with innocence, and so truly thankful, that I could never ever hold onto any ill feelings toward Eddie. For those few minutes I saw his soul and liked what it held inside.

That night at Studio 54, everything was fine between Eddie, his managers and the dozens of comics, half of which were drunk. The club was larger and more open than I expected, but not much fancier than the Improv, which is like saying eating the food at Poacher's wasn't much better than eating the waiters (I guess it'd be vice versa since the waiters were at least fresh). I didn't see as much drugs as I had read about, but I will say I saw a few stuck-up girls either snorting coke or trying to inhale their reflections. The comics I was with, who usually don't drink very much, were very much drinking, not that I noticed them swallowing the booze—all I had to see was how they were dancing. And that was more easily done than I would have liked, because I was one of them. Yes, me, "Mr. Rhythm and Booze" was dancing, although it might have looked like my body was trying to catch up to the beat, but was slowed down by convulsions. Before I could wonder why I got up to dance, I saw Buddy Mantia on the dance floor, either dancing or suffering from his every reflex being activated at once, which made me start wondering why he got up to dance. Normally, I might have called my shrink, but seeing Buddy on the dance floor while disco music was playing within earshot of our galaxy, I felt like I was in Timothy Leary's mind, watching a Fellini musical. Buddy likes a slower form of music—music where you have to travel forward in time to get to the next beat.

After several rounds of drinks that I attempted to sweat off by dancing, but would lose more as a result of perspiring from embarrassment, I left the dance floor with Kelly Rodgers and went to the men's room to rid myself of any lingering fluids. Kelly, who resembled a much younger, better looking Hugh Hefner, was dressed in a stylish white suit with a dark shirt. He had a loud, loose voice that was a few pebbles short of gravely. His laugh (like him) was hearty, full of warmth and mischief and ended with you wanting a lot more. He loved doing and saying things that would startle or confuse people. He'd answer the telephone, by saying "broccoli" or "cabbage." In fact, during his sets, it wouldn't be uncommon to hear him start repeating an odd sounding word a few dozen times. There would be nights when we'd be walking toward or away from a large crowd of people and he'd yell out, "Hey, Bob!" or some other common name and we'd watch people turn to see who was calling. Then he'd duck into other parts of the crowd and launch the name again, driving the designated person crazy. So in line in the men's room of Studio 54, Kelly very loudly started to broadcast how he couldn't wait to get to the urinal and how much he liked looking at guys' penises so he could see how small or funny looking they were. He'd blurt out things like, "Someday I'm going to collect them." Now we're in the men's room of Studio 54, which had a large crop of gay men, which could have been treacherous, but his boisterous blabbering actually stunned them. When he arrived at the urinal he'd look over and start laughing and yelling to me, "John, you got to see this one!" or, "I don't know how this guy even has sex! Maybe he likes midgets!" He was so blatant and uninhibited that all the guys in the men's room probably thought that he was too crazy to mess with, or just too damn funny. The annoying guys who worked in the men's room, handing out soap, towels, etc. were too freaked out to deal with this and backed away from Kelly. I exited as fast as I could, but Kelly just took his time and strolled out of there laughing with the comfortable ease of a good natured dictator.

After that incident, I can't recall much more about that night at Studio 54. I was too drunk. The next day I had a hangover that made me wish I was being water boarded to distract me from the nausea. That night, the comics were only a few hundred erratically churning limbs and several thousand wisecracks away from acting like normal (if not slightly defective) hip human beings.

Following the Crucifixion

During the late 70's, the showcase clubs became as popular as lawyers turning lies into a form of negotiation; people thought disco was soul music and swore, "I'll never get hooked on cocaine."

In the Catch bar I literally bumped into the actress who I spent most of my teenage years lusting after, Carol Lynley. I barely managed to say excuse me, part of that may have had less to do with nerves and more to do with a mouth full of drool.

One Saturday night at Catch, I worked an audience that included David Bowie, Michael Caine, Margaux Hemmingway, Sylvester Stallone, John Kennedy Jr. and Caroline Kennedy. I'm proud to say that without having to call my shrink, or downing several Tequila shots, or changing my name before and after going up, I actually had a good set, got big laughs and walked off to the sound of applause.

But the guy who followed me completely destroyed the room (in comic talk, the more violent the description, the better the set). No comic would ever want an audience to die of natural causes. Lenny Schultz was the absolute craziest guy, maybe ever, in standup comedy or Attica. Had he gone there, he would have scared guys on death row into skipping their last meals A star pitcher in high school and a major league prospect, he blew a chance with the Yankees. In front of their scouts, he fired his first pitch straight up in the air and then later hit a home run and circled the bases trotting backwards.

"It was a full house. Lenny Schultz decides to bring his young girlfriend up on stage. He lifts her blouse and started fondling her breasts. When he's done, she leaves the stage, sits down next to me and went back to her crossword puzzle. A few seconds later she turns to me and says, 'I hate when he does that,' then went back to her puzzle."

-DENNIS MILLER

Lenny, who was soft-spoken and gentle—a gym teacher by day— was 6'2" and two hundred pounds of solid muscle with arms so long that if he ever wore a gorilla suit they'd have to take out the sleeves. He controlled the room like a newspaper strike controlled a man's bowels. Lenny would start his shows prancing around the room like a chicken making weird faces, egging (no pun intended) on the crowd until he heard them chant, "Go crazy, Lenny!"

He'd start off slowly, doing his famous dueling cheeks bit, each cheek inflating and deflating like a condom on a schizophrenic with multiple personalities to the song "Dueling Banjos." Then he'd set two bowls of water side-by-side and dip each hand in a bowl and juggle water, soaking the first two or three rows of patrons. For Lenny's set, the tables were protected with plastic sheeting. From that point on in his set, the gloves came off and anything could happen. Boxes of cereal, cartons of spaghetti, cans of whip cream, motor oil—everything except nerve gas would be sprayed. He put a banana in places that are illegal in most states. He ended his set to the sappy song, "Send In The Clowns," surrounded by a room that looked like Las Vegas after the entire city threw up, standing in his blue jockey shorts, arms spread wide. There were some shows where he'd bring a midget (I know I should say small person, but the M sound is funnier) as a prop and sometimes played him like an accordion and I'm too embarrassed to tell you what else he did or simulated, but I'll give you a hint: my father would have poked both their eyes out.

To follow Lenny's act or The Untouchables was like following the Crucifixion. I did it a few times and the audience was so blown out, I felt worse than the small person Lenny had his way with—although at least the small person got laughs. The crowd didn't have the strength left to even utter the "B" in "boring."

The Untouchables were the current version of Marx brothers. The group's members included Marvin Braverman (the Groucho of the group), who at the time had enough hair and nerve to wear it like John Denver coupled with a New York accent strong enough to blow a rat out of a pothole; Bobby Alto (the Harpo/Chico of the trio), who could make you laugh with just a look from a face that was a cross between Lou Costello and Sarah Jessica Parker, on a body that was pure Lou Costello; and, of course, there was Buddy Mantia—the guy who hit himself in the head with his bat, but somehow never damaged his movie star good looks. He was their Dean Martin and Bud Abbott with a singing voice that stretched four octaves. Their "Italian Wizard of Oz" was their funniest piece and the inspiration for *The Wiz* (admitted by its writer). In *The Untouchables* bit, as a radio pitchman might say, "Bobby Alto <u>was</u> Dorothy"—that is if you think a hairier James Gandolfini in a schoolgirl skirt and saddle shoes would be cute. They performed pieces that were structured to not look structured and allowed room for improvisation. At any moment you could expect almost anything to happen from any place on stage and they made it seem like everything was happening at once. The audience's attention was taken and thrown, and taken again and thrown until they lost themselves on a comedic adventure that ended in pandemonium and a standing ovation. Although I saw them perform only at Catch, their act was formed from fooling around on the Improv stage backing up Robert Klein and then later harmonizing in a nearby alley.

The Untouchables: Buddy Mantia, Bobby Alto and Marvin Braverman

Because of a dispute, The Untouchables left the Improv and went to Catch A Rising Star, where Rick Newman credits them with saving the fledgling club.

The Untouchables had just performed on the Dean Martin show and were working a club in Chicago. After the show they were invited to the local Don's house—Don as in mobster, or, to us Italians, our rich uncle who won't take "no" for an answer unless the question is "Is there such a thing as the Cosa Nostra?" Just as the boys were about to leave, there was a knock on the door and in stepped an immaculately dressed man, dignified in the mold of Ricardo Montalban. He introduced himself as Joselito, Mexico's greatest bullfighter. Joselito was so charming, the guys asked him to come along.

In the limo, Joselito pulled a flask out of the jacket pocket of his glistening white suit and after the boys declined a nip, he took one that turned from a swallow into a chug making him one very happy bullfighter. Raising the near empty flask, he told the boys that back home they don't let him do this in public. To the boys, that statement raised a bigger red flag than Joselito ever used fighting "da bull."

Before they entered the mansion the boys reminded Joselito to behave, to act dignified, respect the Don and not to refill his flask from the Godfather's glass. After they were led inside, the boys waited until they were given the okay before they respectfully shook the Don's hand. Joselito, on the other hand, charged forward like a test car dummy hitting a wall, giving the Don a bone crushing bear hug. The boys managed to pull him off before the Don lost his balance and patience and turned Joselito's white suit red. The Don tried to ignore the crazy Mexican bullfighter who'd turned from a handsome bullfighter, to a drunk with a voice like a bullhorn. The Don asked Buddy to sing, "Sorrento." Joselito immediately rose and started screaming for Buddy to sing "Granada" instead. Before a pistol was fired, Buddy wisely started to sing and Joselito quieted down. Buddy sang a very emotional "Sorrento," not picturing Italy, the home of his ancestors, but thinking that Joselito was going to get them all killed by someone probably *related* to his ancestors.

When the song was over, the boys noticed that Joselito had left the room. Now the boys were beginning to panic, and as inconspicuously as possible, started searching the mansion for the great Mexican bullfighter. One of The Untouchables glanced out the window to make sure their car was running and spotted Joselito's shadow. The boys excused themselves and raced into the front yard, dodging marble statues of the top ten Ancient Roman chicks. And there, in the moonlight, was Joselito, Mexico's great bullfighter, pissing on the Don's brand new Cadillac! They grabbed the bullfighter, threw him into their limo and took off, hoping if the Don's henchmen saw a stream of urine on the Caddy's fender they would finger the tallest dog in the neighborhood.

By now Joselito had gotten so crazy, the boys stopped the limo in the middle of nowhere and dumped Mexico's greatest bullfighter on a deserted road. They left him standing there like a forgotten comic trying to find his way home from a Jerry Stanley Jersey gig.

Mayhem and Mobsters

"The Improv audience consisted of everyday people. Catch A Rising Star was more like the everyday Mafiosi."

-ANONYMOUS

Gilbert Gottfried stopping someone from picking up a dime

At Catch A Rising Star, comics and gangsters often crossed paths. They were always giving us advice like, "Do that joke again and I'll break your fucking legs." When you get a threat like that, you cower, apologize, stay home a couple of nights and wait for another comic to get beat up before returning. Actually, most of the mobsters' threats were harmless, although Jerry Seinfeld had a mug thrown at him on stage and Richard Overton had either a knife or a gun or both put to his head. Al Wiedan, the bartender who was a black belt, had to stop a hoodlum from beating me up—and there were rumors that Belzer was thrown down a flight of stairs. Now this might seem like a lot of incidents, but this is over a 5 year period, so we only averaged about one threatened comic a year.

There was one other time I almost got every bone in my body broken. I was the MC and Maurice (we never knew his last name: e said it was stolen in his sleep), known for being disgusting for the sake of being disgusting, had out-bad-tasted himself with a joke that was embarrassed by its own punch line. The guy sitting across from me at the MC's table, the type who considered the electric chair a family heirloom, commented that he didn't think the sick stuff was funny. Foolishly, I rebutted by saying, "He didn't get a laugh, because his sick joke was just not funny. Watch, I'll do a sick line and get a laugh."

Maurice finished his act, which, if it lasted any longer, could have finished him. I went on stage and did my usual opening line that I think is a funny sick joke. You've heard it in this book before. I told the audience apologetically, "I'm sorry the show started late tonight. I had a flat tire on the way here. It was one in a million. I ran over a guy with a glass eye."

The joke got a huge laugh from the audience. I brought up the next act and proudly went back to the table to stare this killer in the eye and gloat. That's when I noticed his extreme displeasure. Turned out, the mobster had a glass eye! Before I could beg for my life or offer up Maurice as a substitute, he leaned across the table and foully said, like he was *ordering* my last rites, "You fucking knew I had a glass eye, you little fuck! And you did that fucking joke to fuck with me, didn't you?" As I was about to deny it and explain his use of the word fuck wasn't what Lenny Bruce had in mind, he pulled out his glass eye and crushed it in his hands and then burst out laughing. He dropped the splintered ball on the table and left, saying, "You may not have brains, but you got fucking balls." Okay, maybe I *am* slightly exaggerating here, but when I brought the next act off stage, I did a long clean set with one eye on the audience and the other eye, which I hoped to keep that night, on that table, praying it remained empty.

Maurice, who would be unique in a sideshow touring Sodom and Gomorrah, was African American, with a laugh that was a cross between laughter and a dog panting. We all joked about him, but I don't know anyone who didn't like Maurice except maybe the one-eyed mobster and most of his audiences. Maurice claimed he was in the Army and tried to use the Army jacket he wore to prove it. Unlike Maurice, who never used a last name, his jacket did. Right above the pocket it read, "O'Neil." When Larry David and Gilbert Gottfried told him that his claim of being a soldier was a lie and that his last name wasn't O'Neil, Maurice quickly admitted that the name was not his, but still claimed he was in the military. He said that at the end of boot camp, when soldiers threw their hats up in the air, his troop didn't have any hats so they threw their jackets and he caught the one with O'Neil's name on it.

We never believed Maurice's story, nor did I believe him when he told me he didn't get my message because his dog ate his answering machine. But at Catch we did learn that the bigger the gangster, the lower the profile, except for their girlfriends who were usually taller than their mob boyfriends even before they put on six inch spike heels. They all had hair so puffed up that you could use their heads as silencers and wore dresses so tight you could count the ribs they had removed to fit into them. In fact, the mobsters that were bosses were actually incredibly supportive, appreciative, polite and respectful. They could laugh about themselves and didn't wear suits that were a polyester neon blend. It was the lower rung wise guys who were out to prove they were the next Al Capone that you had to watch your peas and zucchinis with. Bob Shaw was actually threatened outside the Improv for making fun of zucchini. And then there was the saga of Joe Piscopo and Johnny Rip.

I was the MC at Catch one night and had just brought Joe on stage. Joe wasn't a member of the SNL cast yet, made great popcorn from scratch and still drove a car cops mistook for an unmarked police car.

His standup act often included him getting laughs by talking to the audience, not just by wearing his nerdy New Jersey outfits. Well, that night he asked a guy, who would be Italian-looking even if Italy never existed, sitting with a small-time wise guy, Johnny Rip, "What do you do for a living?" The guy sat silently and gave Joe the kind of stare that creates a vacuum, or can give you a non-evasive frontal lobotomy. Despite that "warning," for some reason, Joe asked, "What are you, a hit man?" Although accurate, as far as things you shouldn't say to a mobster go, that question is rated right below "I would have used a condom if I knew she was your daughter." So when Joe came off stage, Johnny Rip, fearing that Joe had insulted his peer, cornered Joe in the coatroom, where his fists repeatedly bonded with Joe's face. Now, for a comic, Joe was tough, but that's like saying, "For a guy in a coma, he's a hell of a partier." Joe stood his ground, but his nose didn't. In seconds, Joe's nose had lost two dimensions and he was about to lose a few teeth and consciousness when Johnny held Joe's shirt in order to steady his target...that is, until I stepped in. Oh, I wasn't foolish enough to throw a punch, which, if he felt it in the first place, Johnny would have killed me with a bitch slap. Nor did I ever demand that Johnny stop beating Joe to a pulp. Instead I did the comic thing and tore Joe's shirt off his back and said, "Run, Joe, run!" which Joe wisely did—and lucky for him, Johnny's fists were faster than his legs, which were slower than Joe's legs. In the next month, while Joe's nose healed, Johnny Rip was told in no uncertain terms never to beat up a comic again or he'd suffer the consequences—of paying for his own drinks.

Intentions Were Good

"One night I brought my brother Bruce and a couple of his friends with me to Catch, to see myself and Larry David perform. I raved to them before the show how great and brilliant Larry was. So Larry goes onstage and the audience stares at him as if they were in the planetarium and were gazing at the universe, something that was not uncommon with Larry. After the show my brother's friends were saying, "This guy is the worst, horrible, he'll never amount to anything..." Twenty years later when Larry was a huge star and mulit-millionaire, those same guys were saying, "Geez, I don't know how he made it, he was horrible!"

-BOBBY KELTON

As I've explained, no one had more of a love/hate relationship with the audience than Larry David. There were nights when the audience understood his offbeat brilliance and he'd blow the room out (in a good way); and there were other nights when they couldn't grasp his "out there" concepts and they would blow him out of the room (not in a good way).

On one unforgettable night, I brought Larry up as a cabaret singer named Sidney Gulkis, which is David Sayh's real name, and probably one of the reasons he became a comedian. LD pranced proudly onto the stage in his green army jacket, full of artistic dignity, and started his musical set with a very animated almost gallant "Cabaret," pumping his arms like he was using two fly swatters to accent the lyrics of the song. When the song ended, the audience gave him polite, if not stunned, applause—the kind where people's claps are almost singular and a few beats apart, instead of on top of each other. Undeterred, Larry rocketed into a moving "The Girl From Ipanema." By "moving," I mean Larry moved to the song, making himself smaller, fading away and then coming forward when the lyrics called for it. When Larry's flamboyant rendition was over, the audience wasn't quite as polite. Their claps, hoots and shouts became nasty and sarcastic. Larry, never leaving character, challenged the audience, proclaiming that his inspired singing was that of a professional—a true artist. I think he even named famous venues he insisted he'd performed at. The exchange of unpleasantries went on for a few minutes before Larry stylishly finished his set with a triumphant "Oklahoma." By then, we comics were laughing so hard we didn't even look to see if Larry left the stage threatening to slug someone in the audience.

It wasn't that Larry couldn't sing. He could and can. What had us on the floor was his prideful attitude, his bold, exaggerated movements, both facially and bodily—arms and legs spastically waving like a drowning drum major—and the way he interpreted a lyric, which was so deliberate he looked like a deaf mute learning to pronounce new words. This wasn't unusual. Whenever Larry went on stage, the comics would sit in the back of the room and wait to hear a crazy, funny new bit he was doing, which he did often; or we'd sit there in the hope that he would bomb, which he did often. It's not that we wanted to see him bomb, we just loved to see what craziness his anger would produce. He would say and do things we all thought, but had self-restraint preventing us from actualizing our vengeance on two hundred drunk, paying customers. We were more chicken than angry, while Larry was more angry than chicken.

LD was in the middle of a bit about French Impressionism—Manet, Monet and his fictional character, Tippy-Tippy-Day-Day—when he started getting big laughs, the kind that comics at that time of night question. As LD went further into his bit the laughs exploded, this time LD saw in the mirror that ran along the back wall of the showroom, a circle of red light on his crotch. He stepped forward so he could see under the spots and there was Richard Gerstein, otherwise known, as Richard T. Bear, pointing a laser pen on what used to be Larry's private parts. LD took it in stride by diving off the stage and charging Bear, nostrils flaring beneath his steaming glasses. The struggle to hold Larry back was easier than the struggle to keep from laughing, because no one in the world is funnier than Larry when he's angry.

When I look back at pictures of us at the Improv, Catch, The Comic Strip, playing softball in Central Park, at the Catch picnics, where comics could be seen playing Tug of War (many with the rope wrapped around their necks) or just standing at the bar laughing, it hits me even harder now—especially as I age—that all the comics, singers, musicians, bouncers and bartenders were just kids. Even the club owners, Budd Friedman, Rick Newman, Bob Wachs and Richard Tienken were in their thirties, and the rest of us in our twenties, except Gilbert Gottfried, whose financial idol was Jack Benny, and still lives on eight dollars a day (or maybe less) who was in his teens. You have to love Gilly. He'd be the first one to tell you that he's the cheapest person alive or in a coma. And he'd be bragging.

One night outside Catch, Buddy Mantia and a few others had seen Gilly leaving the club not only with a woman, but a pretty woman. Yet most startling of all was that he was taking a cab! Yes, a cab. And he wasn't hiding in the trunk or in someone's luggage! When Moses parted the Red Sea, Gilly would have been the first one through, fearing Moses might start to charge a toll.

After a few hours of complaints and a debate on what has expanded most, the universe or their egos, the guys got curious, so they called Gilly and asked him if the girl was still there. Gilly told them that she had left. In normal people, survival, food and sex are their primary drives. I can't repeat this enough, in comics, the primary drives are survival, but only after noon; food if it's free and preferably at a diner and sex as a way to get material, since that's all they'd get. To a comic, being sexy is wearing no underwear under your underwear.

Buddy asked what happened and Gilly told him that he was on his couch with the girl, making out (not a pleasant thought, even for Gilly), and suddenly she stopped and demanded money. Gilly, of course, wouldn't pay. So, she left. After Buddy stopped laughing and the other guys laughed more quietly, Buddy empathized with him, or maybe it was more like sympathy and told him it must have been disappointing. Gilly replied that it wasn't so bad; in fact, it had worked out well because when the girl was on the couch, her pocket book spilled and Gilly had found change in between the cushions.

A few years ago, I was at the opening of the AMC 25 on 42nd street with Gilly. All the movies were free as well as the concession stands. Gilly got a trash can-size garbage bag from a kid who worked there and then went to all the concessions stuffing the black bag, so he left looking like a hit man bringing his work home with him. Jack Benny would be proud, if not envious. Gilly may be cheap, but his ability to laugh at himself makes him worth his weight in gold. Don't tell Gilly that though, or he'd sell himself.

A Cast of Characters

"One night, I got completely naked, grabbed a bottle of Champagne, went into the showroom and I started serving it. Elayne Boosler was on stage and my wife, JoAnne, was in the audience... As I poured the champagne I noticed that I was shriveled up. I started yelling, 'I'm bigger than this, but I'm nervous!"

--MARK LONOW, co-owner of the Improv and former member of "Off the Wall" comedy troupe

Guys who I mentioned in previous chapters such as Lenny "Go Crazy" Schultz, who may have been the most insane; Gilbert Gottfried, the cheapest; and Larry David, the most neurotic (or at least tied with Richard Lewis) were only a few of the innumerable oddball, lovable characters that hung out in the showcase clubs.

One of the funniest guys in the clubs, and not by design, was a singer, Joe Rock. He was a big, muscular, good natured guy and our catcher—a position he chose because he could check out the girls, who he always assumed were checking him out. He possessed a high sweet singing voice; sort of like Neil Young with the soulfulness of Kermit the Frog. (Actually he had a very nice voice, but the description of it is not as colorful as the above metaphor). Kelly Rodgers, the MC at Catch, told him that he should change his name, because Joe Rock didn't fit his high sweet voice. Two weeks later, Joe strutted in and told Kelly, "I changed my name; bring me up as Sergeant Rock."

In the late 70's, roller skating was a big craze, but not for me. I lose my balance when I put on two different socks. For weeks, Joe Rock had been telling me that he was writing a roller skating song in which I was tempted to suggest a chorus on ball bearings. On the night he debuted his song, he glided into Catch wearing shorts small enough that you could tell he wasn't Jewish, a guinea t undershirt, and of course, roller skates. I brought him on, announcing his soon to be hit song. With his arms raised in triumph, Joe roller skated onto the stage and then immediately slid across it, knocking over the piano player, the microphone ended up on his ass under the fallen, ancient piano, whose loud crash was the closest it's ever been to being in tune.

When I first started auditioning at Catch, there was one thing I feared more than the audience and that was Terry Columbo. Terry was one of the managers and had a voice that rumbled like an earthquake before his words reached your ears. When they did, it was as if a subway train had collided with your eardrums. Terry would stand at the door and hand out numbers like he was tossing out scraps of bread to lepers. He didn't make us feel unwanted, he made us feel like we were under arrest and were about to be slowly pushed through a wood chipper. There was nothing to fear but fear itself, which was Terry.

Only when you became a regular did Terry start to treat you regular, and that's when you realized that Terry was not just regular, he was one of the kinder people at the club—almost the exact opposite of how he presented himself to the scummy auditioners. He was protective of the comics and always made sure that we were being taken care of. He gave us food (when they had it), cab fare, drinks and he gave the evil eye to dissuade a humiliated heckler.

When I first arrived at Catch, the management was Rick Newman, Big Ritchie and Terry Columbo. Rick and I see each other often and he hasn't changed much, still good looking and charismatic. Big Ritchie and I saw each other about a year ago at a book signing. He still had a voice that sounded like seven loud deaf people trying to harmonize to a Rod Stewart song and he wasn't nearly as big, but much happier. Terry and I haven't seen each other in awhile. Unfortunately, he passed away a decade or so ago. I'll always remember him standing outside Catch with a voice that was more canon than human, scaring the neurosis into psychosis of the would-be and never-be young comics while laughing inside his gentle soul.

Uncle Dirty was probably the most fascinating conversationalist in the clubs. Despite performing on several dozen "Tonight Shows" in the 60s, he remains a relatively unknown and unappreciated comedic figure. Most of my memories of him were of us sitting at the bar talking about something that at that moment seemed urgent if not critical.

Dirty, even to new comics, never acted imposing or intimidating; he lured you in by being self-depreciating in a positive way. In another words, he'd lift you up so you stood above him under his spell. Dirty was about ten or so years older than us, his hair was mostly brown, except for a few outer layers of gray that seemed to be climbing its way to dominance. A full beard surrounded his face, like a working class halo, cut short enough that it mimicked his face's contours. He had olive sized eyes that were bright enough to be blue, but could have been any color that liked being the center of attention.

Uncle Dirty could show you a menu and make you think it was a biblical metaphor. Baseball and football weren't sports—they were existential American puzzles solvable only by Buddha-like insights. He found importance in unimportant things and the unimportant sides of important things. He was passionate about his theories and could find the hidden depth in just about anything, including jugglers. He was smart enough to make a killing in the stock market, but deeply appreciated the gift of cab fare. Now if you know Uncle Dirty at all, you immediately realize he's one of the most liberal-minded, least prejudiced people you'd ever meet. But he's also a comic with that defective gene that rates getting a laugh much higher than the consequences.

Uncle Dirty was sitting in a bar next to a few black men the day Martin Luther King Jr. was assassinated. His first words were the opposite of what he really felt and merely a way to deflect the pain of the moment—and he couldn't help himself, since he thought what came to mind was funny. Dirty, looking up at the TV, said, "Damn. If it would have happened on Thursday, I would have won the pool." The brothers sitting around him weren't comics and didn't laugh, chuckle or understand comic defense mechanisms and beat the hell out of him. When Dirty tells this story, there's not a hint of anger at the pummeling he took, nor any regret at having made such a tasteless joke. I believe he prided himself in thinking he performed a service, becoming a vehicle for his black brothers to vent. Dirty was for equal rights before most of us sheltered comics even heard the term and he admired Dr. King and all he stood for, but he was a comic to the core—core that saw humor in the worst of times and never saw the difference in the shade of a man's skin. I'm sure he would have done the same if it had been one of the Kennedys, Lincoln or even me.

Sheldon Biber, with a full beard a junkie Santa Claus might sport, wasn't an outlandish person. But for some reason during his act he drank out of a quart carton of milk. A punch line followed by a mouthful of milk that dripped down the sides of a spongy beard was not a pleasant sight, or even funny, but it seems to be permanently stuck in my memory, like an imprint of a scene on the screen of a plasma TV.

Warren Bloom was Kelly Rodger's best friend. With his light brown afro, now enhanced by a breeze of gray, a wiry build that would need the use of a microscope to find fat, looked almost exactly the same today as he did then. Kelly and Warren have known each other since college, where Warren kept everything he owned—a set of keys and an extra T-shirt—in a tennis ball can. So I guess it wasn't much of a surprise when Warren Bloom removed the stove, refrigerator, and all the cabinets in his kitchen so he could have more room. Warren called the roaches in his place his friends, gave away Kelly's guitar to someone he thought needed it more and he could make a meal out of anything left in your refrigerator like, oh… pea soup and chocolate. He was fired from working at a deli for playing touch football with whole chickens and explained to us that he shouldn't have been fired because he never fumbled the chicken. He also wrote some great songs that, had he had any kind of ego and wasn't so kind hearted, could have been hits.

Mark Schiff

One of the strangest and funniest comics was Mark Schiff, whose everyday outfits looked like he was dressing for the Antarctic and Hawaii at the same time. Mark would commonly ask people if they had four dollars for a five. He once stopped to pay the toll at the Lincoln Tunnel going into New York with a few thousand dollars spread everywhere in the car—the dashboard, seats and floors—and pretended he couldn't find his money. When the toll collector told Mark he couldn't go into the city with money strewn all over his car, Mark replied, "Don't worry, I'll roll up the window." At a gig, he covered the entire outside of the comedian's bungalow with chicken bones. And once, when I shared a hotel room with him at a gig at Garvin's Grill in Washington, I noticed the funny looks we kept getting from room service. I didn't realize until I left for the show that he had put a heart-shaped sign on the door that read, "Just married, Mark and John." At least he didn't carve it in a tree, get a tattoo or blackmail my parents, who wouldn't have paid.

Jack Graiman

Jack "Shecky" Graiman may have been the most unique among us. Depending on your IQ and age, Jack either looked like a rubber Kurt Vonnegut, or a lecherous Captain Kangaroo with eyes that would make the peepers on the obsequious black porters from the 1940's Hollywood movies look small. Jack grinned and grimaced at the same time. He either yelled or scoffed away his jokes with a playful disdain that made the nasty absurd and the absurd such a flavorful delicacy that left the audience always wanting more, yet fearing that he might actually give it to them.

He'd slowly, as if in cubist stages, creep on stage like he wasn't sure he was moving in the right direction. He'd stop at the microphone, pick it up in his right hand and then he'd scream, "My wife's a big fat pig. I told her to get the fuck out of the house." I said, 'Get the fuck out of the house.' She went on a water diet. She drinks eight glasses of water a day. Now she's not fat, she's bloated. I told her to "get the fuck out of the house." The comics loved watching Jack because, like Larry David, anything could happen to anyone at any time. One night, out of sheer boredom he performed in a southern accent (which gave a new dimension to his bit about teaching musical theater to pygmies and marrying the chief's daughter, Yaboo) and another night he did his entire act dressed as a giant Quaalude.

Jack once borrowed Larry David's tape recorder and when he went out at night, hid it in his oven. You can guess what happened. Jack forgot it was there and baked it until it looked like a plastic toupee. As nuts as Jack seemed with those big blue eyes that seemed permanently widened and forever shining with misadventure, he was, unlike many comics, quick to do a favor and kind hearted to those who society pretends aren't one of us. As I stated earlier, Hell's Kitchen, where Jack lived, was hooker rich. In the morning, Jack would leave donuts and coffee in the hallway on a table for the working girls finishing their shifts. And he never partook of their favors, since he believed it was better to give than receive, especially since he was a heterosexual and they were...?

Probably my favorite story in which I played a part took place at Catch A Rising Star with Jack. I was the MC that Saturday night. During the second show, Rick Newman, the owner, called me and asked which comics were at the club. When I mentioned Jack Graiman, he said, "Don't put him on until I get there."

That Saturday night, Jack was downstairs in Rick's office, absorbed in self-absorption, and I was on stage soaking the crowd in my self-absorption, when Rick Newman came in, so neither of us saw who he was with. As I ran offstage, Rick told me to bring Jack up right away. That's exactly what I did and exactly what I should not have done. Jack didn't know that Rick was bringing in a special guest and Rick sat this person in the back, at a table you can't see from the stage.

Now before I spill the beans, what Jack said was really meant in jest. As you should know by now, comics will say things for a laugh

211

even if it adds to a false perception. As Jack was building toward a strong finish, he pushed a stubby hand through his short Anglo-afro and paused, his big eyes growing and sending out sparks of mischief. Then said. "I've got a riddle for you. What's a dog with Wings?" He paused again and then proclaimed, "Linda McCartney." As Jack started into his next bit (I think about the man who invented the enema), a woman stormed out of the room with Rick chasing her, reaching for her jacket and apologizing more than even the most inadequate comic would. Of course, it was Linda McCartney. Jack finished his set to terrific applause and nonchalantly walked into the bar area where Rick, who mistakenly thought Jack had somehow found out it was Linda McCartney, dived on him, both of them tumbling over the waist high divider near the end of the bar, like Boris Karloff and Lon Chaney in the *Wolf Man Meets Frankenstein*. Rick was hanging upside down trying to choke Jack to death and almost did before three or four of us pulled him off. I think somewhere down the line, Rick made up with Linda McCartney, explaining the circumstances and Jack's remark. And that "Shecky's" joke was taking advantage of people's unjustified disappointment and ignorance concerning Linda marrying the eligible handsome ex-Beatle and then joining Wings. It really had nothing to do with her looks or talent—she was far prettier than any of the girls we dated at the time, except maybe for some of the women in Richard Lewis's harem.

If I dug in slightly deeper, I could probably think of several more characters that were members of our club, but the point is that we were all characters in our own peculiar way. It's fair to say that our neurotic weirdness might be annoying or aggravating to everyone but ourselves. To us it was that very insistent absurdity that kept our insanity in check. We were an odd bunch who gave that very special time an extra layer of color that will always keep our memories of those days fresh and vibrant.

My Wedding

It was near the end of a show at Catch A Rising Star when I first saw DJ, my now ex-wife, who with her sassy short hair, reminded me of Shirley MacLaine in "The Apartment." I invited her to the show at SNL after which we dated for a few months (and I spent nearly a hundred bucks on her) before she moved into my apartment. A year later we got married.

My place wasn't exactly a love nest. She'd arrive home at three or four in the morning after tending bar all night to find comics playing video games, laughing loudly; comics unable to take hints such as "Get the f&*k out already!"

DJ knew a lot of people in the restaurant business and got an incredible deal for the wedding reception at Tavern on the Green. Fifty bucks per person (unfortunately they counted comics as people). Even at that price it was an expensive wedding with over 300 people, almost half were my brothers and sisters of comedy (most which hadn't heard of checking accounts).

I insisted on a tame bachelor party with just the guys. Most of the party took place at Lenny Maxwell's apartment. From out of one of Len's bedrooms, Steve Mittleman emerged, all six foot-five of him dressed like a woman, swishing and swaying as he stripped off his bathrobe to display stockings and garters long enough for a Giraffe's neck and a bra filled with big balloons. Then, swiveling his hairy body like a dying lava lamp, gave me a lap dance. I laughed and hid my face from the video camera. Yes, there is a video of this nasty exhibition of exposed flesh, but it's being saved for blackmailing purposes, so don't look for it on you tube. Of course, Len didn't make it to the party. He had a date with a woman who was surely the type a real bachelor party would employ, because the next day he showed up at my wedding in crutches. When Steve finished his dance, Piscopo, Ronnie Shakes, Ken David, Glenn Hirsch, Mark Schiff, Buddy Mantia, Howie Klein, Kelly Rodgers, Dennis Wolfberg and several other comics said especially cruel, slanderous things about me into the camera, but oh so lovingly. A few wisecracks later, Mark Schiff broke one of Len's expensive vases so the bachelor party moved quickly over to The Comic Strip where eight or nine of us took the stage with the show still in progress, making fools of ourselves, our profession and causing the Strip to return the cover charge. I ended the evening more embarrassed than drunk, wearing my sweater inside out over my sports jacket and two other people's shoes on opposite feet, one of which was surrounded by a dog's offering to the city.

My wedding party included best man Buddy Mantia, Steve Mittleman, Glenn Hirsch, Kelly Rodgers, Tony Darrow, two of my ex-wife's brothers and Larry David's brother Ken. I would have asked LD and Bobby Kelton to be in the wedding party but Larry was working in L.A. and Kelton was opening for someone whose last hit single was on a 78 record. They did manage to attend the wedding, however, arriving just before the ceremony.

Joe Piscopo, Glenn Hirsch and Mark Schiff

Tony Darrow through some business "acquaintances" got a too good to be true deal on a limo to take my wedding posse to Tavern on The Green. Unfortunately it really was too good to be true and the limo never showed. Glenn Hirsch flagged down a hotdog stand, which carried us for a half a block, before tipping over and the vendor nearly dying of a heart attack—he'd obviously eaten too many of his own hotdogs.

The wedding ceremony took place at the restaurant and was performed by a minister from the Ethical Culture Society. On a religious scale, the organization is rated just below the Church of Immediate Gratification. In actuality, the minister was much more to my liking then my ex's childhood priest with whom I had a shouting match when he insisted that any of our kids should be brought up

Catholic. I don't understand why I was kicked out of the rectory just because I called several popes murderers.

The highlight of most weddings is supposed to be the bride graciously walking down the aisle, and it would have been as my ex looked lovely in my mother's satin wedding dress, but she was upstaged by Tony Darrow spontaneously chasing me down the aisle with a baseball bat. It killed. He drew mammoth laughs and applause that drowned out the wedding march and lasted throughout her entire trip to the altar.

The minister, or hitting coach, or whatever you called him, delivered the eulogy—I mean the ceremony, while I loudly jingled the change in my pocket. For a few seconds my hand stopped shuffling the coins and I heard suppressed laughter coming from the ushers lined up against the floor to ceiling windows overlooking the traffic cutting through Central Park. Boredom had set in quickly for the comics in my wedding party. Glenn Hirsch broke up the monotony by exposing himself to the passing automobiles. I started to laugh. Hey, funny is funny. Only marital terror stopped me from clapping.

Dennis Wolfberg volunteered to be the MC at the reception. As always with Dennis—and unlike the groom-- he was enthusiastic and upbeat. His eyes lit up like fireworks, every word accentuated with Dennis' contagious delivery. Electricity sizzled through all his introductions, which made it seem like the marriage actually had a bright future. The words "til death do us part" were overly optimistic by several decades.

Rodney Dangerfield arrived on the ten degree November night wearing Bermuda shorts and a Hawaiian shirt. The outfit didn't deter one of my aunts from following him around insisting that he looked exactly like her dead husband, who died only a couple of weeks earlier. Rodney didn't make a wise crack; he just kept politely murmuring, "Sorry." His last "sorry" was said as he was closing the bathroom stall door. Realizing where she was, she finally got the hint and left him in peace.

Mark Wiener, who was years ahead of the wedding video curve, taped the event. He captured several entertaining moments: Bobby Kelton, Glenn Super and Mark Schiff delivering my material; Ronnie

Shakes confessing to the world, "I'm gay. John's gay. We're both, gay. We're lovers! The whole thing is a sham;" Larry David frowning in pretentious deep thought, then self-consciously laughing at himself (yes, I have footage of him smiling *before* he made several hundred million dollars); Lenny Shultz doing things with his tongue that were barely legal in Tijuana petting farms; and Rick Newman and his girlfriend dropping a bottle of wine in the middle of the dance floor, then trying to pick up the pieces under people's feet, causing several seniors to hit the deck. The tape included several standup bits as well as Mark Schiff passing a hat to raise money so we could continue the party, which went on for two extra hours. Rick Newman and Rich Tienken (Comic Strip owner) stopped Mark and offered to pay for the extra time. Both were so drunk they forgot about their offer but we never reminded them. The main reason for extending the event was because the comics who'd eaten everything, including the table treatments and the parrots on Rodney's shirt, were actually having fun, aided by a great band hired by Mr. Jersey gig-meister, Jerry Stanley.

Of course we lost a ton of money on the reception. As Rick Newman recently told me, "None of the comics had jobs, except me, and I fed them all."

Neither my ex-wife nor I slept on our wedding night, not because of romance or passion. We were packing everything we owned, including a dog and two cats, in order to make our flight to L.A. the next day. But a fresh start in L.A. is like getting a heart transplant from a guy who died because he had a bum ticker.

Crystal-ized

About a week before my wedding Chris Albrecht called and asked me to hold for Billy Crystal's manager, Larry Brezner, who informed me I'd been hired as a staff writer on "The Billy Crystal Show." Great news, huh? Well, it should have been, except that they wanted me—no, ordered me—to be in L.A. the following Tuesday, the day after my wedding. I put my powers of persuasion to work and managed to stretch it out to two whole days, if you count flying time and finding my luggage and a motel that would fit a cat sized dog and dog sized cat. I was on a roll. In a certain very selfish sense I was. We were supposed to go some place tropical for our honeymoon, full of sun, heat, sand and half-naked people lying around sipping drinks with toys sticking out of them. I tried to look disappointed, but it's difficult to do when you're screaming out, "Yes, there is a God!"

I'm not a great vacationer. To me, sitting in the sun between innings was about the limit of my vacationing abilities and the only sand I need to stand on is the stuff that hardens to make cement. At least then you can get traction and don't have to worry about getting splashed, unless the cement is a pair of new shoes the mob just gave you. When people say, "You should get out of the house, it's nice out today," I say, "It's always nice indoors, so why should I go out?"

Well, the day after being told I definitely had the job, I ran into Billy Crystal and Larry Brezner at Catch A Rising Star. I was introduced to Billy as the writer they had just hired. It was the first time I met Billy, who I was surprised to find out was quiet—almost shy. I figured they might show up at one of the clubs so I came prepared. After they welcomed me aboard, I gave Larry an envelope of my writing samples. Yes, I already had the job, yet I managed to turn a bird in the hand into a bird in the hand of the warden for the department of Fish and Game. Larry B. said it was the only time he'd ever had someone audition for a job they'd already gotten.

A day later, still hung over from our wedding party, we boarded a plane headed for L.A. Since we were newlyweds we decided to upgrade to first class, but were denied because a guy had reserved (what would have made the requisite second empty seat) a place for his dog. The experience emotionally prepared me for the esteem a writer is rewarded in Hollywood.

We had a great staff on what could have been a great show. Much like the "standup guys," we all got along great and were mutually supportive. This is atypical of Hollywood, where being supportive of someone means not voicing out loud that you hope they fail.

Richard Crystal, Billy's brother, known to all of us as Rip, shared an office with me. It was the best office on the show not because it was large, had a decent view of the NBC parking lot and was far enough away from the producers that we could actually have fun; what made this office special was it had an air-conditioning vent in the ceiling that all the other vents in every office led to and we could hear everything the producers said. For the first several weeks it was fun because we heard only good things. That soon changed.

I learned a lot on that show—more than I learned at SNL, which was too tiring, competitive and not nearly as cutting edge as I hoped it to be. Years later I had lunch with Hal Wilner, one of the music composers for SNL. He told me of another very good writer, like myself, who had difficulty getting really funny pieces on the show because they were too offbeat and edgy. Of course, the other writer turned out to be Larry David. The staff writers on Billy's show had worked on some of TV and radio's classic shows and were secure enough to appreciate my offbeat thought process.

Jack Rollins, Woody Allen's manager (and truly a show biz legend for discovering not only Woody Allen, but for putting together the two comics that formed the great Nichols and May comedy team), once told me not to go to California because I was too serious a writer. They wouldn't appreciate or understand my humor and they would try to tear me down. The Billy Crystal Show is where I got my first slight tear in my comic's silver lining.

After a few weeks on the show, Billy and I became friends. In fact, since I knew very few people in L.A. at the time, he had invited us over to his house for New Year's Eve. It was a small party of just a few friends, but I got to meet Tom Poston and Bruno Kirby, both now deceased. Maybe my karma affects other people, too.

I also attended a birthday party for Billy, where I sat on the floor with Robin Williams, a network executive, the birthday boy himself and Rob Reiner, who was telling us about a low budget, fake rock and roll documentary he was going to direct called *Spinal Tap*.

My birthday followed Billy's a week later and he took me out to Himi's, a great fish restaurant and bought me a coffee table size book on the Yankees (at Billy's birthday party, a week earlier Bruno Kirby, had given me a large chocolate bar with the Yankee insignia). As we were leaving the fish restaurant, some guy approached Billy and told him, "I'm your biggest fan. I watch you every day." Billy politely thanked him and said, "You watch me every day?" Soap wasn't rerun daily, so it couldn't have been what the fan was talking about. Billy repeated, "You watch me every day?" Billy had a pretty good sized Afro at the time and the fan enthusiastically replied, "Yeah, every single day I exercise with you Mr. Simmons." Billy never burst the guy's bubble and I think even autographed the menu for him as Richard Simmons.

Billy and I started writing sketches together, and the further out I got, the further out he got, and our pieces started getting pretty edgy. One of the producers, asked me to take a walk with him down to the set. On the way there, he told me that I was a terrific writer but I'd be even better if I learned to write pieces that were less original, less funny and more mainstream. That should have been my clue to leave town. I was to learn in Hollywood they don't want anything original unless it's been done before.

"I can't believe that I could have gotten Al Jarreau or Jack Lemmon as a guest and they insisted on Nell Carter."

-BILLY CRYSTAL

It was in his production office that Billy started to do his Fernando Lamas character. He'd walk around from office to office having long Fernando chats with the staff. I remember Richie Crystal telling Billy that his Fernando character would someday become a famous bit, which it of course did, a half decade later.

"You look Marvelous."
–BILLY CRYSTAL as FERNANDO LAMAS

About the fourth or fifth week into production, Richie and I knew that a big meeting was taking place, so we climbed on our desks and listened through the vent. That was how I found out the producers were trying to split Billy and I up, because they thought my offbeat style was having a bad influence on him. That was when I really began to feel Hollywood operating without a license.

Just about every day Billy and I, at some point, would meet in his office and let our imaginations loose, coming up with wild sketches. We were going to do a semi-documentary about a fictional Picasso, which confused his everyday life with his paintings. Of course, we never got a chance to write that piece, but we managed to get a few off the wall, but toned down sketches on the air. It's always sad when you work on a project and you see what it might have been had it been left to run its natural course, untouched by people who have never been. But then again, in Hollywood, implants are considered natural (that is, if you could afford both. I knew an actress who only got one implant because it made it easy to remember which was her good side).

The real shame of it was that we not only had a talented star and a great writing staff, we had a staff that worked well together. I remember the first sketch I wrote was a take-off on "Love Boat," called "Love U-boat," that sort of combined "Love Boat" with *Das Boot*, the German film about a crew on a Nazi submarine. I'd done a first draft and brought it into the office of writing team, Arango and Duran. They quickly saw places to smooth it out, and I watched them punch up, add story beats, and trim out the fat. These guys were a rarity in Hollywood, pros who were willing to teach and show the new guy how the process worked. Another time, we were assigned, because of budget constraints, to write a sketch around an existing set of an inside of an airliner. I watched how they figured out how to build a situation and add odd characters to make the piece work and how by throwing ideas at each other they found a story line that had an odd twist. Had I not

221

been in that room, I would have never known they had to write a sketch based on a set.

A few years earlier, they'd been up for a writing gig on "The Richard Pryor Show." These guys had the balls to show up to the interview with Richard in blackface. Richard, being a true standup, didn't see anything racist in their prank. He thought it was hysterical, practically falling off the chair laughing and they got the job.

There were days when we would have to figure out how to write for a particular guest or discuss what tone the show should have, but instead of sitting in an office, we'd all stand out in the open production space, throwing a ball around, until we either hit someone, broke a piece of equipment or came up with an idea.

About eight or nine years later, I worked on a staff run by Paul Haggis, Oscar-winning writer/director of *Crash* and several other terrific movies. He was the kind of boss standup comics love—a forty-something year old with the mind of a twenty-something and the maturity of a ten-something. We would come in to work around ten or eleven, and get nothing done because Paul would decide that our time would be better spent shopping for stereo equipment for the office. Then, around six or seven at the earliest, we would order food and debate which Leonard Cohen album would be better to bust our eardrums with while we wrote. At about nine, we'd blast Leonard Cohen songs like, "Everybody Knows" or "I'll Take Manhattan" and we'd write til two or three in the morning.

In order to buy a satellite dish from a network executive to get the Yankees, I sold Paul half of my CD collection, so we had plenty of music to choose from, but somehow we would always end up writing to Leonard Cohen's album, "I'm Your Man." The writing room, at its quietest, was frenetic—like being in an insane asylum where they mixed up everyone's meds.

Billy's show had a calmer atmosphere, like writing inside a white summer cloud—a cloud that was about to burst and catch Billy without an umbrella. The day before it happened, Billy had gotten a vote of confidence from Brandon Tartikoff (then in charge of programming at NBC). I arrived to work at ten, the usual starting time for comedy writers everywhere except "The Tonight Show," which started an hour or so earlier. That morning everyone on the staff and on the NBC lot had read in the *Los Angeles Times* that Billy's show had been cancelled, which the producers confirmed with a call to the NBC brass. A few writers, although unhappy for Billy, weren't too upset, since we still had about four weeks left on our contract. They said one of the best jobs they ever had was on a show that got cancelled the second week and they got paid for not working another eleven.

Back then, no one had cellphones that weren't attached to something that weighed slightly less than the satellite it took to send out the signals. Billy had gotten up that morning and had come to work before reading the newspaper, by then everyone on the lot including the guards knew his show was cancelled. He drove past all the security guards and walked through the halls and into the production office thinking about that week's show. He greeted his staff, got coffee, and as usual, asked if he could bring us anything. We had no idea how to react. Before Billy could figure out why most of the staff were missing the balls being tossed at them, he was called into the producer's office and told about the cancellation.

I don't know what his reaction was in the office (his brother Rip and I didn't listen in, allowing him his privacy), but his attitude toward us was great. He was sad, but handled it all with smiles and class. We all felt awful about how Billy was treated, this being one of the few times writers actually felt worse for another human being than themselves. Comedy writers are still comics after all, only without the overriding need for immediate gratification or retribution.

My next writing job was due to the shrewd maneuvering of Jim McCawley, the talent coordinator of "The Tonight Show" (i.e. the man who picked the comics for Johnny Carson). Jim loved my material, but thought I wasn't quite ready to do standup on the show yet. I agreed with him because it went along with my basic philosophy that I was never ready for anything except the worst possible scenario.

One of the most popular segments on "The Tonight Show" was Johnny having fun with the new products that came out for the Christmas season. Jim's idea was to hire me for that, so I could meet Johnny, get my left foot in the door and if the segment was successful he would get Johnny a sample of my material.

The segment went great. Johnny even thanked me during the show on camera, which he apparently never did. A few days later, Jim McCawley gave "Tonight Show" producer Freddie DeCordova samples of my writing material. About ten the next morning I received a call from Freddie DeCordova saying that Johnny Carson loved my material and was even reciting jokes to him (yes, Johnny Carson was saying *my* jokes out loud to another human being) and when they got back from hiatus, I had a job writing on "The Tonight Show." I just had to have a meeting with Johnny, which Freddie said was merely a formality. Signing my name to bankruptcy papers was merely a formality. Having a meeting with Johnny Carson was like Jesus' girlfriend being introduced and left alone to have a chat with his father.

"On one of my Tonight Show appearances, Pavoratti was a guest, and before the show he changed into a tux in my dressing room, putting his huge oversized pants on a hanger. After the show, he left the studio and never retrieved his pants. My friend Barry Marder said, "Hey, Pavoratti left his pants, we should take them." So he did and on the way home decided he didn't want them, leaving me with Pavoratti's pants. I spent a year trying to decide which comedy club tee shirt would go best with them."

-BOBBY KELTON

So two weeks later, I found myself sitting in a small, square office, surrounded by framed covers of every magazine Johnny Carson had ever been on. And this was only the outer office, the place where you wait to be summoned by the man whose face is scrutinizing you from every angle and dimension possible. I felt Johnny's eyes behind the photos trying to find my most vulnerable cells. After ten minutes that seemed like ten years on a chain gang with homicidal hecklers that I had once destroyed from on stage, I was called into his office.

The door opened and Johnny Carson was standing before me, holding out his hand, not to push me away or cover his body in anticipation of an assassination attempt, but to shake my hand. Yes, he wanted me, a kid from a dead end street in New Jersey, to shake the hand that gave the okay sign and playfully tossed pencils over his shoulder as he nearly fell off his chair as comedians sent him into hysterics. Now, I know I had met Johnny before when I had done the Christmas special, but that was only a quick serf-like acknowledgement with other people around. Now I was alone with the King in his private chamber. He pointed to a spot near the black leather couches that were at right angles from each other. Of course I obeyed, trying to remember that I didn't have to bow my head. That's when I noticed that Johnny was holding a small black binder which distracted me from the fact that he sat on the near end of the other couch, our knees not only on the same physical plain but almost touching.

He smiled at me—the same approving smile he had given comics like Rodney Dangerfield, Richard Pryor, and Robert Klein. Then he said to me in words that I can never forget and grow grander with each passing year, "Kid, I really liked your material. It was hysterical. We need guys on our staff who think like you."

"Uh, really, thank you," I managed to stammer.

He followed my blathering by opening up the binder of my material and laughed as he pointed out pieces and jokes he liked. I wasn't only speechless; I couldn't even manage a stutter. Words, syllables, letters—even guttural sounds escaped me. My mouth hung there like it had just landed on my face and I had no idea what to do with it.

Then Johnny asked a question I should have considered more carefully, realizing that my writing talent was worthy of his accolades and answered with my true feelings. "What would you like to do, write sketches or monologue jokes?" he asked. The master had given me a choice. And I reverted to my wimpy nature and said something that I will always regret. Had things come harder for me in the beginning, had I struggled for years on staffs and worked in an atmosphere of competition instead of the world of Standup Guys, where I was supported and left unarmed and uncalculating, I might never have spoken the following words, "Whatever you want me to do."

"Whatever you want me to do." What the hell was I thinking? This was Hollywood. I was given a choice—a chance to shape my own destiny by the most powerful man in comedy, a chance at the most cushy, sought-after job in town (Tonight show monologue writer) and I didn't take it. It was a mistake I would regret some six months later. Johnny smiled, nervously winked and said, "Well, we really need someone with fresh ideas to write sketches. We'll put you there then." My witty reply was "Okay." He said, "Great. Welcome aboard," and extended his hand once more. I shook it with the same enthusiasm I had the first time, but instead of being totally thrilled and full of wonder, the seeds of regret started to take root. As I look back on things, it was probably the moment I regret most in my show business life.

At the time, Chris Albrecht was my agent and negotiated my deal. He was thrilled that he was able to get me scale plus ten percent—the ten percent to cover his agent's fee. I, of course, being the trusting, desperate soul I was, thought it was a great deal. A few months later, when I was on "The Tonight Show" staff, one of the writers told me that Johnny would have paid almost anything to hire me. By then I had realized that scale plus ten was the minimum that the Writer's Guild would accept. In all fairness, Chris wasn't privy to that inside information and didn't want to chance blowing what could and should have been a golden opportunity. Years later, Chris made it up to me by hiring me to write a pilot for HBO and paying me way above scale.

You see, writing monologue jokes on "The Tonight Show" consisted of handing in sixteen jokes a day to Freddie DeCordova, which you could write at home—easily the best writing job invented by man. Instead, I found myself in an office carved into a cold corridor about a quarter of a mile from "The Tonight Show" set.

I also found myself in a no-win situation as I was deemed a threat to the jealous, head writer. I'm not going to mention his name because, even though I felt I was treated horribly, his reaction was not uncommon. He was constantly fighting off ambushes by writers schooled in Hollywood ambition, driven by the motto: "You're only as good as the men you step on." The head writer resented the fact that Johnny, even though it was his show for almost two decades, had the audacity to hire a writer he liked without the head writer's permission or consultation. I remember shaking the head writer's hand and feeling like I was exercising the hand that was about to plunge a knife into my back.

I have written on several shows since "The Tonight Show" and learned how to efficiently use a writing staff. This was easily the most inefficient use of a staff I'd ever witnessed. There was another show that I worked on some years later that was close, but the producer was a hard working, megalomaniac idiot—(and I say that with all due disrespect) whose only previous work had been game shows. If he had been a baseball manager, he would have worn out his pitching staff in spring training. Every day, the head writer would meet with Johnny, go over premises (that I was never given the opportunity to contribute to), and select a few. Then, he would assign every writer to write the same sketches that would be handed back in to him and he would create a hodgepodge of what he thought was funny. This is why, for the last several years, Johnny's sketches became disjointed bits, interrupted by jokes that protruded from a premise like the jagged lines of a guilty man's lie detector test. Johnny never saw what each writer had handed in, only the mutant bit that the head writer had patched together.

It took me one day to realize that I should have chosen to write monologues, so that night I decided to be assertive in my own passive way. I went home and would write thirty or so jokes. The next day I gave them to the head writer, who thanked me like a guy on the electric chair thanks the warden for paying the electric bill on time. He told me that, from then on, I should give him any monologue jokes around 3 o'clock each day and he would take them to Johnny.

I may lack confidence in most areas of my life, but one thing I know is that I'm a good joke writer. Each night, I'd watch the show and wouldn't hear any of my jokes. After a couple weeks, I had a feeling that something was really wrong (one of the few feelings I'd actually been able to process before therapy). I ran into the producer, Freddie DeCordova, in the main office one afternoon. He asked me how it was going and the answer, which slipped off my tongue like it was jumping to its death, made Freddie bring me into his office for a closed-door chat. I told him that I'd been handing jokes into the head writer just as he asked at 3 o'clock every day. Freddie DeCordova, despite being a tall man with a deep intimidating voice, was by nature a kind man, and everyone in Hollywood liked him. He was old school, which meant that he told the truth—and honestly. For an instant I saw a flash of his angry side (and it made me fear for my life, which at the time still retained much of its value). He quickly squelched his anger and softly told me that Johnny gets his monologue jokes at noon and they're all selected before one each day. Freddie told me to give him the jokes and he would see to it that Johnny got them. I could see the head writer sharpening the knife I would soon be stabbed with.

The next night, I began to see Johnny doing my jokes. I felt vindicated and, yet at the same time, indicted. Suddenly, the head writer told me to be at work before nine. The compliments I never received became farther away from ever being handed out. My workload grew as I was being told to do rewrites, even though the sketches had already been slapped together. As a staff writer on "The Tonight Show," you only saw Johnny the day he hired you, during the taping of the show (when you can't talk to him) or on the TV later that night. I knew I would never last on "The Tonight Show" long enough for it to amount to a career move—or even lunch at Musso and Franks.

There was one "Tonight Show" perk that I took advantage of, besides getting bored relatives into the show,. Back then (I refuse to say back in the day), local football games were "blacked out" (television's equivalent of the national security term, redacted). The Raiders (who were still in L.A.) were playing the Jets (who weren't in New Jersey yet) in a playoff game, which was broadcast on NBC (who at the time had ratings that were almost in the toilet). I told the producer, Freddie DeCordova, that I wanted to see the game and he kindly told me exactly where I'd be able to find an empty room, with a gigantic color TV (which was probably 21 or 27 inches) and how to get in.

That Sunday, I was on the NBC lot, when I ran into Budd Friedman and Danny Aiello stealing tape players out of cars in the parking lot (that's a complete lie but it's more exciting than the truth), and I told them I had a place to watch the game. Budd made a big deal about me writing for "The Tonight Show" and Danny was incredibly complimentary as both of them glanced at their watches. I led them toward my TV room, when a guy carrying two pizza boxes said he had a delivery for NBC. And by pure coincidence, he was also a Jet fan. We let him in to look for whoever the pizzas were really not meant for, which lasted two minutes before he gave up his search and offered us the pizzas if we let him watch the game. I'm a comic, Budd is a club owner and Danny is a former bouncer at the Improv, so free food definitely entitled him to a seat right in front of the then massive, 21-inch, color TV. We all knew that the pizza bit was a ruse to get to see the game, but we never mentioned it. Some, who were more trustful of their fellow man, might say it was mere synchronicity and he really had a pizza delivery. But I'd say it was one hell of a con, and it matched the size of our stomachs and the depth of our pocketbooks perfectly.

About ten weeks into "The Tonight Show" gig, I was offered a writing job on a Dick Clark-produced variety series called "The 1/2 Hour Comedy Hour." Dick Clark's offices were just across the street from the NBC lot, so I took the gig, knowing my "Tonight Show" days were dwindling and that I could sneak out of NBC and across the street for meetings. By then, the head writer had worn me out so much that I had stopped writing monologue jokes at night. Writing jokes, at least for me, takes intense concentration, and when you're tense and overworked, the ability to write jokes is severely compromised. However, that didn't mean I wouldn't happily write off-beat sketches of my own design for someone else's show. And no one on either show ever found out I was working for the other.

I loved working for Dick Clark. He was the kindest, most thoughtful producer I had and would ever meet in Hollywood (or at least on equal footing with Andrew Solt and Loren Frohman). I remember I had missed one of the early meetings where Dick showed people around the studio. I had a legitimate excuse, which I'm pretty sure had nothing to do with working on two shows at the same time, so when I finally arrived at Dick's office, he took me for a personal tour. And if food were brought in for the show, Dick would stand behind the catering table, serving everyone. When the show wrapped, Dick threw a huge wrap party, but not at his house, which was in Malibu. Instead, he used a friend's place, which was centrally located in Hollywood, because he was worried that people would drink and drive.

Working the two shows was confusing. I felt like I was in a bad sitcom or a French bedroom farce, sneaking off one lot and onto another to go from meeting to meeting, not knowing where I was half the time. I became friends with one of the writer's assistants on "The

1/2 Hour Comedy Hour," who showed me how to write on a computer. It was a Morrow, which ran on a cpm operating system with a black screen the size of a playing card that was the background for the white specks that formed letters. The assistant left the computer in my office at Dick Clark's show so I could become more proficient in its uses. I felt like a state-of-the-art writer, able to make instant corrections, while leaping from one studio lot to another in a single bound.

"The Tonight Show" gig ended a month or two later. The head writer got his way by manipulating Johnny into allowing him to not pick up my option. Shortly after that the head writer almost lost his job when a writer who he thought was his best friend on the show tried to have him fired. Had I just spoken up when Johnny had asked what I wanted to do, I would have spent several years on "The Tonight Show," writing monologue jokes and never once having to deal with the head writer, who wanted to have my head from day one.

A few years later, I worked on the first "Joe Piscopo Special," where I was hired as one of two writers and wound up being the Supervising Producer for the ACE Award-winning HBO show. Now, without digging up dirt that I wouldn't want anyone to throw in my face, I'll just say that there were some production problems, like an unseen shot list, a shooting schedule that didn't exist in more than one person's head, 22-hour long shooting days, one of which involved a smoke machine that produced poisonous gas and scenes where the sets grew larger and more complex with each take. For its time, the show was groundbreaking because of the style in which it was shot. We shot on 35 mm film stock and it was brooding and Noirish. The special was made up mostly of vignettes driven by music rather than comedy, which is why only a few pieces hold up today.

In one segment, Joe played Frank Sinatra doing a rock video of his standard "Witchcraft." For the band, we used a then unknown group who became White Snake. They spent most of the day high or drunk and I don't think they ever realized their instruments weren't turned on. We used two of the girls from the ZZ Top video, "Legs," but we needed three more. We reluctantly held auditions and saw as many actresses as our limited time and Joe's wife would allow. One of the girls, during her audition, threw a *Playboy Magazine* down on the table in front of us open to her centerfold. Joe was completely embarrassed. His face submerged in innocence, he turned to me then back to the girl and said, "Johnny and I are from New Jersey. We've never seen beautiful girls before."

While I was working on the Dick Clark show, I had watched about 30 seconds of a comedy actress's video, but I knew instantly that this girl was special. Her name was Jan Hooks. A year or so later, I was an editorial producer on a daytime news and entertainment show called "Breakaway," and I hired her to do comedy segments. She went on to do TV and movies and was a regular on "SNL" and "Designing Women." She had the kind of comic instincts that couldn't be learned. She always went where the material was meant to go without being told to—always with the right attitude and perfect timing. As we neared production on the "Piscopo Special," I introduced Jan to Joe, and after a short interview she was hired. Besides acting in some of the bits, Jan played an interviewer, who became the loose thread that connected the vignettes.

At one point during the shoot, Joe decided to elevate me to supervising producer. He said that he couldn't pay me anymore, but he would give me half of his profits. Of course, being the shrewd businessman I was, we went over-budget and I was thankful to receive my Writer's Guild minimum.

"Why do they call dead people late? They're not late, they're never going to get there."

-RICHARD MORRIS

While I was on "Breakaway," I also hired the late Dennis Wolfberg. Dennis was one of my favorite characters, as well as comedians. He had blue-green eyes that rose separately, spiking every accent, word or gesture. He talked with an inner delight tinged by a playful devil, so that even we comics, who like to hear ourselves carry on every side of a conversation, hungered to listen to Dennis. As mentioned earlier he was the impromptu MC at my wedding and made a stressful day enjoyable

231

enough to put aside my premonition of the doom of that other "D" word.

I had used Jan Hooks as a bunny at the Playboy Club, where she drove the male clientele crazy, by bringing them food when they wanted drinks and drinks when they wanted food. Just about every time she tried to bend down like a bunny to serve food or drinks, while trying to bend in the tight outfit, she'd spill their drinks, drop their food and tumble off her high heels occasionally landing on the table practically knocking it over. From that segment came the idea of a comic stripping at Chippendales. Dennis and his inner light of insanity immediately came to mind. When I asked him, I thought it might take some convincing, but I was fooled. Dennis agreed immediately.

We waited to put Dennis on until three or four male strippers had performed—the tall hunks of perfectly carved male flesh taking the female audience at Chippendales to a peak of hormonal frenzy. Dennis, all five feet, eight inches of him, came strutting out like he was a hunk among skinny boys, his eyes bobbing and weaving around with a your-in-for-a-treat smile. His stunted afro swayed with the music, like a few thousand limp metronomes. The women at first broke out in laughter, but as Dennis showed no mercy and dove into his role as the greatest male stripper of all time, they began to boo. Dennis translated their Bronx Cheers into encouragement, so that the more they jeered, the further he dived body first into his strip, swinging his shirt and kicking away his pants, which kept sticking to his shoes, his eyes buzzing in sexual bliss. He strutted up to the women who lined the inner rims of the floor, gyrating all he had as the females leaned away like he was the wrong end of a distasteful magnet. Nothing they could scream or do could discourage this comedic trooper from maximizing the comic potential of the situation, not by acting funny, but by being Mr. Chippendale himself.

I went on to write for several television shows, produced and helped develop a few. The most fun I had was on a syndicated show called "D.C. Follies," produced by a close friend, Loren Frohman. The show was about a bar run by a former Ace Trucking Company member and improvisational comic, Fred Willard, where all the politicians and

Hollywood superstars (being played by puppets) came to unwind after a hard day of being important.

Fred Willard had the genetic makeup of a true standup comic, even though during his standup days he was a member of a comedy Improv troop, "The Ace Trucking Company." I had briefly met Fred at the Improv a few years earlier and spent about a half hour talking baseball. Fred was a throwback to a different era, he drove old classic cars (nothing fancy), listened to Elvis, was shy, quiet and best of all respected the written word. He'd literally ask permission to change the word "the" to "a." As tiny as his outward ego was, his talent was the exact opposite and more. He had the ability to ad lib when needed and make puppets seem so damn human (more human than any of the humans they were standing in for). He made writing for TV what it is not meant to be, enjoyable. At the end of each show, we'd put Fred on stage with John Roarke, a former standup comic and a great impressionist, who did the voices of two of our favorites: Reagan and Nixon. We would just give them a premise and let them ad lib. Afterward, I'd take what we recorded, get it transcribed, smooth it out, and give it back to Fred and John, who would take that and expand on it until we absolutely had to stop the cameras.

A few years later John Roarke, after Thanksgiving dinner at my house in Canyon Country that was filled with several stuffed comedians, waited his turn while they all told embarrassing, funny stories. John, intimidated by all the fast talking standups, waited to tell his stories until last. And they were the funniest. John had grown up across the street from a Catholic Church, thus was drawn to the religion, at one point was even in a seminary. He talked about his first confession and that he didn't quite know how to confess and how certain terms like masturbation should be counted. He thought a good Catholic should count the strokes. Thus, he had the priest almost jumping out of the box to strangle him, when he told the father that he had masturbated some five or six hundred times that week. He also so had us on the floor when he told us about trying to uphold the Catholic belief (which he took literally) that a person should stay clear of his own private parts. He demonstrated how he urinated without touching his penis, by opening his zipper and leaning forward against the wall with his head, so his private part dropped out and he could pee. I was laughing so hard I don't remember how he got it back in. It's not something I want to spend time trying to figure out.

"D.C. Follies" was produced by the Krofft brothers, Sid and Marty. Sid was gay, quiet and passive with a soft almost pleading voice that could barely be heard above his brother's breath. Marty was heterosexual many times over—a tall, no nonsense (except for his own nonsense), ex-used car salesman with a voice that would make a megaphone buzz with envy. He could be crude but in a very forgiving way because of his sheer extroverted audacity. I've always said the reason why Marty had gotten so many women was because when he talks he spits out a higher class of food.

During the second week of our shoot, we had to replace one of our voiceover guys, who had another gig or something. His replacement was a great impressionist but that first night he wasn't as sharp as he normally would be, and Marty wanted to fire him. Sid explained to Marty, "But Marty, his father was just murdered." Marty replied, "I know, Sid, but we didn't kill him!" Another time during the show, the artist who drew the sketches that were used to make the puppets asked for a raise, because his supplies had gotten more expensive. Marty's responded, "Use less lead."

Between our first and second year, there was a long writer's strike. We were lucky that the show was being rerun a few times a week and we were receiving residuals. Sometime during the third or fourth month the residuals stopped coming, because Marty, feeling our pain, stopped paying them and used the money to go to Cannes and suffer for us on the French Rivera. We wound up getting most of it back through the Writer's Guild. Even at the most painful moment during that strike, and during the battle to get the money back to feed my family, I never stopped liking Marty. He had an incredibly kind side to him. When one of our writers was taken to the hospital with chest pains, Marty went with him, ordering doctors and nurses around, screaming, "They killed my mother here! I won't let anything happen to you!" You got to love a guy like that; or at least I do. I'd work for him again in a heartbeat, if Marty was not in need of a new ticker himself.

"D.C. Follies" was a great show that would have gone on for years if the Kroffts didn't get into a dispute with Cannon, the distribution company. Both accused the other of stealing, which they probably both were doing.

I spent fifteen years in Hollywood, writing on shows, a few of them working with and for old Standup Guys. And no matter how many years I took off to write, I always managed to go back to standup. In fact, during a brief stint back in standup, I produced, with my comic pal, Glenn Hirsch, a special on standup comedy for ABC, called "Comedy Club Superstars." We wanted to call it The Comedy Boomers, but the network nixed the name. Our guests were Richard Lewis, Richard Belzer, Bill Maher, Jerry Seinfeld, Paul Reiser, Larry Miller, Rita Rudner, Carol Leifer, Tim Allen, George Wallace, John Mendoza and Paula Poundstone. Not one comic we asked to do the show refused. I only wish the network would have allowed us to use other comics and make the show the way we imagined it, but with the help of Andrew Solt's production company and leadership, we produced what competing networks said was the best show ever done on standup comics.

It was the first show Glenn had ever worked on the producing side and he had the attention span of a comic, which is about equal to the length of time between a speed freak's blinks. So Glenn and I worked out a system to keep ourselves from giggling. During long, boring meetings, Glenn and I did weird things like jump up and curse each other out or accuse one another of doing hideous things. I'm pretty sure I mentioned this earlier, but no comic off stage makes me laugh harder then Glenn.

We once went to some trendy restaurant in New York and smoked a joint on the way. One of our producing partners was to meet us there, but at first couldn't find us, as we had both literally fallen under the table laughing. That same night, we decided to roll another joint, but it was so windy, we needed a place to duck the gusts. We found an indoor ATM, which we decided was the perfect place to pull out our stash of weed and roll a nice thick joint. Glenn had the steadier hands, so it was his job. While I stood next to him, I figured this was the perfect time to get some cash out. Now, had we been in a state like Texas, I'd probably be writing this from jail. Not only were we on tape in possession of marijuana but they had my name and address since I stupidly took out cash.

One time, right before I entered Glenn's office, he decided to take off his pants, leaving on his underwear and sat at his desk. His plan was to ask if I was warm and then get up and open the window so we could get a laugh out of me seeing him in his underwear. That part of his plan went off perfectly, but before Glenn could put his pants back on, there was a knock on the office door and as it swung open, Glenn quickly sat down at his desk. The room was suddenly filled with the production staff, consisting mostly of women, and I suggested that Glenn should point out and explain the show's segments, which he had put on index cards and pinned to his bulletin board. He avoided it at first but soon realized that by getting up in his underwear in front of the group without making mention of it would get an even bigger laugh from me. I did the best I could not to laugh, but with Glenn, that's impossible for me under most circumstances

The comics we used on "Comedy Club Superstars" were all great to work with. They got paid scale and they happily took the extra eight bucks we gave them for cab fare. We even had them sign for it like we did at the clubs. My comic friends were wonderful to interview and it was like old times again, talking about old times. Many of my fellow standups are writing and producing television shows today, making real bucks and I'm sure improving what I wish I hadn't become too jaded by Hollywood to watch.

The Bond

We still have it. We always will. It's there, imprinted on us like an un-evolved, genetic code left over from the prehistoric age. Perhaps it mutated in some, but if you search beneath the deviations, it'll be there. If there is such thing as a soul, comics have one, only ours are attached by a spiritual cord full of knots.

It took a very sad occasion to bring us all together—Dennis Wolfberg's funeral, where our bond was left out in the open for the world to see.

I've described Dennis earlier, but even the most comprehensive exacting description, could never fully explain the way we felt about Dennis and the unique, lopsided corner that he left sparkling inside us all. That day, we felt a one-of-a-kind loss. I've been told it was the same when Ronnie Shakes died, unfortunately I couldn't attend the funeral (and because of that, I don't know if I've ever had complete closure). When Glenn Super died, I'd seen him a few days earlier and his joking at his own diminishing expense had started the healing process. I didn't make it to his testimonial because I got lost. I'm sure Glenn, who had driven with me many times, would have expected nothing less. There have been too many deaths from among our group and those before us who we admired. I wish I could have been there for all of them and can be around for every single one of their deaths in the future (and I mean that both emotionally and selfishly).

The day of Dennis Wolfberg's funeral, the sun was in a great mood. It wasn't just throwing off light, it was bear-hugging everything it touched. And to most of us, who didn't normally like to be touched, it gave comfort. We were a group that could be blended, but never homogenized. There were hundreds of mourners, nearly half were comics or show business people who had been captivated by Dennis's charm.

When I arrived, I almost immediately ran into Larry David. As in the most emotional times you're drawn to the people who will least judge your awkwardness. Of course, LD and I started discussing trivial things like his new green sports coat and then smoothly segued into insults. We traveled through the crowd together, me shaking hands, Larry, who is a bit of a germaphobe, evading handshakes. He instead gave a waist-high fist bump to those of us who understood, and with others, he used his superior physical avoidance skills.

It was Larry's singular perspective of the mundane, his bared neuroses about all the things that made him uncomfortable (which includes everything natural or man-made), pooled with his unrivaled ability to avoid the uncomfortable by confronting it that made him a great success. I always say if you're going to sell your soul, don't go to L.A., it's a buyer's market. In situations when most people would not only have sold their soul, they would have included the first right of refusal in their next life, Larry's artistic integrity and comic soul would go untouched by the sun-glassed serpents of Hollywood. At this time, I'm proud to say, he could buy all their slimy, shrunken souls out of pocket, but I think he'd rather smile all the way to the golf course.

Not being one whose greatest gift is feeling normal emotions, I couldn't put up enough walls to shake the sadness, nor could I block the magnetism that drew us all together that day, despite the varying degrees of our success, like the surviving members of a depleted platoon.

In most cases, deep down, somewhere within our pliable cores, comics feel like we were meant to be on life's losing side. Some of us, of course, have the resume and financial resources to prove it. Larry David and Jerry Seinfeld had very recently received their first syndication checks rumored to be $80 million apiece—a mere microbe in the universe compared to what they'd eventually score. And although there was a buzz about their amazing good fortune going around, it played no part in how we dealt with each other.

Larry and I wound our way through the crowd, talking about nothing that was meant nor destined to be memorable. At one point, everyone stopped their pilgrimage to listen to the eulogy, introduced by Mark Schiff and delivered by Hiram Kasten.

This was not one of those comic's funerals or testimonials where every comic tries to out-tribute the other. Hiram delivered a soulful eulogy that moved the unmovable. It was warm, heart-felt and laced with funny anecdotes, mixed in a way that left out the ego and replaced it with Dennis. I can't say I didn't see a dry eye in the house, because this house was full of comics who respond to most jokes not by laughing, but by saying, "That's funny." I think we did the same here. In our minds, we were all saying, "That's sad," or, "I could see crying here." Hiram's eulogy was so moving that Budd Friedman gave him spots at the Improv for the next three weeks or so.

What came next was the most gut-wrenching moment. No, Larry and Jerry didn't show us their checks. Dennis's coffin was being lowered into his grave and Jeannie McBride, his wife, was holding their twin boys. One of the boys screamed for his daddy while reaching out towards the coffin. It snatched at our insides and tore apart the bricks that we used to wall-up the entrance to the inner sanctum in all comics, that at times, can be touched; but is always quickly shuts off again, so no one can ever see its contents.

I don't remember where Larry had gone or if he'd gone anywhere, but I found myself next to Paul Reiser, both of us nodding acknowledgement for our mutual pain. Then, fittingly, sharing a shovel, we scooped up dirt and slowly dropped it on Dennis's coffin. If you knew Dennis's act, you would agree that it should have been yogurt we dumped on his coffin, as "American Pie" played in the background.

After that, we all split into small groups, individuals moving from one gathering to another, spreading greetings, telling stories and laughing. The sun was losing interest in the day, but stayed long enough to leave an orange and yellow goodbye that rested on the faces of the comics, giving us a clear view of our everlasting bond.

A Generation Of Laughs

Top Row: Ronnie Shakes, Steve Mittleman, Larry David, Keenan Wayans. Second Row: Joe Piscopo, Brant Von Hoffman, John DeBellis, Jamie Evans. In Front: Mark Schiff

"The comedians from 1975 to 1982 had a camaraderie and history with each other, the likes of which will never be seen again."
-RICHARD TIENKEN (owner of The Comic Strip)

Although we were aware of CBGB's, Studio 54, Plato's Retreat, the disco scene, Son of Sam, the race riots, and even survived one of the hottest summers on record, these things had very little to do with our lives and occupied only a tiny space in my memory.

We lived in our own space, where our only reference points in regards to time were what spot on what show we were working and when the Yankees were playing. I look back at movies that depict that era and say, "Wow! That happened then?!" or, "People really dressed like that?!" The music, TV shows, spiked hair and especially the wild sex and drug scenes eluded me completely. I was never a child or even a foster child, of the 70s. I was a child of the Improv, Catch and The Comic Strip, with 30 or 40 brothers and sisters who were brought up in the same small residence, on 8 bucks a day. Everything I am today and will be tomorrow as an artist, originated in those showcase clubs that grow loftier by the moment in my memory.

In most cases, for a comic to describe a period of time as the best five years of his life, it would be the equivalent of a guy in prison discussing the best five years of his solitary confinement. As I've stated several times before, comics feel alone and isolated by nature. Back then we had the comfort of being alone together. Our generation of comedians was fortunate to have gathered, lived and grown up in the time of the Standup Comic. That extraordinary half decade allowed us not only to storm over our walls, but it also built common barriers that protected and nourished our individual insanities to form a fortress. A place that encouraged us to be part of something bigger and better than our fragile egos could ever silently proclaim.

"It was a non competitive atmosphere for the most part, and we were happy to see each other do well. We became friends, there was no jealousy. And for the first five or six years, we were together every night."

-JERRY SEINFELD

We were an unusual collection of what I guess you could call "people," bonded together initially not by love for each other and certainly not by money, but by our needy souls all craving essentially the same, at times, elusive goal. For all our likeness and individual differences we had one thing in common, besides similar mental disorders: the pure love—no even more than that—the absolute obsession with standup comedy, not just as a profession, or a way of life, or a way to avoid life, but as a valid important art form. An art form that we wanted to be part of so badly that the choice was no longer ours, like swimming downstream, being aided by a powerful current carrying us in the direction of our creative compasses; but we no longer had the will nor the control to ever get out of the water. And even if we drowned, at least we drowned in a place where we belonged. Our lungs filled with water, through mouths that were opened wide from laughing.

W.C. Fields had the best definition of a comic. He said, "The difference between a regular person and comic is, if a regular person saw an old lady walk down the street and fall down a manhole they'd laugh. A comic would laugh, but only if it was a real old lady." Well, the difference between a comic today and the comics I came up through the ranks with is this: today when a comic comes offstage after a good set, his peers might pat him on the back, and say, "Good set," or, "Great job." When we came off the stage after a good set, our peers would come over, pat us on the back and say "Good set, great job, but if you change this joke around, or add this punch line, or a topper, or take a word out of the set up, you can get a better laugh." We respected and learned from each other. Some of us might have been so selfish, if it were possible, we wouldn't exhale, but when it came to our fellow comics, Mother Theresa couldn't have given out more punch lines.

No matter how big of a laugh we ever received on stage, the best laughs were always the laughs we had together. I never laughed harder, longer and with more heart than I laughed back then.

John DeBellis, Joe Piscopo, Brant Von Hoffman

We were each others' best audience, and I would give back all the cab fare I ever received and all the dinner food I threw up to be part of that audience again.

"I don't think any of us would have become the comedians or entertainers that we've become without passing through that crucible. And also I wouldn't trade anything for the fun we had. God we had fun. We were too stupid to know how hard it was. I miss seeing everybody all the time."

-BILL MAHER

Group includes: Rick Overton, Glenn Hirsch, Brant von Hoffman, Sue Giosa, Liz Giosa, Roger Sullivan and John DeBellis

The End

Acknowledgements

*I'd like to thank everyone who helped me with this book. You know who you are.

I especially do not want to thank Bill Mazeroski, Curt Schilling, and Luis Gonazlez. You know what you did!

*I was afraid that I would leave someone out.

Author's Bio

John originally started his decent into helplessness as a standup comic before turning to writing because he needed another way to express his depression. He wrote jokes for the likes of Rodney Dangerfrield, Johnny Carson, David Letterman, Gabe Kaplan, Elayne Boozler, Billy Crystal, and Joe Piscopo before joining the writing staffs of "Saturday Night Live," "The Tonight Show," and "Politically Incorrect." He was the head writer for critically acclaimed D.C. Follies and has written for sitcoms so bad, to this day, he's too embarrassed to cash the checks. He was, however, the supervising producer of the ACE Award winning "Joe Piscopo Special" on *HBO and* also produced what the competing networks, said was the best special ever done about standup comedy, "Comedy Club Super Stars" on *ABC*.

In recent years John wrote and directed, "The Last Request," a feature film starring Danny Aiello and T.R.Knight, due in the theaters sometime before his next reincarnation. John considers himself very sexy for a writer/standup comic; he wears no underwear under his underwear. He currently lives with his dog and cat in New Jersey, but soon plans on moving out of the kennel.

Photography Credits

Group picture at Elayne's apartment – Morty David
Baby DeBellis – John DeBellis
Chris Albrecht and Judy Orbach – Debbie Rene Duperrieu
Glenn Hirsch eating like dog – Debbie Rene Duperrieu
John DeBellis on stage – John DeBellis
Rodney and Wuhl – Debbie Rene Duperrieu
Ronnie Shakes – Debbie Rene Duperrieu
Ronnie Shakes' phone book – Jerry Stanley
Melanie Chartoff – Melanie Chartoff
Rita Rudner – Rita Rudner
Marisa, Jamie, Barbara – Debbie Rene Duperrieu
Larry David and Debbie – Debbie Rene Duperrieu
John, Gilly, Piscopo – John DeBellis
John, Larry and Kelton – John DeBellis
Joe Piscopo and John – Debbie Rene Duperrieu
Glenn Hirsch and Kenny Kramer – John DeBellis
Mittleman, Brant and John – John DeBellis
Larry David, Schiff, Provenza – Mark Schiff
Thanksgiving dinner – John DeBellis
Larry David shortstop – Morty David
Judy Orbach singing – Debbie Rene Duperrieu
Paul Provenza at the Improv – Debbie Rene Duperrieu
Mark Schiff and Jerry Stanley – Jerry Stanley
Laughing Stock poster – Jerry Stanley
John Piscopo batting – John DeBellis
The Untouchables – Bert Torchia
Gilbert Gottfriend gun – Mark Schiff
Mark Schiff batting – Mark Schiff
Jack Graiman – Debie Rene Duperrieu
Piscopo, Hirsch, Schiff – John DeBellis
Guys at Brants wedding – Mark Schiff
John, Piscopo, Brant – Debbie Rene Duperrieu
Group closing picture – Glenn Hirsch

CPSIA information can be obtained at www.ICGtesting.com
Printed in the USA
BVOW031153290413

319393BV00001B/2/P